FUGITIVE MINDS

FUGITIVE MINDS

*On Madness, Sleep and
other Twilight Afflictions*

Antonio Melechi

WILLIAM HEINEMANN : LONDON

First published in the United Kingdom in 2003 by William Heinemann

1 3 5 7 9 10 8 6 4 2

William Heinemann
The Random House Group Limited
20 Vauxhall Bridge Road, London, SW1V 2SA

Random House Australia (Pty) Limited
20 Alfred Street, Milsons Point, Sydney
New South Wales 2061, Australia

Random House New Zealand Limited
18 Poland Road, Glenfield
Auckland 10, New Zealand

Random House (Pty) Limited
Endulini, 5a Jubilee Road, Parktown 2193, South Africa

The Random House Group Limited Reg. No. 954009

www.randomhouse.co.uk

A CIP catalogue record for this book
is available from the British Library

Papers used by Random House
are natural, recyclable products made from wood grown in
sustainable forests. The manufacturing processes conform to
the environmental regulations of the country of origin

ISBN 0 434 01007 3

Typeset by SX Composing DTP, Rayleigh, Essex
Printed and bound in Great Britain by
Biddles Ltd, Guildford and King's Lynn

The imagination of the waking consciousness is a civilized republic, kept in order by the voice of the magistrate; the imagination of the dreaming consciousness is the same republic, delivered up to anarchy; it should be said, however, that passions are themselves frequent offences against the authority of the law-giver, even when his powers are fully exercised.

Diderot and d'Alembert
Encyclopédie (1767)

For my everloves
Silvie, Tilly and Lana

Contents

Pasts Imperfect

De La Trance

The Big Sleep

Alien Infirmities

The Alchemy of Emotion

Mystical Maladies

List of Illustrations

Introduction

Several years ago, while visiting family in southern Italy, I arranged to meet a friend I had not seen for some time. Before meeting Enzo, I was warned that he was *nervoso*. Not easily translated, *nervoso* is a catch-all term, a pliable idiom which may suggest anything from petulant irritability to exhaustion and breakdown. My cousin, who lived one village on from Enzo's home town, relayed the gossip she was privy to – Enzo had split with his long-standing girlfriend, his business had foundered and left him in considerable debt, and, of late, he had worked fitfully. There was, it seemed, good reason for him to be *nervoso*. I prepared myself for a difficult evening.

Enzo was waiting on his doorstep. His face was thin, his hair cropped close. He asked after my family, told me how his youngest brother was still trying to evade military service and took me down the road to see the beginnings of his latest venture: a garage packed full of surfboards and windsurfers that he planned to hire out over the summer. Nothing in his demeanour suggested that he was *nervoso*. As we drove out to the coast, I asked if he had been ill. He told me that he had begun to suffer from headaches and been unable to concentrate or sleep after separating from his girlfriend. Feeling weak and listless, he started to lose his hair. He visited his doctor, then consulted specialists in Naples and Rome, but it was only after finding his way to a *fattucchiera*, a local folk healer, that his mystery affliction was diagnosed to his satisfaction. His ex-girlfriend had, the *fattucchiera* revealed, placed a spell on him using a potion containing her own menstrual blood. By way of antidote, Enzo was instructed to deliver a small package (the contents of which he was not entirely certain of) to her home. From that day on, he began to recover.

Enzo's story surprised me as much as the large triangular abracadabra tattoo that he now wore on his forearm. From childhood stories, I knew a little about the traditions of popular magic that were once practised throughout the Salentine peninsula. I had also quite recently explored the history of tarantism, the much misunderstood 'dancing mania' that had until fairly recently functioned as a form of popular healing in this part of the world. Among Enzo's generation, these beliefs and practices were generally dismissed as superstition, but their vestiges survived. Enzo believed – and, it soon transpired, so did his family – that the rancour of separation had spurred his girlfriend to take revenge by poisoning him. To translate his malady into an affective disorder or a fanciful delusion of persecution was to ignore its personal meaning and its social function. Enzo's understanding of his sickness may well have allowed him to displace other preoccupations and concerns, or to avoid the stigma attached to mental illness, but it was nevertheless a meaningful response to his circumstances. It was only by unravelling his experiences from within, by placing them in a personal and cultural context, that an outsider could begin to understand how and why he had become ill. It was a valuable lesson to have learnt – one which has shaped the way I have approached all the mental states discussed in this book.

The fifty or so phenomena that I discuss in *Fugitive Minds* include forms of classical and modern madness, neurological disorders, trance and sleep states, varieties of emotion and memory, the so-called 'culture-bound syndromes' such as *amok* and *koro,* and a spectrum of mystical and spiritual experiences, from alien abduction to solitude. The one common denominator they share is that they have all been framed, rightly or wrongly, in terms of their pathology. The Ancient Greeks considered sleep and dreams as a nocturnal insanity. Nineteenth-century medicine examined trance and possession as forms of hysteria, mysticism as epilepsy, nostalgia and *déjà vu* as disorders of memory. Visions and voices are today still regarded as the prime symptoms of psychosis, while addiction has become a biological craving. The questions I have asked of these and other 'twilight afflictions' are essentially those raised by Enzo's malady. How are the symptoms of illness culturally manufactured? What happens when societies move from a supernatural notion of illness as sin or possession to the disease model of modern medicine? Have deviancy, eccentricity, revolt, normative emotions and alien behaviours been wrongly medicalised? Which afflictions have been most misunderstood or neglected by the biological and clinical approaches?

To answer these questions I have drawn much from auto-biographies of the insane and the inspired, on spiritual confession and dream diary, and assorted testimony from synaesthetes, alien abductees, drugged poets and manic novelists, not to mention the odd 'werewolf' and 'zombie'. But these primary sources are only a starting point. To trace the history of all these moods and maladies, to examine the clinical and cultural spaces in which they thrive, one needs to move beyond these private dispatches. This has required a fair amount of jumping between disciplines, including anthropology, psychiatry, sociology and neuroscience. Working this broader canvas has meant that the parallels between many apparently remote phenomena have often come into sharp focus. The similarities between accounts of sleep paralysis and alien abductions are striking. Glossolalia shares much in common with patterns of psychotic speech and primitive incantation. Near-death experiences bear some comparison with the ritualised transports of shamanism. The experience of being 'unmanned' in the context of schizophrenia contains uncanny echoes of *koro*, a form of genital retraction generally found in China and Southeast Asia. Psychologists and anthropologists have tended to deride such comparisons, often rightly. The conflation of the primitive and the pathological, or the primitive and the infantile, does mask vital differences. Nevertheless, it is useful to commute, to counterpoint and juxtapose, if only to understand what is essential to each.

* * *

While writing *Fugitive Minds*, I have been struck by the extent to which naturalistic psychology has been overshadowed by its experimental and laboratory cousins. A little over a century ago, the philosopher and psychologist Henri Bergson closed a lecture to the newly formed Institut Psychologique in Paris by predicting that the coming century would expose the vagaries of the waking and sleeping mind. Bergson's optimism was understandable. In Vienna, having just published *The Interpretation of Dreams*, Sigmund Freud was turning his attention to the psychopathologies of everyday life. In London, Frederic Myers was about to synthesise twenty years of psychical research into his theory of the subliminal self. And in Boston, William James was tidying final drafts of his Gifford lectures on *The Varieties of Religious Experience* (1902).

Sure enough, the discoveries came, but it was the biological sciences that stole the thunder. First, cellular biology identified the brain's neurons and synapses. Soon, physiologists began to isolate its chemical transmitters. By the 1930s, the first recordings of electrical activity in the human brain allowed researchers to chart the sleep cycle graphically. These breakthroughs had a retrograde effect on psychology, infecting it with the materialism that Bergson would dedicate much of his career to dismantling. The first signs of laboratory fever emerged in Baltimore, where behaviourism, as championed by John B. Watson, proposed that the language of inner consciousness, introspection and mental states was now redundant. The observable and the quantifiable were to become the touchstones of the new psychology. The extent to which psychology attempted to model itself on the physical sciences, particularly in the United States, was quite remarkable. In 1941, the year of Bergson's death, Gordon W. Allport published a dull mission statement, *The Use of Personal Documents in Psychological Science*, which gave qualified defence to the use of prima-facie reports and testimony. The first-hand reports that were so vital to nineteenth-century psychology had been effectively consigned to the dustbin of anecdote and gossip.

The history of psychology offers a great corrective to the notion that science is progressive and incremental. Behaviourism was not enthusiastically embraced in Europe, but there was nevertheless a decline in experimental studies of dreaming, hypnosis, telepathy and automatic writing. The clinical description of epileptic fugues, migrainous aura, glossolalia, somnambulism, synaesthesia and many other anomalies also fell by the wayside. While psychoanalysis bucked the trend and continued to explore these and other recesses, its approach and conclusions were blighted by what Carl Jung called 'monotony of interpretation'. Psychology in fact never recovered the roving sensibility of the *fin-de-siècle* researchers who, like Bergson and James, described and experimented, who kept abreast of advances in the humanities and sciences, who were not averse to speaking in the first person. Consequently, many of the mental states with which this book is concerned have in recent decades been rather more thoroughly studied through the prism of biology and neuroscience. Four stages of dreaming and almost ninety disorders of sleep have been logged. Brain scanning technologies have identified the cerebral signatures of trance, epilepsy and schizophrenia. A technique known as *transcranial magnetic stimulation* has thrown considerable light on the production of auditory hallucinations, depression and mania. By stimulating parts of the temporal lobe, one Canadian neuroscientist even claims to have located the centre of the 'God Experience'.

More than a century ago, in *The Varieties of Religious Experience*, William James was already warning of the dangers of this 'medical materialism', lampooning 'simple-minded' clinicians who retro-actively diagnosed Saint Paul an epileptic, Saint Teresa an hysteric and Saint Francis of Assisi an hereditary degenerate. James quite rightly maintained that the biology of mystical states was, at best, only half the story. These elusive forms of consciousness could not, he maintained, be reduced to a flurry of electrical activity, to the rushing and damming of neurotransmitters. James's argument is more apposite than ever. The maps that brain science continues to generate, the diagnoses that modern-day medicine and pathology arrive at, should not be allowed the last word on any mental state, mystical or otherwise. As much as neuroscience has been able to trace the base characteristics of dreaming sleep, of mental illness and the emotions, *Fugitive Minds* is written in the conviction that it has been less successful in grasping *what* these twilight afflictions are and *why* they come about.

Aldous Huxley once described visionary experiences as the 'mind's antipodes', 'the mental equivalent of Australia'. In a more recent essay, Susan Sontag reminds us that: 'Illness is the night-side of life, a more onerous citizenship. Everyone who is born holds dual citizenship, in the kingdom of the well and in the kingdom of the sick . . . sooner or later each of us is obliged, at least for a spell, to identify ourselves as citizens of that other place.' As seductive as both these analogies are, this picturesque geography of the mind is, like the argot of 'altered states', a touch too exotic. The borders between sickness and health, delusion and rationality, dreaming and wakefulness are, as I have tried to show, rather less fixed and clearly defined than we might assume. Indeed, fear and love, shame and solitude, fantasy and memory – everything that Huxley curiously dismissed as the furniture of 'everyday consciousness' – are just as fugitive as their more feverish counterparts.

Unholy Turmoil

The Schizophrenic Sentence

In March 1903, Professor Paul Flechsig received a bulky package from a former patient of his psychiatric clinic at the University of Leipzig in Germany. In an open letter accompanying a copy of *Memoirs of My Nervous Illness*, Daniel Paul Schreber made his motives for writing clear. 'I don't harbour any personal grievances against any person,' he wrote. 'My aim is solely to further knowledge of truth in a vital field, that of religion.' While few theologians are familiar with Schreber's autobiography, it has become a seminal document in the history of psychiatry. Of all the first-person testimonies of madness, none has proved more influential. As Freud wrote in a letter to Jung, 'the Wonderful Schreber' ought to have been appointed a professor of psychiatry and director of his own mental hospital.

Given Schreber's claim that he had been used 'as an object for scientific experiments', it is doubtful whether Flechsig responded to Schreber's request to examine his memoirs and to confirm the role that he had played in the 'miracles' to which he had been subjected. However, Dr Weber, director of the Sonnenstein public asylum from which Schreber had been recently released, expressed an opinion which many *fin-de-siècle* psychiatrists would have shared:

> When we survey the contents of this document and consider the mass of indiscretions in regard to himself and other persons which it contains, when we observe the unblushing manner in which he describes situations and events which are of the most delicate nature and indeed, in an aesthetic sense, utterly impossible, when we reflect upon his use of strong language of the most offensive

kind, and so forth, we shall find it quite impossible to understand how a man, distinguished apart from this by his tact and refinement, could contemplate taking a step so compromising to himself in the public eye . . .

But not all clinicians agreed. To understand the true nature of insanity, as opposed to its nosography – its definition and place in the general scheme of mental infirmities – personal testimonies were vital. On these grounds, the first German reviewers commended Schreber's undertaking. Fellow psychiatrists were advised to clear a small space on their bookshelves (at this time dominated by successive editions of Kraepelin's *Textbook of Psychiatry* (1883)). However, it was Freud who was responsible for bringing Schreber's *Memoirs* to a wider audience. His 'Psycho-analytical Notes on an Autobiographical Account of a Case of Paranoia' appeared in 1911, the year in which Schreber died. Freud's defence of the *Memoirs* was more emphatic than his inter-pretation of Schreber's paranoia as a repression of a passive homosexuality. 'Surely we can hardly expect that a case history which sets out to give a picture of deranged humanity and its struggles to rehabilitate itself should exhibit "discretion" and "aesthetic" charm.'

Born in 1842, Daniel Paul Schreber was the son of a well-known physician whose child-rearing manuals urged a regime designed to produce healthy and obedient children through exercise and discipline. At the age of forty-two, Schreber, the younger of two sons, had his first breakdown. Within six months, he had recovered from an 'attack of severe hypochondria' and resumed his legal career. In 1893, some years after becoming a high court judge, the same affliction returned in more acute form. This time the first intimations of serious illness came during a bout of insomnia. Unable to sleep, Schreber became attuned to the crackling noises that he would eventually recognise as divine 'interferences'. With morphine and chloral failing to cure his insomnia, a desperate Schreber returned to the university clinic where Professor Flechsig had previously treated him. Anxious and suicidal, he was referred to Flechsig's private asylum. His

4

condition failed to improve. In February of 1894, there 'appeared the first signs of communication with supernatural powers, particularly that of nerve contact with Professor Flechsig'.

Schreber considered 'nerve-language' to be a form of subvocal thinking of which all individuals are ordinarily unaware. In his case, the nerve-language was controlled from without: Flechsig had succeeded in 'imprisoning his will-power, such as occurs during hypnosis', and was responsible for the 'unholy turmoil' in his head. When 'voluptuous sensations' began to enter his body, Schreber believed that Flechsig planned to 'unman' him, so that the asylum attendants could sexually exploit him. Although Schreber never abandoned the belief that Flechsig had taken part in his 'soul murder' – well after his release in 1903, he continued to hear voices that shouted Flechsig's name – the conspiracy to transform him into a woman soon assumed a more grandiose dimension, with his emasculation considered a divine necessity. Once he had been turned into a woman, Schreber thought that divine rays would impregnate him, leading to the creation of a new race. If the world was to be restored to a lost state of blessedness, this was a fate to which he could reconcile himself. In his last years at Sonnenstein, Schreber did exactly this: keeping tight lipped about his clandestine mission, he impressed doctors with his worldly table talk and easy manners.

Much of Schreber's *Memoirs* was preoccupied with the spiritual and philosophical insights that his illness afforded him. Having spoken with trees, birds and God himself, having had to share his skull with other souls, having felt the stirrings of a human embryo within his body, Schreber wrote as an authority on the miraculous. Whether affirming the Immaculate Conception, taking issue with Kraepelin's views on the 'faulty judgement' which invariably accompanies delusions or offering arguments against cremation, he had one objective: to defend the truth of the supernatural against the follies of 'naked materialism'. His *Memoirs* were not an apologia for the errors or excesses of madness.

In 1910, with only one year to live, Schreber was diagnosed as suffering from dementia praecox, a degenerative condition that Emil Kraepelin had distinguished from manic-depressive insanity in 1896. 'Dementia praecox,' wrote Kraepelin, 'consists of states the common characteristic of which is a peculiar destruction of the internal connections of the psychic personality.' Apart from the delusions and hallucinations that composed its primary symptoms, Kraepelin observed an array of emotional and bodily disturbances which led him to identify three types or subcategories of the disease: catatonic, hebephrenic and paranoid. The most notable characteristic of patients suffering from dementia praecox was, for Kraepelin, an inability to engage in a meaningful rapport; however, an alternative diagnosis for the disease that Schreber had fallen victim to was now emerging – schizophrenia. When Eugen Bleuler published *Dementia Praecox or the Group of Schizophrenias* in 1911, the symptoms and outcome of dementia praecox were partially redefined. Stressing that morbid deterioration was not a necessary outcome of schizophrenia, Bleuler listed the primary symptoms, the so-called 'four As', as disturbances of *association* (disordered thinking), *affect* (lack of emotion), *ambivalence* (contradictory emotions) and *autism* (remoteness or retreat into fantasy).

Almost all the symptoms which Kraepelin and Bleuler catalogued remain central to the modern picture of schizophrenia. Excluding the repetitive movements that both psychiatrists observed (in patients who might in fact have been suffering from certain strains of encephalitis lethargica), the symptoms of schizophrenia remain as diverse as ever. As Louis Sass notes:

> Schizophrenics can be hypersensitive to human contact but also indifferent. They can be pedantic or capricious, idle or diligent, irritable or filled with an all-encompassing yet somehow empty hilarity. They can experience a rushing flow of ideas or a total blocking; and their actions, thoughts, perceptions can seem rigidly ordered or controlled . . . but at other times chaotic and formless. They will sometimes feel they can influence the whole universe, at other times as if they can't control even their own thoughts or their limbs – or, in what is one of the supreme paradoxes of this condition, they may have both these experiences at the same moment. They may be extremely negativistic, responding to requests by doing the exact opposite or by refusing even to

6

acknowledge the requester's existence; yet it is inaccurate to characterize them, as is often done, as simply oppositional or even as out of contact with their social environment. For, at other times, the same schizophrenic may be afflicted with 'suggestion slavery' – veritable 'fits of servility' in which he complies instantly with every request (although sometimes exaggerating his performance to a ridiculous degree).

While there now exists a substantial body of first-person literature which testifies to most aspects of the psychotic experience, Schreber's fame rests on the fact that he was the first patient whose writings were received as prima-facie evidence. To place the *Memoirs* in historical context, it is important to remember that psychiatry was barely fifty years old. The classification of the mental disorders had been achieved by scrupulous examination of the onset, course and outcome of each illness. As detailed as Kraepelin's case histories were, they were focused exclusively on the natural history of symptoms, providing little or no space to consider the life stories that Freud or Aleksandr Luria might have brought to the fore.

That there might be an expressive aspect to psychosis was not seriously considered before the end of the nineteenth century. In 1900 and 1913, London's Royal Bethlem Hospital staged exhibitions of 'psychotic art'. In 1907, Paul Meunier published *L'Art chez les fous*, drawing on the much-publicised collection of 'mad art' at Villejuif. Soon afterwards, the Heidelberg psychiatrist Hans Prinzhorn began systematically to collect 'the productions of pictorial art by mental patients, which are not simply copies of existing images or memories of their days of health, but intended as expressions of their personal experience'. Prinzhorn's remit did extend to collecting the writings of the mentally ill, but it was in their picture-making and their constructions that he sought to trace the 'decisive turn inward upon the self'. Although some of the artists featured in his *Artistry of the Mentally Ill*, such as August Natterer and Adolf Wölfli, also wrote or combined words and pictures in their compositions, interest in schizophrenic writing remained limited to André Breton and a number of his fellow surrealists.

Before the *Memoirs* were translated into English in the 1950s, few autobiographies had approached the vicissitudes of psychosis with the meticulous clarity of Schreber's. Besides the nineteenth-century asylum writings such as Urbain Metcalf's *The Interior of Bethlem Hospital* and John Perceval's *A Narrative of Treatment Experienced by a Gentleman, During a State of Mental Derangement*, which were principally works of protestation rather than introspection, only one biography stood comparison to Schreber's *Memoirs* – Thomas Hennell's *The Witnesses*, published in 1938. Hennell, a young art teacher, had been living in London for two years when he began his gradual descent into psychosis. Unrequited in love, seeking solace in the Book of Revelations, Hennell, like Schreber, began to feel the undertow of 'habitual and partly unconscious processes' carrying him away. With new ideas and pictures constantly stirring in him, Hennell felt himself being ushered into 'unforeseen possibilities', into 'faith – far beyond reason'. In this first phase of manic excitement, Hennell gives away his belongings and withdraws all his savings. In his work, he is particularly productive. To anyone who will listen, he is happy to expound the prophecies and insights to which he is subject. But time and space, dream and reality, begin to merge. Hennell is exposed to more signs and portents. Memories now burst into view. Everything he sees assumes an eerie or malign quality.

The horror begins its feverish crescendo when, while out walking on a country road, Hennell is arrested by three men who appear to him as pimps disguised as policemen. Waking in a police cell the following morning, Hennell feels himself enter the invisible body of a 'second presence'. 'These sensations are scarcely accurately remembered, yet it was with a grating and numbing pain that my ribs became the inverted ribs of the other being, my left eye became his eye, and at last I could just be aware with my right of the form of the next change as it was adumbrated on the wall. It seemed to be a gigantic body, twice as large as a man's, and sexless.' Admitted to a mental hospital, Hennell is privy to a constant stream of hallucinatory visitors, including dwarfs, Herod and Richard II. For five weeks, he remains engrossed by visions and whisperings. His thoughts are answered immediately. In his

8

dreams, he travels nightly to the ends of the Earth. Sometimes he is awoken by brilliant flashes to find people standing over him. He suspects that his psychiatrist, Dr Gillray, has 'the power to alter the shapes of things, strangely and enormously'.

As much as Schreber and Hennell made sense of their afflictions in terms that psychiatry could not, their accounts of psychosis were limited in at least two respects. First, the experiences they both describe relate principally to the 'positive' aspects of schizophrenia – its delusions and hallucinations, rather than the four As that Bleuler identified. The profound sense of apathy and withdrawal that is so often present in schizophrenia is nowhere to be found in Schreber's or Hennell's autobiographies. Secondly, both these works are reconstructions of schizophrenia, rendered in a language and thinking that is largely alien to it. True schizophrenic writing is rather more difficult to navigate. In 1795, a full century before Kraepelin noted that mental patients were apt to speak or write in 'disconnected sentences having no relation to the general situation', John Ferriar made these observations: 'When lunatics attempt to write, there is a perpetual recurrence of one or two favourite ideas, intermixed with phrases which convey scarcely any meaning either separately, or in connection with other parts. It would be a hard task for a man of common understanding, to put such rhapsodies into any intelligible form, yet patients will run their ideas in the very same track for weeks together.'

This schizophrenic 'word salad' – a jumble of fragmented and partial sentences, shifting subjects and registers – is the most outward manifestation of disordered thinking. One of the more recent theories put forward to explain these defects in schizophrenic thinking and expression is that of overinclusion, which suggests that schizophrenics have lost the ability to categorise. Presented with an assortment of objects and asked to sort them according to type, a schizophrenic will create non-categories. A book and a glove may, for instance, be placed together because they are both 'manual instruments'. Other objects may be united on the basis of equally obscure connection or simply because of similar-sounding names. This absence of any obvious connection between ideas, known as derailment, is just one of the ways in which schizophrenic thinking renders itself bizarre to others.

In a much-cited study of the 'deviant language' of schizophrenia, the psychiatrist Nancy Andreasen has identified at least seven failures of communication, including poverty of content (the tendency to supply too little meaningful information) and loss of goal (a failure to carry a chain of thought to its natural end). Although schizophrenic language has some deficiencies in grammar or semantics, these are usually a consequence of the failure to signpost ideas. For this reason, schizophrenic language gives the impression of being permanently stuck in the middle of an idea or of being carried away by a tide of association:

> I fear fear is fear fear fear itself and the invisible people in the Teddy Bear Lounge. They have all kinds of colors and I fear they are around me everywhere to go back and forth on a dream eddie talking. Where the water goes and a high cliff comes. Church is a living crab. About me and talking back at me. Everyone. They enter my mind and distract me. And I've yes always wanted to enhance myself in the present tense. They have heads and lines for a neck. Two arms and two legs. Like a geeeee!!! Charlie Brown Character!!! Their shape is distorted by . . . By reds and greens and white and yellllllowing the people have a girl curve feminine adventure and are GHOSSTLEY.

It is only through an intimate understanding of patient and illness that this type of schizophrenic writing can become accessible. In *Welcome to My Country*, the psychologist Lauren Slater describes her attempts to decipher the voluminous scribblings of 'Joseph', the chronic schizophrenic patient who was responsible for the above passage. By recognising the tendency to digress and providing contextual detail, Slater was able to 'filter' and 'translate' Joseph's cryptic ramblings – to find the thinking, feeling person behind the most confusing of sentences:

> I fear fear itself
> I fear invisible people

They have all kinds of colors
I fear they are around me, talking back at me
They enter my mind
Distract me
They have heads
A line for a neck
Two arms
Two legs
Like a Charlie Brown Character
Their shape is distorted
By reds and greens, whites and yellows
The people have a girl curve
Feminine adventure and are
Ghostly

The danger of this kind of transliteration is, of course, that it finds rather too much meaning and expression. James Joyce, who considered the poetry of his schizophrenic daughter Lucia as a linguistic experiment akin to his own, was certainly partly guilty on this count. When Joyce consulted Carl Jung in regard to Lucia's illness, the Swiss psychiatrist was struck by her use of portmanteau words and neologisms, but could not ascribe any intention to these linguistic innovations. Jung may have been right to stress the often random and desultory aspects of schizophrenic language, but Joyce was not wrong to think that it might have its rhymes and reasons.

Hearts of Stone

Perched on the gateway of London's Royal Bethlem Hospital, two stone figures – one writhing in manacled anguish, the other frozen in serene terror – once advertised the twin worlds of madness that paying visitors might find within. *Raving Madness* and *Melancholy Madness*, as the sculptor Caius Gabriel Cibber dubbed these two faces of insanity, were as familiar to Enlightenment thinkers as they had been to classical commentators. When the poet Christopher Smart was unfortunate enough to find himself confined at Bethlem in the 1760s, he had little difficulty in identifying these stone figures: 'That on the left is melancholy or sullen-madness, the other down-right distraction'.

The description and treatment of melancholy were, however, about to change. In the latter part of the eighteenth century, the word 'depression' began to be employed as shorthand for all-too-familiar feelings of melancholic listlessness and dejection. In 1818 – a few years after *Raving Madness* and *Melancholy Madness* were removed from public display at Bethlem – the Leipzig psychiatrist Johann Christian Heinroth first used the term 'depression' as a condition in and of itself. By the beginning of the twentieth century, Emil Kraepelin had distinguished 'simple depression' from 'depressive insanity'. What was once melancholia had now become depression. With the new label came subtle changes in the symptoms and meaning of this most ancient of illnesses. As depression placed an increasing premium on physical rather than psychological symptoms, fatigue came slowly to obscure the anguish and dejection of melancholy.

The early classical commentators had considered melancholy a chronic disease of the brain caused by an excess of black bile, one of the four humours. Despite Aristotle's claim that that the disease was the badge of 'all truly outstanding men' – a theme that the Renaissance thinkers would revive and embellish – it was more usually considered a 'commotion of the mind', an 'anguish of the soul', in which fear and sorrow, loss of reason and delusions – the hallmarks of mania – could manifest themselves. In one of the first clinical descriptions of its symptomology, Soranus of Ephesus, who practised in both Alexandria and Rome in the first century AD, listed the following 'signs of melancholy':

> Mental anguish and distress, dejection, silence, animosity toward members of the household, sometimes a desire to live and at other times a longing for death, suspicion on the part of the patient that a plot is being hatched against him, weeping without reason, meaningless muttering, and, again, occasional joviality; precordial distension, especially after eating, coldness of the limbs, mild sweat, a sharp pain in the esophagus or cardia . . . heaviness of the head, complexion greenish-black or somewhat blue, body attenuated, weakness, indigestion . . . intestinal cramps, vomiting.

Soranus also remarked that the disease affected far more men than women, striking principally in middle age. Yet he, like others, only partially endorsed the humoral theory that ascribed its origins to a build-up of black bile. Diet, temperament and other factors were also thought to play their part. The treatment he recommended involved a combination of fasting, bloodletting, poultices, leeches and gentle exercise. With more amenable patients, he also advocated philosophy, whose discourses might help 'banish fear, sorrow and wrath'.

Soranus's contemporary, Rufus, a rather more important thinker on melancholia, stressed the delusional symptoms that could accompany the disease, including transformations of the body (melancholics sometimes felt themselves to be headless or made of metal or earthenware) and bogus prophecy. He also noted that the disease was common in old age, that it could occur in infants and that the very worst cases were associated with women. Rufus's fragmentary remarks on melancholia were routinely invoked by late medieval and Renaissance thinkers. One medical historian goes as far as to suggest that he 'led the way with regard to the medical conception of melancholy for more than fifteen hundred years'.

It is with the Oxford vicar Robert Burton, author of the encyclopaedic *Anatomy of Melancholy*, that the modern history of melancholy begins. While Burton's work, first published in 1621, is in essence a survey of melancholy, its 'grievous passions' and 'immoderate perturbations', through the ages, his own thinking and prejudices are apparent. First, Burton's schema emphasises three subgroups of melancholy: love melancholy, jealousy and religious melancholy. Second, as much as Burton endorsed the humoral theory of melancholy, and laid out other causes such as diet and idleness, the condition was for him a pre-eminently human and spiritual affliction:

> Great travail is created for all men, and a heavy yoke on the sons of Adam, from the day they go out of their mother's womb, unto the day they return to all things. Namely their thoughts, and fear of their hearts, and imagination of things they wait for, and the day of death. From him that sitteth in glorious throne, to him that sitteth in the earth and ashes; from him that is clothed in blue silk, and weareth a Crown, to him that is clothed in simple linen. Wrath, envy, trouble, and unquietness, and fear of death, and rigour, and strife, and such things come to both man and beast, but sevenfold to the ungodly.

Burton's pastoral duties would have provided him with abundant experience of parishioners who were 'afraid that heaven might fall on their heads', but his interest in melancholy was never merely professional. From an early age, Burton suffered from pains in his head and stomach, burning sensations in his hands and knees. Whatever his physician, Simon Forman, recommended, does not appear to have relieved him. When Burton claimed that 'Hypochondriachal or flatuous melancholy is, in my judgement, the most frequent and grievous', we can only presume that he spoke from long and painful experience.

As Burton does not furnish any direct account of his sufferings, or indeed those of his parishioners, his *Anatomy* makes it difficult to assess the medical picture of melancholy in England at the end of the Renaissance. For this perspective, we can, however, turn to the Reverend Richard Napier, an Anglican clergyman and physician whose notebooks (1597–1634) include details of more than two thousand cases of variously troubled minds. Approximately 20 per cent of Napier's cases were diagnosed as suffering from melancholy. The label 'melancholick' was especially reserved for patients of higher social standing, who found solace in the classical associations of melancholy and intellectual and moral greatness. Napier's more lowly patients were likely to be diagnosed as suffering from grief, anxiety or the mopes. In true Renaissance fashion, Napier employed all manner of remedies, including purgatives and emetics, and herbal and alchemical preparations. Some of his patients were also administered the 'spiritual physic' of prayer or given astrological amulets to augment their faith.

With the publication of Burton's magisterial treatise, melancholy was to become an increasingly commonplace diagnosis, particularly among the *bons vivants* of literary society. In 1713, the problem was pervasive enough for the essayist Joseph Addison to describe it as 'a kind of demon that haunts our island, and often conveys itself to us in an easterly wind'. In his 1733 work *The English Malady*, the Scottish physician George Cheyne acknowledged that melancholy and all of its close cousins ('Distempers, spleen, vapors and lowness of spirits') were 'computed to make almost one third of the complaints of the People of England'. The high incidence of suicide was, furthermore, connected to the prevalence of melancholy: 'all self-murderers are first distracted and distempered in their intellectual faculties'. Foreign commentators were, Cheyne concluded, justified in calling the condition the English Malady. Like Burton, Cheyne could also claim to speak partly from experience. Having always suffered from a nervous disposition, Cheyne found his life and health transformed after leaving Edinburgh:

I all of a sudden changed my whole manner of living; I found the bottle-companions, the younger gentry, and free-livers, to be the most easy of access and quickly susceptible to friendship and acquaintance, nothing being necessary for that purpose, but to be able to eat lustily, and swallow down much liquor . . . my health was in a few years brought into great distress by so sudden and violent change. I grew excessively fat, short breathed, lethargic and listless . . . [soon suffering from] constant violent headache, giddiness, lowness, anxiety and terror, so that I went about like a man condemned.

Cheyne's breakdown occurred in 1715, when he was well established as a society doctor. Although he never entirely escaped the cloud of melancholy, a diet of milk and vegetables combined with a more temperate lifestyle helped make it an intermittent horror. This was the very regime he recommended to an illustrious clientele that included John Wesley, David Hume, Beau Nash, the Countess of Huntington and Samuel Johnson – who experienced a 'horrible melancholia' after leaving Oxford in his early twenties. Although Johnson suffered only one other completed breakdown, while in his fifties, he spent much of his life in chronic fear that madness might claim him.

Physicians soon began to plot the particular course of melancholy. Writing in 1799, a London doctor called James Sim noted that 'in the first approaches of melancholy the persons become silent and absorbed in thought, dislike being spoken to or roused, and seem always occupied in some grave contemplation. Jest, laughter, and every species of hilarity seem irksome to them'. There was also loss of appetite, problems in sleeping and all-consuming lethargy. 'When obliged to move, their motion is slow, measured, solemn, or torpid, with folded arms. Their speech is slow.' Yet this despondency was now also known to bring more florid delusions of persecution or guilt, with patients thinking 'all their friends are become enemies' or complaining of 'some crime that they have committed, which can never be forgiven by God or man'.

A more intimate picture of melancholy was, at the same time, provided by members of a profession that appeared more disposed to it than most. The poet William Cowper, for example, described how, in 1773, after bouts of nervous illness that left him 'overwhelmed with despair', he was finally 'plunged into a melancholy that made me almost an infant'. Surprisingly, the experience was a positive boon to his writing. In fact, he was convinced that this 'dejection of spirits, which, I suppose, may have prevented many a man from becoming an author, made me one'.

Cowper's melancholy bears many parallels with that of the Jesuit priest and poet Gerard Manley Hopkins. The 'fits of sadness' that began to plague Hopkins in 1884, on his first visit to Dublin, suffused the last years of his life. In the midst of this worsening depression – punctuated by periods of joyous elation – Hopkins found himself inspired to compose a series of five sonnets, known as the Terrible Sonnets or the Sonnets of Desolation. 'Four of these', he wrote, 'came like inspirations unbidden and against my will.' This strikingly beautiful series of poems puts words to the desolation that is so often mute:

> I am gall, I am heartburn. God's most deep decree
> Bitter would have me taste; my tastes me;
> Bones built in me, flesh filled, blood brimmed the curse.
> Self yeast of spirit a dull dough sours. I see
> The lost are like this, and their scourge to be
> As I am mine, their sweating selves; but worse.

The Terrible Sonnets were composed in a period in which depression was being reshaped through medical emphasis on the physical symptoms, rather than psychic distress. In his 1881 book *American Nervousness*, the New York physician George Beard identified neurasthenia as an organic disease that was a by-product of the heavy burdens of modern 'brain-toil'. Theorised as a simple depletion of nervous energy – 'Men, like batteries, need a reserve force,' wrote Beard, 'and, men, like batteries, need to be measured by the amount of this reserve force' – neurasthenia had none of the hereditary stigma attached to mental illness. Characterised by fatigue, irritability, insomnia, headaches, digestive problems and a truly vast array of somatic symptoms, neurasthenia was common-place, even fashionable, among the American and European middle classes at the end of the nineteenth century. The methods of treating neurasthenia were almost as varied as its symptoms. Beyond the infamous 'rest cure' pioneered by the Philadelphia physician Weir Mitchell, electrotherapy and hydrobaths were popular, although some physicians maintained that suggestion by the physician was paramount in rescuing the patient from her morbid inertia.

While Hopkins never discovered a way through his depression – he died aged forty-four – Russian writer Leo Tolstoy suffered a 'crisis' which led to religious conversion. 'The truth lay in this – that life had no meaning for me. Every day of life, every step in it, brought me nearer the edge of a precipice, whence I clearly saw the ruin before me. To stop, to go back, were alike impossible; nor could I shut my eyes so as to not see the suffering that alone awaited me, the death of all in me even to annihilation.' As insightful as they are, Tolstoy's spiritual confessions do not have the emotional force or immediacy of Hopkins's writing. Nor does he describe the physical aspects of depression, which the American novelist William Styron touches on in his memoir *Darkness Visible*:

> What I had begun to discover is that, mysteriously and in ways that are totally remote from normal experience, the gray drizzle of horror induced by depression takes on the quality of physical pain. But it is not an easily identifiable pain, like that of a broken limb. It may be more accurate to say that despair, owing to some evil trick played upon the sick brain by the inhabiting psyche, comes to resemble the diabolical discomfort of being imprisoned in a fiercely over-heated room. And because no breeze stirs this cauldron, because there is no escape from this smothering confine-ment, it is entirely natural that the victim begins to ceaselessly think of oblivion . . . The pain is unrelenting . . . For in virtually any other serious sickness, a patient who felt similar devastation would be lying flat in bed, possibly sedated and hooked up to tubes and wires of life support systems.

According to the medical historian Edward Shorter, the somatic aspects of depression were first reported in the late nineteenth century. Before then, 'stricken individuals developed pseudo-epilepsy in addition to the standard somatic accompaniments of depressed mood; in the nineteenth century, paralyses, peculiar anaesthesias, constrictions of vision, and catalepsy; in the twentieth century, chronic pain and fatigue syndromes'.

The semaphore of depression, its attempt to somatise abjection and anxiety, appears to be particularly exaggerated in cultures in which emotional expression is impeded, where little or no provision exists for the mentally troubled or where illness is stigmatised. Arthur Kleinman, Professor of Anthropology at Harvard University, has extensively examined 'this bodily mode of experiencing personal and political distress' in relation to Chinese culture, where the diagnosis of neurasthenia has been fully assimilated. According to Kleinman, neurasthenia in China 'provides the legitimation of a putative physical disease for bodily expressions of personal and social distress that would otherwise go unauthorized, or worse, be labelled emotional problems and mental illness . . . [which are] regarded as carrying a hereditary taint of moral failure and constitutional vulnerability'.

The search for the biological basis of depression has tended to overshadow the findings of social psychiatry and medical anthropology, disciplines which have looked to the life events and social factors that variously provoke and shape depression. Yet the sheer variability of symptoms associated with various forms of suffering and distress should serve as a powerful reminder of the dangers of ascribing depression to the depletion of serotonin, noradrenaline, dopamine or other brain chemicals. As Burton wrote: 'melancholy conceits produce diversity of symptoms in several persons. They are irregular, obscure, various, so infinite, Proteus himself is not so diverse.'

The Theatre of the Possessed

With the appointment of Urbain Grandier to the parish of St Pierre-du-Marché in Loudun in 1617, the best documented of all the medieval episodes of possession began slowly to unfold. Grandier, a young and arrogant Jesuit, wasted little time in offending Canon Mignon and other ecclesiastical dignitaries. As he freely indulged himself with the widows and daughters of the parish and, more egregiously, offended Cardinal Richelieu – who had temporarily lost his royal influence – Grandier's enemies waited for their moment. Finally, in 1630, Mignon and his growing circle of allies succeeded in instigating charges of debauchery and impiety. Grandier was eventually absolved after an official inquiry, but Mignon was presented with a second opportunity to vilify Grandier when he was invited to become confessor to the nuns at the small Ursuline convent at Loudun. This time he did not waste it.

Sister Jeanne des Anges, the prioress of the convent at Loudun, had for some years nursed a feverish infatuation with Grandier, known to her only by amorous reputation. Neglecting catechism and prayer, Sister Jeanne dreamed of secret assignations with Grandier. As two young nuns enlisted themselves into her fantasies, Sister Jeanne made her first overture to Grandier in the form of a letter requesting spiritual guidance. His polite refusal turned her passion into vitriol. It did not prove difficult for Mignon to persuade Sister Jeanne, obsessed and sickly as she was, that she had been possessed by Grandier's devils. Thus a supernatural trap came to be laid. If Grandier could not be brought to task for his worldly misdeeds, these charges would prove rather more difficult to evade.

Mignon and three other exorcists lost no time in priming the nuns. In a matter of days, all bar the very oldest reported that Grandier had dispatched his devils on nightly visits to the convent. After the arrival of two other specially chosen exorcists, Mignon allowed the public to witness the grotesque circus to which he played ringmaster. After two unsuccessful attempts, Barré, the most notorious of the six exorcists, reduced Sister Jeanne to blasphemous convulsions. Seven devils were eventually found squatting in her tiny body. The first, who identified himself as Asmodeus, required forty-eight hours (and one quart of holy water delivered by enema) before taking his leave. Despite the fact that Sister Jeanne now claimed that she was not possessed, and that visiting physicians considered this a textbook case of *furor uterinus* (sexual frenzy), the exorcism continued.

Grandier was accused of sorcery; however, when official witnesses reported 'a vehement suspicion of trickery and suggestion', the plot seemed to be backfiring. In December of 1632, after the Archbishop sent his personal physician to investigate, Mignon was barred from taking any further part in the ensuing exorcisms, which would now be obliged to take place under strict supervision. The conspiracy against Grandier was only revived when Henri de Condé, the princely supporter of Cardinal Richelieu, took a belated interest in the possession and encouraged Louis XIII to reopen the investigation. Once again, Sister Jeanne and the other nuns were thrown into the paroxysms of heresy. As she had before, 'Sister Claire fell on the ground, blaspheming, in convulsions, lifting up her petticoats and chemise, displaying her privy parts without any shame, and uttering filthy words. Her gestures became so indecent that the audience averted its eyes. She cried out again and again, abusing herself with her hands, "Come on, then, *foutez-moi!*"' Visiting sightseers, who had came from abroad as well as from the cities and provinces, were as shocked as they had hoped to be.

In moments of quiet contrition, the sisters appealed to the crowds, explaining that lies were being fabricated against Grandier. The exorcists nodded knowingly – to what lengths Satan would go to protect his own! On 18 August 1634, Grandier was found guilty of *maleficia*, of causing demoniacal possession, and condemned to be tortured and burnt at the stake. Mignon was allowed to perform his twice-daily conjurations on Sister Jeanne after Grandier's execution, but the task of finally exorcising Sister Jeanne and the other possessed sisters fell on four Jesuit fathers who arrived, by royal summons, in Loudun in December of 1634. Among this group was one Jean-Joseph Surin. More disposed than others to believing that the sisters at Loudun had fallen foul of the Powers of Darkness, Surin was a man of acute melancholy and infinite patience. With Sister Jeanne having now decided that she would do her utmost to deter any new exorcist, his endurance was to be severely tested. Within a few months, he had 'fallen into a state far removed from anything I could have foreseen'.

Exorcism was clearly not easy work. Within a month of leaving Loudun, the exorcist Father Lactance had died a delirious death and two others, Father Tranquille and Dr Mannouri, would meet the same end. Surin now appeared to be succumbing to the same spiritual malady. However, his appetite for suffering, his total commitment to the sanctification of Sister Jeanne, eventually reaped rewards. In the summer, she began to confide in him privately. She confessed, meditated, took communion. She experienced the ecstasies described by Saint Teresa and other divine brides. As her demons departed, the miracle that Surin had prayed for occurred: bright red stigmata bearing the legend of Saint Joseph appeared on her arm. Within a year, Sister Jeanne had reinvented herself. Travelling from Loudun to Tours, to Paris and Moulins, Nevers and Lyons, she was received by bishops and met with royalty. Everywhere she went, crowds jostled to see her saintly stigmata and touch her holy chemise.

Less than ten years after Surin's miraculous exorcism, Sister Jeanne decided that it was time to reflect on her possession. 'At the commencement of my possession,' she wrote in her *Spiritual Autobiography*, 'I was almost three months in a continual disturbance of mind, so that I do not remember anything that passed during that time . . . My Mind was often filled with blasphemies and sometimes I uttered them without being able to make any thought to stop myself. I felt for God a continual aversion and nothing inspired greater hatred than the spectacle of his goodness and the readiness with which he pardons repentant sinners.' Unable to distinguish the desires of the demons from her own, she recalled the violence with which she had refused communion, the fury with which evil spirits physically attacked her, her relentless rages and fits.

In his classic study *Possession*, F. K. Oesterreich cast doubt on the validity of Sister Jeanne's account, suggesting that because it comes from 'a highly hysterical person of somewhat weak moral nature, it must be accepted with great reserve'. Oesterreich has a point. Certainly her possession involved duplicity and self-delusion. At times, it is indeed difficult to gauge from her account whether she was participating in a charade or enduring a nightmare. But this ambiguity underpins rather than undermines the nature of her possession. As the Jesuit historian Michel de Certeau points out, the possessed traditionally benefited from being victims. 'They are accomplices of the chastisement that returns them to religious "society" . . . the nuns derive the privilege of being victims, subjected to the hard law of purifying theatre.'

If the fidelity of Sister Jeanne's *Spiritual Autobiography* is, as Oesterreich suggested, questionable, her exorcist and confessor, Jean-Joseph Surin, proved a rather more reliable guide to the afflictions he suffered. In a letter to his old friend Father d'Attichy, Surin described the process through which 'God has permitted the devils to pass out of the possessed person's body and, entering into mine, to assault me, to throw me down, to torment me so that all can see, possessing me for several hours at a stretch like a demoniac'. Surin had become a deeply divided spirit. On one hand, he would experience 'great joy and delight'; on the other, he would shudder and wail in complete desperation, feeling damnation in every fibre. In May of 1635, the month that Surin wrote his letter, royalty arrived to witness the devils at first hand. The exorcist and the possessed had apparently traded places. Surin could now be found writhing at the feet of the impassive prioress.

Had the nature of these illnesses been misconstrued under demonology, being recognised as possession rather than hysteria?

As nineteenth-century physicians looked back on the history of possession, this view became increasingly commonplace. When Gilles de la Tourette, whose family was from Loudun, reviewed the case of Sister Jeanne in his 1886 essay, he concluded that she was an hysteric spurred on by unrequited love. A few years later, after having spent considerable time studying the famous Boston medium Mrs Piper, William James remarked, 'History shows that mediumship is identical with demon possession.' More recent commentators have continued in this vein, drawing apposite and dubious parallels between possession and multiple personality and schizophrenia.

The possession of Christoph Haizmann provides a good example of the dangers of this kind of retroactive diagnosis. Haizmann, a minor Bavarian painter, fell ill after the death of his father in the late 1660s. Eventually, a pact with the devil – whom he claimed to have encountered in human guise while walking in his local woods – allowed him a nine-year reprieve. In 1677, shortly before he was contractually bound to turn over his soul, Haizmann began to experience unnatural convulsions. Travelling to the shrine of the most Blessed Virgin in Mariazell, Haizmann sought the services of Father Sebastian Meitinger. The three-day exorcism at first appeared to have succeeded in purging his demons, but they returned within a few months, and Haizmann was now subject to a series of grandiloquent and grotesque hallucinations that allowed him to perceive 'what great bliss and indescribable pain there was in eternity'. Before a second exorcism finally succeeded in restoring his sanity, Haizmann recorded his visions in a diary and painted a series of nine portraits of the devil in the various forms he had appeared to him.

Two centuries after being deposited at the Austrian National Library, these manuscripts were brought to the attention of Freud. His 1923 case study of Haizmann, 'A Neurosis of Demoniacal Possession in the Seventeenth Century', selected aspects of Haizmann's experience which best suited Freud's concept of neurosis as a sexual repression. The British psychiatrists Ida Macalpine and Richard Hunter took exception to Freud's reductionism. In *Schizophrenia 1677*, they argued that the true source of Haizmann's affliction was pre-oedipal, yet their more detailed examination of Haizmann and his strangely androgynous devil, his birth fantasies and his various fixations was, as Roy Porter has noted, no less myopic. 'All these psychiatric techniques of isolating figures like Haizmann, putting them on a couch and diagnosing their problems can indeed become positively perverse. For doing so withdraws attention from the social, cultural, institutional and linguistic environments which give their actions meaning.'

Haizmann's possession was not, as one contemporary psychiatrist claims, 'madness, simply perceived from a different world view'. Nor was that of Sister Jeanne or Father Surin. The spiritual crises that overcame them were derived and expressed in terms congruent with the religious culture of the age. Haizmann's Faustian struggle with his devil was never understood as a delusion. His treatment never required him to achieve psychological insight: it tackled the demons head on. For these reasons, medieval possession was in many ways less alienating than the secular insanities of today. 'During this time,' Haizmann wrote in January of 1677, 'several people watched over me, who were also so horror stricken that they became seriously ill and saw visions.' For all its torturous symptoms, possession was an incorrigibly social illness.

Multiple Minds

The afflictions that Father Surin and Sister Jeanne des Anges suffered belong to a world that was disposed to the advances of the supernatural. After the Enlightenment called time on demonology, cases of possession became increasingly rare. With this demise there emerged new ways in which the self could be divided, interrogated and reunited.

Double or alternating personality, the first of these phenomena, differed from possession in two respects. First, only one personality was experienced at any one time. Secondly, the new sub-personality which revealed itself was almost always more intellectually and socially adept. One of the first cases to be reported in the medical literature was described by the German physician Eberhardt Gmelin, in the 1790s, as an instance of *umgetauschte persönlichkeit* (exchanging personality). The young woman in question had been impressed by the aristocratic refugees that had fled the French Revolution and taken up residence in Stuttgart, and 'suddenly "exchanged" her own personality for the manners and ways of a French-born lady, imitating her and speaking French perfectly and German as would a French woman'. This transition occurred regularly. 'In her French personality, the subject had complete memory of all that she had said and done during her previous French states. As a German she knew nothing of her French personality.'

Echoing Gmelin's case of 'exchanged personality' was that of Mary Reynolds, whose 'two-fold consciousness' was first reported in the *Medical Repository* of New York in 1817. 'This young lady', the physician S. L. Mitchell noted, 'is naturally of cheerful disposition but thoughtful. In her second state, her imagination glows, her wit is keen, her remarks are often shrewd . . . her prejudices sometimes very strong'. Mitchell observed that this 'astonishing transition' always took place during sleep. On her first 'severe visitation' in 1811, Mary awoke to find herself blind. She recovered her sight, but her home and family remained unfamiliar to her. For five weeks, she was a flamboyant and cheerful stranger. Then, without warning, she awoke as her usual self, retaining no memory of the events just passed. A week later, she returned to the second state, remembering every detail of the previous weeks. For the next fifteen or so years, Mary continued to lapse and recover, spending varying amounts of time in her second state. The process was dynamic and therapeutic. At the age of thirty-six, when she stopped commuting between these two states, she had apparently become a joyful and loving woman.

The case of Mary Reynolds did not immediately capture medical or public imagination. After Mitchell's brief summary in the New York *Medical Repository*, her case history was footnoted by the Glasgow physician Robert Macnish in his highly popular 1830 book *The Philosophy of Sleep* – which, in successive editions, made European psychologists aware of 'Macnish's lady'. Then, in 1860, six years after her death, Reynolds's story was featured in *Harper's Magazine*, but it was not until the end of 1880s, when the vicissitudes of hysteria had in France already blurred into multiple personality, that Weir Mitchell and William James effectively reopened the case. Reynolds's time had finally arrived.

The French reports of *dédoublement de la personalité* added a number of crucial dimensions to the phenomenon. While the early-nineteenth-century cases had involved personalities that were mutually oblivious, the wave of French multiples often involved a secondary personality (B) that was aware of the primary personality (A). According to the psychiatric historian Henri Ellenberger, the prototype for this one-way amnesia was Félida X, a patient of the Bordeaux surgeon Eugène Azam. From the age of thirteen, Félida had been subject to a daily 'crisis' which would carry into sleep, from which she would for a few hours afterwards emerge as an altogether happier, healthier and more 'brilliant' person. In this second state, Félida was aware of both aspects of her split life. As Félida's ailments became worse in later life, the periods of her secondary state became protracted and predominant.

In 1885, two years before Azam finally published his case history of Félida X, medical science had already reported 'a beautifully clear example of spontaneous *déroulement* of several personality states'. The patient in question, Louis Vivet, displayed each and every symptom of *grande hystérie* – from constipation and headaches to catalepsy and paranoia. Bourru and Burot, the physicians who treated Vivet in military hospital, only 'discovered' his various personalities after employing hypnosis in conjunction with magnets, metals and drugs. Vivet responded well to suggestion, apparently regressing and demonstrating signs and symptoms which Bourru and Burot took as memories of previous experiences. The conflation of memory with personality came all too easily. Memory had by now become the touchstone for the psychological exploration of personality. In all, Bourru and Burot found that Vivet had six discrete personalities, each corresponding to different periods in his life, each easily recognisable by the particular contractures of his body.

Multiple personality in France was essentially an exotic offshoot of the disease category of hysteria. Like Félida X and Louis Vivet, almost all of the French multiples had been initially treated for hysteria, and most had found their secondary personalities developed through hypnosis. When the medical framework of hysteria began to be dismantled in the 1890s (see next chapter), there was a rapid decline in the diagnosis of multiple personality. However, in Harvard, it was still about to flourish under the auspices of Morton Prince and the Boston School of Psychiatry.

Having studied in Paris, Prince was familiar with many of the well-known cases of *dédoublement de la personalité* described by Azam and Pierre Janet, to whom we owe the concept of dissociation. In his 1906 book, *The Dissociation of a Personality*, Prince introduced the English-language prototype of multiple personality, 'Miss Christine Beauchamp'. When first consulting Prince in 1898, the prim New England student had complained of headaches, insomnia and lassitude – the classic symptoms of *fin-de-siècle* neurasthenia. To treat this rampantly middle-class form of depression, Prince began a course of hypnosis. Initially, his patient appeared little changed. However, after a month or so, Prince found that two distinct trance 'personalities' were beginning to emerge: the first was a caricature of the reticent and timid Miss B; the second was the exact opposite – happy, energetic and free of all her usual symptoms.

The relationship between Miss Beauchamp and her two alters was complex. Only one of the bizarre triad, 'Sally', was fully cognisant of the others, and she did all she could do to shock and embarrass. 'The personalities', wrote Prince, 'come and go in kaleidoscopic succession, many changes often being made in the course of twenty-four hours. . . . Miss Beauchamp, if I may use that name to designate several distinct people, at one moment does and plans and arranges something to which a short moment ago she most strongly objected, indulges tastes which a moment before would have been abhorrent'. When a fourth personality, whom Sally referred to as 'the idiot', eventually broke through, Prince concluded that an emotional trauma suffered some years previously was responsible for this multiple dissociation.

Prince's racy monograph described the methods through which he succeeded in suturing Miss Beauchamp's subpersonalities. With 'malice aforethought', the 500-page drama was aimed primarily at the general reader. Soon, other cases of multiple personality were reported in Prince's *Journal of Abnormal Psychology* and in *The Proceedings of the American Society of Psychical Research*, but the bandwagon was brought to a premature halt. With psychoanalysis and its model of repression in the ascendancy, the dissociated personality was dismissed as a vestige of *grande hystérie*, and so it remained for more than fifty years. Between 1922 and 1972, fewer than fifty cases of multiple personality appeared in the medical journals.

In his recent study of multiple personality, the philosopher Ian Hacking locates three factors that combined to create a new wave of American diagnoses in the 1970s and 1980s. First, Flora Rheta Schreiber's 1973 book *Sybil* (a fictionalised account of how the psychotherapist Dr Cornelia Wilbur uncovered the sixteen subpersonalities that 'Sybil Dorsett' had fragmented into after suffering childhood abuse) offered a guiding template to practitioners, while pushing multiple personality into the glare of daytime television. Second, the psychotherapy movement claimed a mounting catalogue of multiples (typically women who had spent several years in the mental health system and who came, via psychotherapy, to abreact buried memories of childhood, to discover alters or past-life incarnations) and successfully urged the American Psychiatric Association to list multiple personality disorder in the 1980 *Diagnostic and Statistical Manual of Mental Disorders* (DSM). Thirdly, and perhaps most importantly, as feminism and the recovered memory movement combined to bring child abuse and trauma into public discourse, multiple personality became widely identified as a natural mechanism of repression. By 1990, more than 20,000 diagnoses had been made across North America, and some members of the multiple-personality movement claimed that at least 10 per cent of all psychiatric disorders were wrongly diagnosed cases of multiple personality.

While the American multiple-personality movement is rather less influential than it was ten or fifteen years ago, it continues to campaign for wider recognition through its journal *Dissociation*, self-help groups, bulletin boards, annual conferences and regular media exposure. Critics of multiple personality have pointed out that the condition never occurs spontaneously, that the process through which alters and memories are identified is less than impartial and that the 'personalities' are neither separate nor autonomous. All this may be true, but the more general claim that it is iatrogenic, physician-made, is far from justified. This interpretation overlooks the extent to which the wider culture sponsors the search for, and disclosure of, secret memories and hidden alters. For this reason, Ian Hacking considers multiple personality as an ongoing chapter in the 'secularisation of the soul'.

Written on the Body

For the Ancient Greeks, hysteria was a female malady the myriad symptoms of which, from palpitations and breathing difficulties to convulsive fits and phantom pregnancies, were all linked to displacements of the womb. Like so many aspects of classical learning, this notion of hysteria remained largely unquestioned until the seventeenth century, as the uterine theory began to cede ground to nervous and chemical explanations. The range of illnesses and afflictions that hysteria was thought capable of mimicking was, at the same time, vastly expanded. Writing in 1682, Thomas Sydenham claimed that hysteria was 'of the chronic diseases, unless I err, the commonest'. 'Few of the maladies of miserable mortality are not imitated by it.' Those suffering from hysteria, a disease that too often deceived physicians, were not, argued Syndenham, only women and the feeble-minded. All bodies were potentially hysterical; all could succumb to its treacherous influence. Its symptoms were now thought to vary according to the part of the body the disease attacked.

The modern history of hysteria begins with the neurologist Jean Martin Charcot, who began to treat and investigate this strangely amorphous malady in the 1870s. Charcot's twice-weekly lectures at the Salpêtrière in Paris drew an international audience which was spellbound by the insights that Charcot, 'the Napoleon of Hysteria', brought to the diagnosis of patients. For Charcot, the 'permanent symptoms of hysteria, hysterical stigmata, as we are accustomed to calling them,' were blindness or narrowing of the visual field, anaesthesia of the skin, paralysis, convulsions and somnambulism. These stigmata were, he thought, all triggered by trauma, but had an underlying pathology that was specific to different hysterogenic zones of the body. In the case of female hysterics (who comprised about 90 per cent of the thousand or so he treated), Charcot found that the ovaries were chiefly responsible for seizures. By applying pressure to them, Charcot found that seizures could be inhibited. To this end, he developed his own instrument, an ovarian compressor, which could be attached to the patients for days at a time. With rather less success, Charcot also experimented with compression of the testicles on his male patients.

Hypnosis was also employed by Charcot to both induce and relieve attacks in his patients. Many of the female patients he hypnotised during his public demonstrations became minor celebrities. Hysterics such as Blanche Wittman and Elise Duval were painted and photographed while in the throes of acrobatic convulsion or majestic pose. Despite Charcot's insistence that hysteria was not a sexual disorder or limited to women, he and his colleagues were continually beguiled by its overtly feminine qualities. Other stereotypes were also attached to hysteria. Many of the patients who travelled to Paris for consultation with Charcot were of Jewish origin, and Charcot himself made much of the connection between race and hysteria. In 1891, one medical paper blithely endorsed his assertion, 'The Israelite is nervous.'

While the vast majority of patients treated at the Salpêtrière were cases of *petite hystérie* without seizures, Charcot constructed an idealised iconography of hysteria that was built around the most florid and theatrical of spasms, convulsions, paroxysms, catalepsies, ecstasies and comas – of which patients retained no memory. Through sketches and photographs, the spectacle of the hysterical body was tabulated, its positions and poses organised into a four-stage typology of '*la grande attaque hystérique*'. In *Études cliniques sur l'hystéro-épilepsie ou grande hystérie*, published in 1881, Charcot's student Paul Richer graphically illustrated these stages, showing the transition from epileptoid seizures to the contortions of *clownisme*, and from the '*attitudes passionelles*' through to the final '*période de délire*'. Charcot conceded that the four-stage version of the hysterical attack was relatively rare and that it was far more common for hysterics to experience partial fits and minor twitches and tics. As Mark Micale points out in *Approaching Hysteria*, however, his baroque taxonomy 'brought a useful but largely artificial clarity to the subject'.

It was while studying at the Salpêtrière in the 1880s that a pupil of Charcot, Sigmund Freud, began to develop his own theory of hysteria as a forgotten *psychological* trauma. Developed in tandem with Josef Breuer in *Studies on Hysteria*, this theory originally coincided with Freud's adoption of hypnosis as a therapeutic tool. Freud's emphasis on the sexual roots of hysteria – pursued rather less literally than Charcot – proved even more controversial. Turning Charcot's organic theory on its head, Freud and Breuer announced, in 1895, that the 'hysteric suffers mainly from reminiscences' often relating to childhood sexual experience. These experiences of 'seduction' or abuse were, Freud originally thought, the real trauma that hysterics sought to represent through their afflictions. This theory, however, was soon abandoned. Increasing doubts as to the veracity of the memories that his patients confided in him, and limited success with hypnosis, led Freud towards a fantasy-driven theory of hysteria.

Freud's 'Fragment of an Analysis of a Case of Hysteria', the most famous of all his case studies, offered 'solutions of hysterical symptoms' suffered by his young patient 'Dora' and proposed a broader 'sexual-organic basis of the whole condition'. Dora (Ida Bauer) was the eighteen-year-old daughter of a wealthy Viennese Jew, whom Freud had treated for a 'confusional attack' in 1896. Suffering from depression, aphasia and a nervous cough – symptoms that Freud considered characteristic of *petite hystérie* – Dora was treated over a three-month period in 1900. Using dream analysis, working as the 'conscientious archaeologist' he considered himself, Freud unearthed a complex of confused emotion, which, he thought, reflected her ambivalent affection for her father and Herr K, the husband of her father's mistress. Almost all the evidence he marshalled to support this conclusion came from two dreams. When Dora abruptly announced that she would not be returning to visit Freud, his 'hopes of a successful termination of the treatment were at their highest'. He considered this an 'unmistakable act of vengeance'.

Freud was right to think that his study of Dora would 'produce an even more horrifying effect than usual', but he could not have anticipated the lasting controversy that would surround his treatment of Dora and his more general theory of hysteria. Freud has been accused of various manipulations. A number of critics have suggested that Dora's treatment was initiated by her father so that she would not divulge the details of his affair and that Freud was active in this subterfuge; others have pointed out that Dora is, above all, a literary creation, with Freud, its unreliable narrator, employing techniques of plotting and characterisation that can be compared to the plays of Ibsen or novels of Henry James.

Another of Charcot's pupils, Josef Babinski, was also partly responsible for overturning the Salpêtrière's model of hystero-epilepsy. Arguing that its symptoms were not organic, but rather transmitted by doctors, patients and expectation, Babinski exposed the implicit contract on which the disease was based. 'Hysteria', he wrote in 1906, 'is a pathological condition mani-fested by disturbances which in certain subjects can be produced with complete exactness and are apt to vanish under the influence of persuasion (countersuggestion) alone.' As fewer and fewer cases of hysteria were diagnosed or discussed, psychiatrists and anthro-pologists found that its natural habitat was among traditional or displaced communities. 'Conversion hysteria' was, for example, seen to afflict front-line soldiers throughout Europe. In Southeast Asia, folk illnesses such as *latah* and *amok* were claimed as exotic examples of hysteria. Further afield, the arctic hysteria of the Inuits extended the range of symptoms associated with the hysterical attack.

In 1928, celebrating the fiftieth anniversary of Charcot's version of hysteria in *La Révolution Surréaliste*, Louis Aragon and André Breton proposed their own alternative definition: 'This mental condition is based on the need of a reciprocal seduction, which explains the hastily accepted miracles of medical suggestion (or countersuggestion). Hysteria is not a pathological phenomenon and may in all respects be considered a supreme means of expression.' The surrealists' attempt to rehabilitate hysteria was a serious prank with a sound premise. Aragon and Breton, physicians *manqués*, understood as well as anyone what Charcot and Freud appeared to forget – that the symptoms of hysteria were always shaped by the 'reciprocal seduction' of doctor and patient.

One-Track Minds

Yayoi Kusama paints dots. For more than forty years, she has daubed walls and canvases, furniture and inflatables, mannequins and naked bodies with a second skin of dots that swarm in kinetic indecision, that bob and float like drifting photisms. Having spent much of her adult life in psychiatric care, the dots have been her 'self-therapy': they alone have saved her from the 'strange, uncanny things, which come in and out of my soul'. 'The psychiatrists I saw were in my opinion a mess, with their heads muddied and brainwashed by Freud. . . . All I needed from them was a piece of information about how to cure myself, which they never gave me.' Kusama discovered this antidote herself. The dots became a protective grille with which she attempted to shield herself from intrusive thoughts, from persistent experiences of unreality.

The symptoms of obsessive neurosis, the condition that Kusama has been diagnosed with, were described centuries before Freud and the great nineteenth-century theorists. Christian demonology in the late Middle Ages maintained a distinction between possession and obsession, regarding the latter as a 'besiegement' that even the most virtuous of souls might succumb to. Robert Burton described a man 'who dared not go over a bridge, come near a pool, rock, steep hill, lie in a chamber where across beams were, for fear he be tempted to hang, draw or precipitate himself.' And according to many of his con-temporaries, Samuel Johnson was no stranger to such obsessive 'particularity'. James Boswell observed that:

> [It] was his anxious care to go out or into a door or passage by a
> certain number of steps from a certain point, or at least so that his

right or left foot . . . should constantly make the first actual movement when he came close to a door or passage. Occasionally, he
would suddenly stop, and then seem to count his steps with a deep
eagerness; and when he had neglected or gone wrong in this sort
of magical movement, I have seen him go back again, put himself
in a proper posture to begin this ceremony, and having gone
through it, break from his abstraction, walk briskly on, and join his
companion.

All the obsessions and compulsions listed in today's psychiatric
textbooks, from rituals of checking and counting to preoccupations with cleanliness and symmetry, have a considerable
history. The first detailed clinical description of obsessive thinking
or behaviour belongs to the early 1830s, however, when Jean-
Etienne Dominique Esquirol, the great systematiser of the mental
illnesses, began to profile cases of 'monomania'. In this case study
of Mademoiselle F, he outlined a form of 'reasoning monomania'
which he considered as having a particularly acute and chronic
course:

> One day, at the age of eighteen, without any known cause, on
> going out of the house of her aunt, she is seized with disquietude,
> lest she might unintentionally carry away in her apron, something
> belonging to her relative. From henceforth, she makes her visits
> without wearing her apron. At a later period, she spends much
> time in completing the accounts and invoices, being apprehensive
> of committing some error; of substituting one figure for another;
> and consequently of wronging customers. Later still, she fears that
> by handling money, she shall retain *something of value in her fingers*. . . .
> Her apprehensions gradually augment and become general.
> When she places her hand upon anything, her disquietudes are
> renewed, and she washes her hands in much water. . . . During the
> paroxysms, she neither reads, labours or writes, but in presence of
> her waiting woman; and if accidentally alone, even in her apart-
> ment, she chooses not to sit down before the servant comes in, and
> assures her that there is nothing upon the seat, to prevent it. . . .
> She is never irrational; is aware of her condition; perceives the

ridiculous nature of her apprehensions and the absurdity of her precautions; and laughs and makes sport of them. She also laments, and sometimes weeps in view of them.

Seventy years after Esquirol described the case of Mademoiselle F, Freud argued that such cases of 'obsessive neurosis' were essentially a dialect of hysteria. Freud's breakthrough was to bring obsessional ideas into 'temporal relationship with the patient's experience'. This psychodynamic approach is often said to have stunted the development of more effective behavioural treatments, but these techniques had in fact already been employed. A contemporary of Esquirol, François Leuret, claimed success with a treatment that is nowadays known as 'differential reinforcement'. Leuret's patient, a wine merchant whose obsessive thinking had gripped him for more than a decade, was instructed to read and memorise passages of literature. Success or failure dictated the food ration he would receive. Within weeks, the patient reported that his usual thinking had been interrupted. Even exposure therapy, the principal clinical treatment for obsessive–compulsive disorders and phobias, which attempts to introduce patients slowly and systematically to objects or situations they typically avoid, had already been used by Pierre Janet before the end of the nineteenth century.

Obsessive–compulsive disorder (OCD) entered the medical lexicon in the early 1980s. The diagnosis of OCD is made when obsessions or compulsions are deemed to cause 'excessive distress'. The American Psychiatric Association's *Diagnostic and Statistical Manual of Mental Disorders* considers obsessions as 'recurrent, persistent ideas, thoughts, images, or impulses that are experienced, at least initially, as intrusive and senseless, e.g., a parent's having repeated impulses to kill a loved child, a religious person's having blasphemous thoughts'. Compulsions are defined, rather less clearly, as 'repetitive, purposeful, and intentional behaviours that are performed in response to obsession or according to certain rules or in a stereotypical fashion'. About 80 per cent of cases of OCD involve some element of both obsession and compulsion. An obsession with contamination and germs will, for instance, lead to compulsive hand-washing, showering and household cleaning.

Obsessions multiply. In the case of Freud's 'Rat Man', morbid preoccupations with the welfare of his father and 'a lady whom he admired' spiralled into a whole series of connected rites. During thunderstorms, he was impelled to count between flashes of lightning. On kicking a stone lying in the road, he was struck by the thought that his lady's carriage might come to harm and was impelled to remove it. A few minutes later, realising the absurdity of his actions, he returned to place the stone in its original position. Later, an 'obsession for understanding' required him to 'understand the precise meaning of every syllable that was addressed to him, as though he might otherwise be missing some priceless treasure'.

The last of these obsessions, known as doubting mania, or *folie à doute*, in the nineteenth century, is today consigned to a sundry list of subtypes on the Yale-Brown Compulsive Scale. Among the other 'subtypes' – which include the overwhelming need to confess or ask questions and the compulsion to pull one's hair out – the most fascinating is the overarching need to know or remember. The case of 'Georgette', as described by the French physician Valentin Magnan, is a particularly good example of this latter form of fixation. Georgette, a twenty-six-year-old alcoholic man, suddenly developed an obsession with recovering lost names. This first manifested itself after reading a newspaper story about a young girl who had fallen into an open sewer. Consumed by the story, but unable to recall the girl's name, Georgette spent a sleepless night racking his brain, consumed by rising, visceral panic. On the following day, Georgette managed to discover the girl's name, but the experience repeated itself. To ensure he would never forget a name, Georgette evolved a complex system of cross-referenced files, the administration of which took up much of his time. The system worked, at first. Eventually, his obsession extended to a morbid fear of forgetting faces, requiring him also to keep photographs in a rapidly expanding archive.

The fact that all the above obsessions and compulsions are encountered in other conditions, from schizophrenia to depression, would suggest that OCD is not an entirely self-contained anxiety disorder. The condition that most overlaps with OCD is Tourette's syndrome, which is primarily composed of motor and vocal tics. While Tourette's is a neurological dysfunction, and its symptoms hence considered *involuntary*, there is a substantial grey area in which it meets and merges with OCD. Comparison of the two conditions has led some researchers to suggest that apparently compulsive acts (of washing, cleaning, checking, etc.) are not necessarily the tendrilous outgrowth of obsession. These compulsions may in fact be complex tics, hardwired automatisms, which are subsequently rationalised.

As well as compulsively counting his footsteps, Samuel Johnson displayed a gamut of convulsive starts and odd gesticulations. Johnson was an inveterate toucher of posts, an utterer of 'pious ejaculations'. He clucked and whistled between his famous soliloquies. He shook and rolled his rather sizeable head. His breathing was often violent. Richard Robert Madden's *Infirmities of Genius*, first published in 1833, began its medical examination of the 'habits and constitutional peculiarities of genius' with a profile of Johnson. Ascribing different aspects of Johnson's character to hypochondria, scrofula and other conditions, he suggested that the physical mannerisms were the product of a nervous disorder that went back to his childhood. While this conjecture has since been extended into a retroactive diagnosis of Tourette's syndrome, Boswell records that none of Johnson's friends 'ever ventured to ask an explanation' for his many idiosyncrasies. Speculation, of course, abounded. While Pope and Boswell were drawn to compare his infirmity with St Vitus's dance, Sir Joshua Reynolds was rather more perceptive in detecting some kind of language in Johnson's odd movements:

> Those motions or tricks of Dr Johnson are improperly called convulsions. He could sit motionless, when he was told to do so, as well as any other man; my opinion is that it proceeded from a habit which he had indulged himself in, of accompanying his thoughts with certain untoward actions, and those actions always appeared to me as if they were meant to reprobate some part of his past conduct. Whenever he was not engaged in conversation, such

thoughts were sure to rush into his mind; and for this reason, any company, any employment whatever, he preferred to being alone.

It would be to easy to claim Samuel Johnson's *New Dictionary of the English Language* as voluminous testimony to the Tourette's sufferer's love of lists, as hardbound incarnation of the obsessive's need-to-know. But like the dot art of Kusama, lexicography and conversation are more likely to have provided the Great Cham with a way of screening his tics and superstitions, of diverting himself from those compulsions he preferred simply to call 'bad habits'.

True Delusions

In one of the first clinical descriptions of a delusion, Phillipe Pinel, writing in 1800, described a patient who had fallen into 'a true delirium brought on by terrors of the revolution'. The man believed that he had been guillotined, but that judges had issued a belated reprieve, allowing his head to be reunited with his body. 'However, by an error of some sort, they put on his shoulders the head of another unfortunate. This idea that his head has been changed occupies him night and day. . . . "See my teeth!" he would repeat incessantly, "they used to be wonderful and these are rotten! My mouth was healthy and this one's infected. What a difference between this hair and the hair I had before my change of head." '

Psychiatrists recognise delusions as the major symptom of psychosis and a myriad of discrete disorders. As far back as 1758, Dr William Battie was arguing in his *Treatise on Madness* that the 'deluded imagination' was the essence of insanity. The madman was one who was 'unalterably persuaded of the existence or appearance of any thing, which either does not exist or does not actually appear to him, and who behaves according to such erroneous perception'.

Despite the diagnostic significance of delusions, their definition and classification remain in many ways unclear. The notion of delusions as 'false beliefs based on incorrect inference about external reality' is misleading. It is not so much that a schizo-phrenic patient believes that air-conditioning is being used to implant thoughts in her head, or that a flickering streetlight is an apocalyptic portent, that defines her as deluded. As clinicians do not investigate the actual bases of these or any other delusory beliefs, it is the *rationality*, not the *reality*, of such claims that is under scrutiny. Absence of evidence and the failure to engage with others' demands for supporting information equally define the clinical delusion. Other qualities that distinguish delusions from normal beliefs are their incorrigibility (their absolute imperviousness to counterargument) and the extent to which the individual is wholly preoccupied with them.

The emergence of a full-blown delusional system is often anticipated by a period of intellectual excitement in which everyday objects and events become invested with considerable but uncertain meaning. There is a sense of foreboding, of ominous significance, a wavering sense of some ineffable transformation having taken place. Sometimes referred to as a pre-delusional state, this period lays the foundation for what is to follow. Television advertisement, song lyrics, car registration numbers, one's own hands – all these things are freighted with insidious meaning. While there is some elation, this is principally a state of inchoate anxiety. Delusions make indirect sense of this confusion. Where there was uncertainty there will soon be absolute conviction.

At least four different categories of primary delusion now traverse the full spectrum of mental disorders. These *primary delusions* are perceived by many psychiatrists as 'random' and 'empty' constructions, devoid of psychological significance. Cognitive psychologists are, on the other hand, more disposed to regard delusions as reflecting or attempting to resolve intrapsychic conflict. They argue that personality factors do have some role in shaping the content of delusions. Delusions of persecution, for example, enable an individual to defend self-esteem by shifting responsibility for negative events on to others. That fact that delusions darkly mirror and distort metaphysical beliefs and cultural preoccupations is rather less contentious. Some comparative psychiatrists maintain that delusions are always linked to culturally critical issues, working the fault lines and stresses in the social fabric.

Delusions of persecution are the most common of all delusory beliefs, being typical of schizophrenia, manic depression, dementia and a number of organic disorders. As the psychiatrist

Ronald Siegel notes, 'Ordinary life is slowly, subtly filled with suspicion . . . It is suspicion in the literal meaning: to look below the surface for details. Scrutinizing everything, the paranoid looks for clues confirming the mistrust and doubt. This requires closed, focussed attention. It requires alertness and hypersensitivity to the smallest details. The paranoid seizes on these minor details, inflates their significance, and then works them into a logical systematic pattern.'

The hidden meanings and intentions that are sensed in paranoid schizophrenia and other disorders are known as ideas or *delusions of reference*. While the paranoid fasten on sinister plans and malicious acts, depressives are likely to be tormented by messages that denigrate and belittle, that make public their shortcomings and mental state. Litter at a bus stop may, for example, be an all too pointed insult. A casual smile, an overheard conversation, makes it known that she will punished. The content of delusions of reference is not necessarily negative, however. In a rare condition known to British psychiatrists as Le Clerembault's syndrome, the subject believes that a person that they are in love with – quite often someone they have never met – reciprocates these sentiments by oblique yet public communications.

Many schizophrenics succumb to *delusions of control*, imagining themselves in bondage to the kind of 'influencing machines' famously described by James Tilly Matthews and Daniel Paul Schreber. In a classic paper, 'On the Origin of the Influencing Machine in Schizophrenia' (1933), the Viennese psychiatrist Victor Tausk interpreted these delusions of mental manipulation as a regression to an 'original undifferentiated state'. As questionable as Tausk's theory is, his study of Natalija A, a former student of philosophy whose delusions of mind control began in her mid-twenties, is nevertheless revealing:

> She declares that for six and a half years she has been under the influence of an electrical machine made in Berlin, though the machine's use is prohibited by the police. It has the form of a human body, indeed the patient's own form, though not in all details. Her mother, like her male and female friends, is also under

the influence of the machine or similar machines. . . . She is certain that for men there is a masculine form representing the masculine form and for women a female one . . . The patient does not know definitely how this machine is to be handled, or how it is connected with her; but she vaguely thinks it is by means of telepathy. The outstanding fact about the machine is that it is being manipulated by someone in a certain manner, and everything that occurs to it also occurs to her. When someone strikes the machine she feels the blow in the corresponding part of her body. . . . The inner parts of the machine consist of electric batteries, which are supposed to represent the internal organs of the human body. Those who handle the machine produce a slimy substance in her nose, disgusting smells, dreams, thoughts, feelings, and disturb her while she is thinking, reading or writing. . . . The man who utilizes the apparatus to persecute her, her rejected suitor, a college professor, is prompted by jealousy.

The kinds of thought disturbance that this machine elucidates are threefold. First, it explains the direct insertion or implantation of ideas that the subject does not recognise as her own: unwanted thoughts that disrupt her thinking, words that she did not intend to say, memories that she has no connection to. Second, it sheds light on her inability to maintain a train of thought or conversation. The machine is siphoning her thoughts. It leaves her unable to recall what had occupied her attention, whom she is waiting to meet, what she was about to say. Lastly, such a machine may also help explain how others are able to read her thoughts. It allows them access to her thinking, makes her transparent to everyone.

These very powers may be also attributed directly to individuals and groups, including psychiatrists themselves. The German writer Unica Zurn, for instance, suspected that her doctors had formed a 'central thought agency'. 'This agency for thought', she wrote, 'unites the suggestible willpower of several doctors. Five or six doctors concentrate, for instance, on the abdomen of the patient and put her in a state of sensual pleasure.' Such agencies may also employ hypnosis, telepathy, state-of-the-art electronics or implants, but more antiquated techniques of mind control such as poisoning and spells are used as and when required. Interestingly, delusions of control are not only passive. Schizophrenics occasionally believe that they are, through their thoughts, gaze or some other emanating force, also responsible for the mental state of others.

The wild, frenetic highs of psychotic illness often steer the individual to an exaggerated sense of their own talents, intellect and self-importance. These *delusions of grandiosity* manifest themselves in claims of royal blood, elevated connection or the assumption of some other equally lofty identity – Jesus Christ, the Dalai Lama, the Virgin Mary, etc. Some manic-depressives and epileptics may experience inspired insight into religious and philosophical matters. The conviction of having discovered a great truth or guiding principle is akin to conversion, having much in common with the so-called 'creative illnesses' that are known to have played a significant part in the making of many spiritual leaders, from Ignatius of Loyola to Gurdjieff, as well as more recent gurus and cult leaders. They share the same absolute conviction, the same ability to assimilate and explain everything in terms of one overriding belief, the same unshakeable sense of destiny. The 'charisma of certainty', as the psychiatrist Anthony Storr calls it, enables these individuals to find support for their beliefs. In doing so, they transform their personal delusion into a collective faith.

While these principal types of delusion are apparent across many mental disorders, others are linked to more specific conditions. For example, in Alzheimer's disease, failing memory leads to delusions of theft. (The subject will often try to prevent these thefts by hiding her belongings. Forgetting that she has done so, she will return to the place that they are usually kept only to find that they have been stolen.) Organic conditions also have a part to play in delusory afflictions such as parasitosis, where the subject is convinced that insects, worms or internal parasites are lodged and crawling under the skin. Particularly common in cases of cocaine or amphetamine abuse, the delusion is a very plausible explanation for the very real sensations caused by blood constriction and thickening of dermal collagen. When dermatological tests are unable to confirm any infestation, subjects may resort to biting, gnawing and even torching their own skin.

Comparative studies of psychiatric symptoms in modern and developing countries have shown delusory thinking to be far more prevalent in modern societies. It has also been observed that Western delusions are principally self-focused, while those in the East are other-directed. A Japanese disorder known as *taijin-kyofu* is a prime example. Characterised by a neurotic concern with the effect of one's thoughts and behaviour on others, the condition caricatures the Japanese preoccupation with propriety and shame. Those suffering from *taijin-kyofu* may believe that their breath and body odours are foul; that they are unintentionally making people feel uncomfortable by glancing at them; or, worse still, that they are offending people by thinking thoughts aloud. In so far as they exaggerate, twist and invert elements of the wider culture, all delusions, from the paranoid to the grandiose, offer a tantalising glimpse of characteristics we so often fail to recognise in ourselves.

Manic Sunlight

Salvador Dalí was a man of many eccentricities, most of them as cultivated as the waxy curlicues of his trademark moustache. But for all his artistic pretensions, Dalí did have a genuine eye for the extraordinary. In the writings of Raymond Roussel, the Spanish painter discovered a talent that was altogether more strange and wayward, more fastidious and complex, than his own. Of Roussel's last verse novel, *Nouvelles impressions d'Afrique* – a book which he retained at his bedside for some fifty years – Dalí wrote that it was 'of all the books of our era . . . the most ungraspably poetic'.

The origins of Roussel's anti-travelogue of Africa – a book composed behind the closed shutters of a custom-built caravan, entirely immune to the elements, landscape and events that passed it by – can, as with all his other equally solipsistic writings, be traced back to the 1890s, when, at the age of nineteen, Roussel suddenly turned from music to literature, believing that he would complete a prodigious work before he reached twenty. The 'curious crisis' that he underwent allowed him to work tirelessly, day and night, while in a vast, luminescent rapture:

One understands by some peculiar means that one is creating a masterpiece, that one is a prodigy; there are child prodigies who have revealed their genius at the age of nineteen. I was the equal of Dante and Shakespeare, I was feeling what Victor Hugo had felt when he was seventy, what Napoleon had felt in 1811 . . . I experienced *la gloire* . . . Whatever I wrote was surrounded by rays of light; I used to close the curtains for I was afraid that the shining rays emanating from my pen might escape into the outside world through even the smallest chink; I wanted suddenly to throw back the screen and light up the world. To leave these papers lying about would have sent out rays of light as far as China and the desperate crowd would have flung themselves upon my house. But it was in vain that I took such precautions, for rays of light were streaming through me and through the walls, I was carrying the sun within myself and could do nothing to impede the tremendous light I was radiating. Each line was repeated in thousands of copies, and I wrote with a thousand flaming pen-nibs. . . . I was at that moment in a state of unheard of bliss, a single blow of the pickaxe had opened up entire seams of marvels, I had won the most dazzling first prize. I lived more during that time than in any other period of existence.

Roussel was in his mid-thirties when he began to visit the renowned psychologist Pierre Janet – who would later include a case study of Roussel (under the pseudonym 'Martial') in his book *De l'angoisse à l'extase*. By this time, the 'seam of marvels' had fallen away, leaving only an underbelly of private obsessions and fixations. Roussel now fasted for days at a time, fearing that eating would spoil his serenity. He refused to travel at night for fear of entering a tunnel. He thought sex was losing the 'charm of taboo' and was preoccupied with the laxity of modern dress. His standards of hygiene extended to using twenty-five handkerchiefs a week and following an elaborate system that ensured no suit or overcoat would be worn more than fifteen times. Socially, he was inept in the extreme: fearing that he might offend or be offended, he assailed new acquaintances with a barrage of purely factual questions.

More than anything, Roussel wanted to recover the diet of 'moral sunlight' that sustained him while writing *La Doublure*. This labyrinthine work, which had failed to make any impact on the literary world, was born of energies and emotions that he had permanently lost. 'I seek it always,' Roussel confided to Janet. 'I will seek it forever. I would give all my remaining years of life to relive one instant of that glory.' Janet, an expert on nervous disorders, considered Roussel's mania to have been a close cousin of the transports of the Christian saints and mystics, whose fervour was now displaced and channelled towards aesthetic ends. Roussel's mood swings and anxieties, his monumental profligacy in financing the staging and publishing of his own work, these were all, according to Janet, the lingering side effects of his first crisis. Roussel's blinkered pursuit of his exalted mania allowed him no sense of what his illness had deprived him of. Far from it, Roussel reprinted portions of Janet's case study in his later writings. And, shortly before his death in 1933, he instructed his publishers that all future editions of his work should include, as a frontispiece, a picture of himself taken in Milan, in 1896, during the long summer of his inspired malady. The same photograph was later sent to a firm of funerary sculptors, with a view to commissioning a final tribute to *la gloire*.

The grandiosity of the manic episode has a long history of clinical description. In *De Causis et Signis Morborum*, the Alexandrian physician Aretaeus described the euphoric trajectory of mania: 'without being cultivated he [the maniac] says he is a philosopher . . . and the incompetent [announce themselves] good artisans . . . he feels great and inspired'. Like Roussel, the ancients also experienced a new-found power and vitality, to the point that 'some refused to urinate for fear of causing a new deluge'. For Aretaeus, mania was 'nothing else but melancholia in more intense form', but it was the latter that continued to claim a genuine association with intellectual and artistic temperament. When mania and melancholia were eventually recognised as the fluctuating poles of the same disease, now known as manic depression, or bipolar disorder, the imaginative potential of mania was finally recognised.

Considering the signs and symptoms of mania, in its major and minor forms, it should come as no surprise that so many artists and writers have found their work propelled by its unbridled momentum and self-possession. Kay Redfield Jamison, Professor of Psychiatry at Johns Hopkins University, writes:

[D]uring hypomania and mania, mood is generally elevated and expansive . . . activity and energy levels are greatly increased; the need for sleep is decreased; speech is often rapid, excitable, and intrusive; and thinking is fast, moving quickly from topic to topic. Hypomanic or manic individuals usually have an inflated self-esteem, as well as a certainty of conviction about the correctness and importance of their ideas. This grandiosity can contribute to poor judgement, which, in turn, often results in chaotic patterns of personal and professional relationships . . . spending excessive amounts of money, impulsive involvements in questionable endeavours, reckless driving, extreme impatience, intense and impulsive romantic or sexual liaisons.'

At its worst, mania can be wildly delusory, giving rise to disturbed and paranoid thoughts, but the more usual signature of manic thinking is exuberant and divergent. The fluency of ideas and expression, the ability to interweave ideas, to simultaneously pursue different associations as opposed to one fixed train of thought, did not fail to impress the early clinical observers. In 1913, the Swiss psychiatrist Eugen Bleuler observed that:

The *thinking* of the manic is flighty. He jumps by by-paths from one subject to another, and cannot adhere to anything. With this the ideas run along very easy and involuntarily . . . Because of the more rapid flow of ideas, and especially because of the falling off of inhibitions, artistic activities are often facilitated even though something worthwhile is produced only in very mild cases and when the patient is otherwise talented in this direction. The heightened sensibilities naturally have the effect of furthering this.

That poets and writers should be so prone to the highs and lows of manic depression might appear to tell us something about the occupational hazards of solitude and prolonged introspection. However, these factors are rarely accorded any *causative* impact on manic depression. Seasonal patterns, family distribution and twin studies provide strong evidence for genetic transmission. If one identical twin suffers from manic depression, there is a 67 per cent chance that the sibling will be affected. In the case of a fraternal twin, this is reduced to 20 per cent. All the same, these and other statistics do not preclude psychological and social influences. Given that almost 30 per cent of individuals who carry the predisposing genes – whichever genes they may be – do not develop the disease, the role of environmental triggers cannot be ruled out.

Recent research into the style and content of 'manic art' describes this oeuvre as 'bold', 'busy', and 'confused', characterised by 'anger', 'sensuousness', 'wildness' and 'ebullience'. These same qualities are apparent in 'manic writing', which demonstrates an increase in the use of rhyme, puns and word associations. Hypomania appears to provide the perfect admix of energy and divergency without the calamitous derailing of thinking that occurs in acute mania. Like many, the British writer John Custance found it impossible to put pen to paper when his manic mood rose too high. When he did manage 'to get it down' the results were disconcerting. 'Unfortunately, when I come to read what I have written in cold blood, after the manic excitement has passed, I can barely make head or tail of it and very often its appalling egocentricity makes me sick.'

Over the past sixty years or so, a number of studies have sought to use biographical material relating to writers, artists and composers to belatedly diagnose and study the effects of manic depression. There are obvious problems with this case history approach: many, if not all, of the symptoms of schizophrenia can occur in manic-depressive illness; letters, diaries and medical records rarely provide evidence for emphatic diagnosis. Well aware of these problems, Kay Redfield Jamison has conducted a study of mood disorders among major British and Irish poets born between 1705 and 1805. Only one in six of this constituency provided no indication of a significant mood disorder. Compared with current rates of manic depression among the general population, Jamison found that poets were thirty times more likely to suffer from mood disorder, and at least twenty times as likely to be committed to an asylum. Despite using different diagnostic criteria, all studies of the psychopathology of writers and artists, past and present, confirm this trade-off. Arnold M. Ludwig's monumental study of the mental health of 1004 eminent men and women, *The Price of Greatness*, found that 87 per cent of poets experienced some form of psychiatric illness. Of these, about 70 per cent experienced a mood disorder, and 18 per cent committed suicide. Explorers and natural scientists were the least affected.

As with so many writers and artists, Virginia Woolf suffered the type of manic depression that is known to have had extensive antecedence, traceable through both maternal and paternal family lines. Woolf's first manic episode occurred at the age of thirteen. This was followed by intermittent periods of depression and mania, each lasting two to three months. In 1914, Woolf experienced her most sustained period of depression, plunging her into a near-suicidal torpor which soon gave way to euphoria. A pattern of alternating depression and mania now established itself. While her depression stalled her writing – leaving her fit only for critical reviews, rather than fiction – her hypomania allowed it to flourish. In these periods, she described herself as 'a porous vessel afloat on sensation; a sensitive plate exposed to invisible rays'. Voices sometimes spoke to her, and she was more than ready to yield to them. These experiences prompted her to search, in her autobiography, for childhood intimations of the same trans-cendent truth – to recover similar moments of 'purest ecstasy'.

Yet Woolf's recurrent 'glooms' were not just the blank punctuation to her creative outpouring. They were, she came to believe, a necessary ballast and counterperspective. This kind of 'critical editorial role', as Jamison calls it, is not uncommon. Many writers have found that depression produces a cold, analytical attitude to their own work. 'Depression', writes Jamison, 'prunes and sculpts; it also ruminates and ponders and, ultimately subdues and focuses thought.' But for every poem or novel that has been burnished through this process of reflection and revision, how many have been permanently discarded?

Even in illness, Roussel was atypical. For all his anxieties and obsessions, he was never to experience the persistent mood swings of Woolf and other literary manic-depressives. His life and work was a non-stop homage to himself: to the magical half-year he had entered into himself most fully. Through his writing, Roussel created a world that was equally self-intoxicated. The humble pun provided him with his secret method. As laborious and convoluted as his technique was – one line could take up to fifteen hours – the lost 'sensations of art' he sought to rescue were more than worth it.

Hearing Voices

The French poet and artist Henri Michaux spent the best part of a decade writing and painting while under the influence of mescaline, cannabis, LSD and other drugs. Of all the experiences he endured during these experiments in 'co-habitation', few were more unsettling than the voices he heard repeating and ridiculing his unspoken thoughts, the foreign voices that jeered him, the surging murmurs that filled the afternoon silence of his apartment. Michaux was no stranger to hallucination. All sorts of drug-induced phantasms had paraded themselves before him – crumpled lizards and mechanical giraffes, trees that heckled, photographs that were spirited to life. The music of oboes and barrel organs had on one occasion drifted in from nowhere, sliding under the door to his apartment. But none of these hallucinations confounded him, left him feeling quite so estranged. The voices were something else: their reality could not be tested. They were 'secondary personages' that inhabited him and could not be eluded.

Michaux's objective was to examine the 'endless hoax' of madness. The types of voice that he experienced broadly corresponded to those identified by the psychiatrist Kurt Schneider in his 1939 classification of the first-rank symptoms of schizophrenia, namely: voices that repeat or anticipate the subject's own thinking; that discuss and comment in the third person; that give running commentary to the subject's thoughts or behaviour. These voices remain the *sine qua non* of schizophrenia, as well as indicating other mental disorders. A covert study of diagnostic practice conducted in a number of American hospitals in the 1970s found that the majority of researchers who presented themselves at psychiatric hospitals claiming to hear voices were quickly diagnosed as schizophrenic. Little has changed. Psychiatrists waste no time in establishing the presence of voices, but tend to be indifferent to their content.

The medicalisation of hallucinations or diseased perceptions began in the late eighteenth century, before the asylum system had begun to establish itself. It was not until the second half of the nineteenth century, however, that Henry Maudsley and his clinical contemporaries would deem virtually all auditory hallucinations as pathological. Saint Paul, Emanuel Swedenborg, George Fox and John Wesley were just a few of the great and good which Maudsley's *Natural Causes and Supernatural Seemings* (1886) considered as having suffered from epilepsy, rather than having been blessed by mystical insight. Like so many thinkers of his day, Maudsley endorsed the belief that hallucinations were more common in the 'savage and barbarous mind . . . occurring more readily in young children than adults.' The one exception to this rule was the visual and auditory hallucinations perceived 'when suddenly awaking out of sleep'.

In *Voices of Reason, Voices of Insanity* (2000), Ivan Leudar and Philip Thomas argue that Maudsley's distinction has become enshrined in clinical practice, with psychiatrists establishing whether voices are heard in clear consciousness or in a state of reduced vigilance. In practice, however, there are few questions that psychiatrists ask about voices. Having established the rudiments of their content, personality and the mood states that they arise in, voices are dismissed. 'In psychiatry,' Leudar and Thomas write, 'voices have little or no meaning . . . the psychiatrist feels that the very act of talking with the subject about the voices may increase their preoccupation with imperative demands, making it more likely that they will act on them.' This partly explains why the voices of schizophrenia remain so misunderstood. The notion that ghostly voices admonish, castigate and impel the schizophrenic, urging him towards desperate action, is not borne out by recent research. This is only part of the picture.

A number of surveys have attempted to measure the extent to which voices are heard among the general population. When

Edmund Parish published his *Hallucinations and Illusions* in 1897, he suggested that between 10 and 30 per cent of people experienced auditory hallucinations or other 'fallacious perceptions'. This went way beyond the 1890 survey conducted by the Society for Psychical Research. Fewer than 10 per cent of the 17,000 persons interviewed in this survey claimed to have experienced 'a vivid impression of seeing or being touched by a living being or inanimate object, or of hearing a voice . . . not due to any external physical cause'. Of these positive responses, only a quarter described auditory hallucinations. The voices were more often than not unidentified, but were, perhaps surprisingly, more likely to be voices of the living rather than the deceased.

A follow-up survey conducted by Mass Observation in 1947 secured 1500 questionnaire responses to much the same questions. Again, the voices were generally attributed to unrecognised or living people. Almost three times more women than men had multiple hallucinations. The most comprehensive survey of vocal hallucinations to date was carried out across five American cities in 1991. Of 18,500 people interviewed, 2 per cent claimed to have heard voices of some description. A 1998 MIND study of childhood voices arrived at the same figure, suggesting that children are in fact no more likely to hallucinate than adults are.

Although the voices of schizophrenia can be a source of permanent distress, all the above studies suggest that they exist on a continuum with those voices reported by the population at large. The similarity is particularly striking in the case of the hallucinations among those who have suffered abuse, trauma and bereavement. Marcus Romme, Professor of Psychiatry at the University of Maastricht, has been a prominent campaigner for the normalising of voices. Arguing that the diagnosis and treatment of voices in schizophrenia may compound and make the symptoms more difficult to manage, he and his Dutch colleagues seek to promote a positive approach to voice-hearing that relies neither on therapy nor on medication. 'We should let people decide for themselves what helps nor not,' says Romme. The Voice Hearing Network that he has been active in establishing has a burgeoning membership who claim ownership of their condition, seeking to better cope with their voices, rather than eradicate them.

The history of vocal hallucination lends some plausibility to the argument that voices are an essential aspect of human psychology. In *The Origin of Consciousness in the Breakdown of the Bicameral Mind*, the late Princeton psychologist Julian Jaynes brilliantly argued that voice hearers are akin to the heroes of *The Iliad* and the prophets of the Old Testament, who were guided by voice of king or god. Jaynes suggests that 'the occasion of an hallucination was stress, as it is in our contemporaries', particularly the 'the stress caused by a son's death'.

Between 3000 and 1000 BC, the bicameral mind – which was able to function as two separate hemispheres, or 'persons' – was, according to Jaynes, on the road to unified consciousness. Jaynes's explanation of the demise of vocal hallucinations has been criticised for being overly neurological, but his argument is in fact more subtle, proposing that any number of environmental changes could have dampened the power of the now speechless right brain. While Jaynes traces the impact of agriculture, cities and dynasties as civilising influences, Professor Walter Ong has good grounds for arguing that Jaynes does not make enough of a case for the shift from orality to literacy. All the characteristics of the bicameral mind can, says Ong, be found in oral cultures past and present.

The frequency of vocal hallucinations among developing populations is well established. DOSMED (Determinants of Outcome of Severe Mental Disorders) studies of psychiatric symptoms conducted by the World Health Organisation in the 1980s and '90s found that auditory and visual hallucinations are far more common in traditional societies. (The same symptoms are, however, more persistent and less favourable in modern societies.) A folk illness such as *ukutwasa* is a good example of the way in which voice-hearing is ritualised in a traditional society. Among the Tembu people of South Africa, the 'illness' begins when the 'River People' are heard calling. As listlessness gives way to anxiety, the afflicted person runs to a river, hoping to obtain powers of healing and divination. All kinds of auditory hallucinations may be present in *ukutwasa*. It is at once a visionary state *and* a mental illness. Its outcome depends on the individual's capacity to learn from his illness, to master it and to convince others of his newly found powers.

Yet the voices that once spoke spontaneously to the bicameral mind are also roused in primitive societies by 'techniques of ecstasy' in which plant intoxicants play an important role. While Chuckee and Tungus healers have traditionally used fly-agaric to invoke the voices of spirits (which would be spoken through him), the Mazatec Indians have employed a different mushroom, *Psilocybe mexicana.* Two conclusions can be drawn from the use of intoxicants to hear supernatural voices. First, orality alone is not enough to explain the capacity for auditory hallucinations – even in societies that have no system of writing, hallucinations are far from the norm. Second, the use of plant drugs to achieve hallucination may, as Jaynes suggests, be a direct consequence of the breakdown of the bicameral mind. This would certainly accord with the religious historian Mircea Eliade's claim that the use of plant sacraments is a belated addition to the shaman's magical office.

Cognitive psychologists understand vocal hallucinations as a failure in the monitoring of inner speech. As Richard Bentall explains, inner speech is what 'we use when thinking and regulating our own behaviour. We use this internal dialogue to monitor our own actions, to make plans for the future, to decide what to do. . . . Even when thinking silently in words, however, small movements of the vocal cords can be detected . . . This phenomenon is known as *sub-vocalization* and reflects the fact that thinking is literally internalized self-talk.' A failure in the ability to monitor 'self-talk' can be easily induced by the use of auditory feedback. This technique involves having the pitch of one's recorded spoken words and phrases altered and replayed via headphones. A 1999 experiment conducted by Louise Johns and Philip McGuire at Withington Hospital, Manchester, demonstrated that schizophrenic patients find it more difficult to recognise their own voices, even when the pitch is only moderately altered. Moreover, they are far more inclined to attribute voices to another person than to demonstrate uncertainty. Interestingly, this externalisation was particularly apparent when the words they heard being spoken were derogatory.

Brain-imaging studies of schizophrenics during auditory hallucinations show, as Jaynes's work would suggest, heightened involvement of the right temporal lobe. To counteract these right-sided hallucinations, low-frequency stimulation has been used as an experimental treatment in small-scale trials. Stimulation of the left tempoparietal cortex, which plays an important role in speech perception, has been shown to have some success in interrupting hallucinations, with some patients reporting total eradication of voices for weeks after treatment.

The very notion of a medical cure for voices is, of course, disputed by Romme and by many voice hearers themselves. To dispel unwelcome hallucinations, voice hearers have developed techniques that are far simpler and often just as effective. Listening to a Walkman or reading aloud can, for example, block out voices without the unwelcome side effects of anti-psychotic drugs. On the other hand, there are others who are more than happy to listen to their voices, to engage with these 'second personages' without being unduly vexed. This might be a useful skill, but it is certainly not, as one voice hearer has recently claimed, a qualification in primitive magic.

Experimental Delirium

In his 1838 treatise *The Mental Maladies*, the French alienist Jean-Etienne Dominique Esquirol remarked: 'A man is in delirium when his sensations are not at all in agreement with external objects, when his ideas are not at all in agreement with his sensations, when his judgements and his resolutions are not at all in agreement with his ideas, when his ideas, judgements, and resolutions are independent of his volition.' Although Esquirol here used the term 'delirium' as a synonym for insanity writ large, the term referred equally to the more transient disturbances of thought and perception witnessed in febrile illnesses. This other delirium was madness in miniature. Known as *phrenitis* to Greek and Roman writers, its occurrence had been well documented in relation to insomnia, hysteria and acute intoxication. From the sixteenth century onwards, medical writing continued to describe the symptoms of delirium in its 'low' and 'raving' forms, always stressing the fundamental connections between delirium and dreaming. Eventually, in the 1840s, Jean-Jacques Joseph Moreau de Tours, a former pupil of Esquirol, began to study and report on delirium from a more intimate perspective.

Moreau, the young alienist, had accompanied patients on therapeutic tours of Switzerland, Italy and the Orient in the 1830s. In Egypt, he discovered *dawamesc*, an aromatic cannabis paste which the local *hashishin* freely indulged. On returning to Paris, Moreau set about using this fabled drug as 'a powerful, unique, means of exploring the subject of pathology', and delirium in particular. To this end, he set about experimenting on himself, making observations and collecting testimonies from fellow physicians.

Moreau first experienced the effects of hashish at a dinner party in December of 1841, in the presence of friends, his wife and young son. His testimony is perhaps the first alienist's account of madness from within. While eating oysters, Moreau is seized by gales of laughter. After watching the food on his plate mutate into a lion's head, he begins to spar with a compote of sugared fruit. He leaves the dining room to find a piano, where he plays an aria from Auber's *Le Domino noir*. After a few minutes, the music conjures an apparition of his brother, who stands upon the piano holding a fork adorned with three coloured lanterns. Suddenly, Moreau feels his body as a dead weight. He kneels, as if to pray, but in a sudden change of mood begins to dance the polka while imitating actors he has recently seen perform. Moving into an unlit room, he feels as if he is choking and falling into a bottomless pit. His cries alert friends, who take him back into the dining room. A million insects begin to devour his head, but he is concerned only with one – the resident on the third hair from the left on his forehead – which he believes to be in labour.

He now begins to reminisce and is transported back to a dinner he had attended five years before. This scene gives way to a vision of his smiling, cherubic son, suspended in a blue and silver sky. Overcome with joy, Moreau plummets from these celestial heights into a 'country of lanterns'. His eyes burn. He quickly concludes that his servant must have waxed them, and that he is now polishing them with a brush.

On drinking a glass of lemonade, he is dispatched down the river Seine and into a swimming pool where he almost drowns. Friends come to the rescue, but while he is being saved he sees his brother crossing the Pont des Arts. Because his ideas are 'too bizarre to be credible', he tries to remain silent, but his antics have already awoken his young son, who was sleeping on his mother's lap. These cries momentarily bring him to his senses. He hugs his child, but is led away by friends who fear that he is in the midst of a crisis. The affront leads Moreau to declare that this is not his son, but the child of a childless woman who has long envied him, and leaves. On his return, an absent friend whose head is adorned with an enormous rat greets him.

Moreau's account of his hashish misadventure echoed many of the features of delirium outlined by Soranus of Ephesus in the first century AD. As the condition developed, Soranus observed that there was:

> quiet or loud laughter, singing, or a state of sadness, silence, murmuring, crying, or a barely audible muttering to one's self; or such a state of anger that the patient jumps in a rage and can scarcely be held back, is wrathful at everyone, shouts, beats himself or tears his own clothing and that of his neighbours, or seeks to hide in fear, or weeps, or fails to answer those who speak to him, while he speaks not only with those who are not present but with the dead, as if they were in his presence.

Yet Moreau claimed even more of his experience. 'There is not a single, elementary manifestation of mental illness', he announced, 'that cannot be found in the mental changes caused by hashish, from simple manic excitement to frenzied delirium.' First, he explained, hashish unleashed a train of uncontrollable ideas. Second, it gave rise to obsessions and delusions. Third, it eroded volition and led to impulsive behaviour. Fourth, it produced the hallucinations and illusions that were characteristic of psychosis.

Moreau insisted that he had retained a wavering insight throughout his fantasia, being at once within and without his delirium. This double state was, he maintained, exactly analogous to a *sleepless dream*, where sleep and waking are mingled and confused. 'The clearest, most alert consciousness cannot distinguish between these two states, nor between the mental operations that characterize either one.' On the edge of delirium, never entirely within it, Moreau was convinced that 'the benefit of self-observation' had allowed him to espy the true nature of insanity. Delirium was, he argued, at root a dissociation of thinking, and this intellectual damage was responsible for the wild excesses of emotion.

Moreau, who went on to co-found the Club des Haschischins, playing the role of Arab-garbed master of ceremonies to the Parisian *haut monde* with some aplomb, was hardly the first physician to suggest a parallel between dreams and insanity. The pathological characteristics of dreaming had been commented on throughout the classical period. However, this analogy was inverted in the seventeenth century, so that, as Michel Foucault observed, 'it is madness which takes its original nature from the dream.' But Moreau's claims were more literal: the delirium of insanity was, he held, a direct intrusion of dream thinking and perception into the waking consciousness. This same explanation of delirium was in turn advanced by Alfred Maury in his 1861 book *Le Sommeil et les rêves*, and again, twenty years on, by Ernest Lasègue in the strangely titled paper 'Alcoholic Delirium is not a Delirium, but it is a dream'. Almost a full century after Moreau's first investigation, EEG technology confirmed that delirium did in fact bear the physiological traces of dreaming within wakefulness.

Moreau's claims for hashish were nevertheless excessive. Leaving aside his attempts to champion hashish as a cure for mental illness – which earnt him the ridicule of Baudelaire – hashish did not reveal each and every symptom of delirium in equal measure. Hashish stirred the milder and more fleeting aspects of delirium, not its fugitive far side. Acute delirium involves profound and extended episodes of dissociation that cannot be recollected. There is no narrative for true delirium. It can be observed only from the outside.

While alcohol and cocaine will, if consumed in prodigious quantities over an extended period of time, give rise to these extremes, plant drugs such as deadly nightshade (*Atropa belladonna*), black henbane (*Hyoscyamus niger*) and thorn-apple (*Datura stramonium*) are the chemical masters of delirium. Having provided the ingredients for the flying ointments of medieval witches, these plants – which Moreau was also interested in – have a long history of purported connections with supernatural and criminal activities. That their delirium is different to that produced by hashish is well established. Discussing the effects of belladonna poisoning, Dr Forbes Winslow, a well-known Victorian physician, noted that:

> One of the marvellous effects of continued doses is the production of a singular psychological phenomenon. A delirium supervenes,

unaccompanied by any fantasia, or imaginary illusion, whose marked characteristic is somnambulism. An individual who has taken it in several doses seems to be perfectly alive to surrounding objects, his senses conveying faithfully to the brain the impressions that they receive; he goes through his usual avocations without exhibiting any unwonted feeling, yet he is quite unconscious of his existence, and performs mechanically all that he is accustomed to do . . . When this state of somnambulism passes away, the individual has not the slightest recollection of what occurred to him; he reverts to that which immediately preceded the attack, nor can any allusion to his apparent reverie induce him to believe that he has excited any attention. The case of the tailor who remained on his shopboard for fifteen hours, using all the gestures which his business requires, moving his lips as if speaking, yet the whole time perfectly insensible, has been frequently quoted. It was produced by belladonna.

There was nevertheless one 'psychological phenomenon' that this family of substances could never have stimulated in Moreau. On the first occasion he took hashish – and, more than probably, on subsequent occasions – Moreau felt a vitality and abundance of certain feelings that he considered inappropriate for discussion in a 'serious work'. 'Plato himself could not have dreamed of purer and more spiritual passions than those kindled by hashish,' he rhapsodised. Even after the effects of hashish had disappeared, Moreau hinted that a newly amplified capacity for love and affection remained with him.

While the spiritual dimension that Moreau struggled to address remains a neglected corner of febrile and toxic states, delirium has performed a minor role in the history of religious illumination. Only a few years before Moreau became intimate with hashish, Cardinal John Henry Newman suffered a near-fatal bout of typhoid fever while travelling in Sicily. He later reflected: 'I had a most consoling and overpowering thought of God's electing love and seemed to feel I was His, all my feelings, painful and pleasant, were, I believe, heightened by the delirium.' Was this the *agape* that Moreau secretly discovered in the madness of hashish?

The Impersonators

Not long after Freud published his essay on 'The Occurrence in Dreams of Material from Fairy Tales' (1913), the French psychiatrist Joseph Capgras encountered a 'fantastic but systematised delusion' that could have come straight out of the Brothers Grimm, not to mention Borges or Philip K. Dick. Capgras's first patient, 'Madame M', believed that she was the victim of a complex plot in which her husband and daughter, her concierge and fellow tenants, were all replaced by doubles. Up to 28,000 people in all had, according to Madame M, been abducted and locked up in underground dungeons and vaults. Each of these had been substituted by doubles 'whose acting is good enough to prove convincing'. The doctors at the hospitals of Saint-Anne and Maison-Blanche had up to fifteen doubles, the sisters had up to fifty, her husband eighty. Between 1914 and 1918, her daughter was replaced by no fewer than 2000 doubles.

At least two clinicians had before described individual instances of this kind of pathological misidentification, but neither anticipated that it might represent a more general delusion. The term that Capgras settled on in his 1923 paper, '*illusion de sosies*' (illusion of doubles), never assumed any currency. By the end of the 1920s, French and German psychiatrists had elected 'Capgras' syndrome' as the preferred appellation. To this day the syndrome remains, alongside Fregoli and Cotard, one of the most enigmatic of all pathological delusions. Whereas the Fregoli delusion involves one and the same persecutor seen in the guise of various strangers, cases of Cotard involve delusions of disembodiment that are typically connected with depressive states. The Capgras delusion, by contrast, sees any significant other derealised, replaced by one or more lookalikes.

Having initially favoured an organic explanation of the delusion, Capgras and his colleagues quickly turned to Freudian theory. The presumption that Capgras' syndrome was a purely mental phenomenon, occurring only in females, led this first wave of investigators to link the delusion to the peculiar development of female sexuality. (Unlike the male child, for whom the mother is the love object throughout the oedipal phase, Freud argued that the female child is twice thwarted: required to transfer her desire to her father.) Feminine psychology was thus thought to account for the denial of identity that occurred in Capgras' syndrome. As a way of regulating and balancing mixed emotions towards any familial member, the delusion made perfect womanly sense to the Freudians. So much so that there appears to have been definite resistance to the idea that Capgras' syndrome was anything other than feminine. When a male case of Capgras was eventually reported in 1936, the patient's latent homosexuality was thought to account for its occurrence.

By the 1970s, when more than fifty cases of the syndrome were extensively reviewed and subjected to more systematic scrutiny, the presumed sexual division of the condition was, along with other long-standing assumptions, proved wrong. Far from being almost exclusively associated with women, about 40 per cent of the cases reported in English-language journals were male. The objects of the delusion were also more varied and shifting than had been previously acknowledged. Besides spouses and children, siblings, employers, pets and virtual strangers were all liable to be perceived as doubles and lookalikes. Furthermore, this derealisation occasionally extended to belongings and other material objects, which the patient claimed a double had replaced with identical fakes.

Combined with the syndrome's increasing occurrence in connection with organic disorders, these observations have led to more cautious theorising. The concept of cognitive dissonance, developed by the social psychologist Leon Festinger, has been used by neuropsychologists to explain the process by which the Capgras patient resolves the tension that arises from this absence of emotional connection to significant others. Festinger described dissonance as the distressing state which arises when individuals 'find themselves doing things that don't fit with what they know, or having opinions that don't fit with others they hold'. Festinger demonstrated that, to resolve this incompatibility, individuals would invariably change their attitudes to accommodate their behaviour. In the case of the Capgras patient, the conviction that there has been some unaccountable transformation in the other appears to be such a strategy for resolving dissonance.

The more radical step taken by the neuroscientist V. S. Ramachandran is to entirely reject any psychological explanation. In his study of 'Arthur', the thirty-year-old son of a diplomat who awoke from a coma to find that his real father had employed a legion of doubles to take care of him, Ramachandran notes some of the interesting anomalies that led him to reject any Freudian-minded interpretation. First, Arthur's delusion was wavering, punctuated by a reluctant, 'intellectual' acceptance of his father's true identity. Second, the denial of his father's identity only occurred in the field of vision – his father was accepted as such when he spoke on the phone. By experimentally testing these and other slippages of recognition, Ramachandran concluded that Capgras' syndrome was best explained as a disconnection of the emotional element of recognition; in neurological terms, a failure in the relay of information from the visual centres to the amygdala.

This did not, however, explain cases of misidentification where the double is actually preferred to the original. More to the point, the neurology of the Capgras delusion could not account for any of the particular delusions and beliefs that emerge as explanations. Although 'Arthur' did not elaborate or rationalise his father's replacement, many cases of Capgras delusion give rise to delusional belief systems. The narratives that attempt to account for mysterious doubling are varied, but in tune with more general paranoiac delusions. One patient believed that his stepfather was a hi-tech android; another patient that his entire family had been killed by Chinese communists and replaced by doubles. In some cases, Capgras sufferers feel themselves persecuted by the doubles, living in fear of being poisoned or sexually or mentally abused. It

is in these instances that family members and attendant pro-
fessionals may be conscripted into the delusion, being accused of
being doubles or of having themselves killed the originals. A
number of these themes are evident in the following account of a
middle-aged woman who admitted herself to hospital, 'to prove to
my husband that I'm not crazy'. There is, however, a less than
clearly developed 'plot' or delusional system. Instead, a series of
random 'clues' leads to the multiplication of husband doubles and
the appearance of new ones:

> . . . she told the staff that her husband's twin brother (there is no
> such person) had been intermittently taking his place since their
> marriage four years ago. . . . The substitution first occurred on
> their wedding day, when her husband went to the men's room and
> an impostor took his place. As evidence, she produced snapshots
> from the wedding, comparing pictures of her husband and his
> 'twin'. When the pictures failed to prove convincing, she claimed
> that the best ones had mysteriously disappeared. Although
> unemployed and living on welfare, she believed that she was
> married for her money and that an attempt was being made to
> drive her crazy. In addition, she complained that her husband had
> been making sexual advances, constantly putting his hands on her
> and even inspecting her genitals with a flashlight. . . . Further
> interviewing revealed that the patient could distinguish the
> impostor by his greater height; she 'could fit her head under her
> impostor's chin but not her husband's'. After one visit from her
> husband, she expressed the conviction that it was the impostor
> who had visited. She noted that the pair of pants he wore had
> always been too long for her husband, but fitted the visitor
> perfectly. She also believed in a *second double* of her husband who
> had a rotten green toenail. Once she event went so far as calling
> the police and demanding that her husband remove his sock. She
> also offered a vague theory that her husband stayed in a motel in
> Canada when an impostor filled his place. During her hospital stay
> she vacillated as to whether or not a third double existed. . . . [A
> few weeks before being discharged] she asked her therapist if he
> had a 'brother' working in the hospital.

69

As an attempt to explain the uncanny feeling of strangeness which familiar people evoke, the identification of doubles and lookalikes is entirely rational. The Capgras delusion is not a failure of *reasoning*, it is an attempt to explain the absence of emotional connection produced by a failure of recognition. In contrast to truly paranoid delusions, there is often a lack of conviction in the working hypothesis that the Capgras patient constructs, and partial awareness of its fabrication. This is clearly evident in the following conversation between a psychiatrist and a Capgras patient who reported that his family had been replaced by doubles:

Doctor: Isn't that unusual?
Patient: It was unbelievable!
Doctor: How do you account for it?
Patient: I don't know. I try to understand it myself, and it was virtually impossible.
Doctor: What if I told you I don't believe it?
Patient: That's perfectly understandable. In fact, when I tell the story, I feel that I'm concocting a story . . . It's not quite right. Something is wrong.

See Me Now

After separating from his wife and family, August Strindberg arrived in Paris in the summer of 1890 half expecting some kind of catastrophe to befall him. Shortly after checking into his hotel, Strindberg discovered that a stranger was occupying the room opposite his writing desk. 'This unknown man never uttered a word; he seemed to be occupied in writing something behind the partition that separated us. All the same it was odd that he should push back his chair every time I moved mine. He repeated my every movement in a way that suggested that he wanted to annoy me by imitating me.' After three days, the stranger appeared to change rooms, but Strindberg could still hear him, 'lying there, stretched out parallel to me. I could hear him turning the pages of a book, putting out a lamp, turning over and falling asleep.'

Strindberg never actually saw the stranger who imitated his every move, but plenty of writers had already described the circumstances under which they had met their doppelgängers. Out riding, Goethe encountered his exact likeness dressed in different clothes. Maupassant, while suffering from syphilis-induced psychosis, listened to his double dictate a section of the short story he was then working on. Shelley, plagued by hallucinations for much of his adult life, observed his double on many occasions. In the summer of 1822, while he was in Pisa, the double spoke to him in Italian. 'How long do you mean to be content?' Three weeks later, Shelley was dead.

'The story of the modern double', writes the literary critic Karl Miller, 'starts with the magical science of the eighteenth century in Europe, when Mesmerists and Animal Magnetists went in for an experimental separation of the second self, and romantic writers went in for its cultural exploitation. Jean Paul Richter invented the term doppelgänger . . . Goethe, Tieck, Kleist, among other German writers of the time, sped the progress of the subject.' The nineteenth-century 'craze for duality' may well have emerged from this confluence of medical and literary sources, but the second self, the double and the doppelgänger are not, as Miller is aware, synonymous. For literary purposes, these phenomena might be justifiably considered alongside each other, but autoscopy (hallucinations of the self), as described by Strindberg, Goethe, Maupassant and Shelley, was never induced experimentally in the nineteenth century, and, moreover, there was only a small body of medical literature on the subject.

Strindberg's intimation of his doppelgänger echoed that of Dostoevsky's Mr Goldyakin, who pursues and finally captures the 'mysterious personage' who appears in the entrance to his flat in *The Double*. The story of Shelley's doppelgänger was, by contrast, very much in the mould of cases reported by German physicians and philosophers who endorsed the long-standing folk belief in the double as a wraith or harbinger of death. In early nineteenth-century Britain, there was, however, no comparable tradition of ghostly investigation. Physicians who considered the nature of apparitions, such as John Ferriar and Samuel Hibbert-Ware, all too quickly ascribed all ghostly visions to melancholy, mania or the study of mysticism and metaphysics. When Catherine Crowe compiled her supernatural miscellany *The Night Side of Nature* in 1843, she was as a consequence largely reliant on German material:

> Dr Werner relates that a jeweller at Ludwigsburg, named Ratzel, when in perfect health, one evening, on turning the corner of a street, met his own form, face to face. The figure seemed as real and lifelike as himself; and he was so close as to look into its eyes. He saw seized with terror . . . Shortly afterwards, as he was passing through a forest, he fell in with some wood-cutters, who asked him to lend a hand to the ropes with which they were pulling down an oak tree. He did so, and was killed by its fall . . . Becker, professor of mathematics at Rostock, having fallen into argument with some

friends regarding a point of theology, on going to his library to fetch a book which he wished to refer to, saw himself sitting at the table in the seat he usually occupied. He approached the figure, which appeared to be reading, and looking over its shoulder, he observed that the book open before it was a bible, and that, with one of the fingers of the right hand, it pointed to the passage – 'Make ready thy house, for thou must die!' . . . He took leave of his friends, and expired on the following day, at six o'clock in the evening.

While Crowe maintained that there was no natural explanation for the doppelgänger, the Brighton physician Arthur Wigan soon claimed to have found a material cause for the phenomenon in the dual structure of the brain, as described in his 1844 book *The Duality of Mind*. But clinical interest in autoscopy was short-lived, and, aside from Freud's speculation on the uncanniness of the doppelgänger (primitive 'assurance of immortality' turned 'ghastly harbinger of death'), the horrors of self-confrontation were explored principally in literature, poetry and paintings such as Rossetti's *How They Met Themselves*. A century on, when medical interest in autoscopy was eventually revived, the double's mythological and literary heritage tended to preclude any analysis of the patient's actual experience of autoscopy. One British psychiatrist endorsed the crepuscular nature of the double despite the fact that only two of the seven cases he reported occurred at twilight. And, as if to confirm this dubious association, another medical commentator suggested that 'the survival of superstition, magic, myth and folklore in our subconscious are partially responsible for this predominantly nocturnal character of autoscopy'.

Myth and folklore continue to shroud the autoscopic hallucination. Most recently, John Lash, author of *Twins and the Double* (1993), gives credence to some rather questionable features. 'Witnesses to their own double', he writes, 'agree upon a number of striking traits: the double has a ruddy, feral, over-energized cast, it glares and casts insolent looks, or laughs with a chilling derisive edge, and it disappears instantly if the witness shows just a little too much agitation at its presence.'

Surveying the clinical literature on autoscopy, one finds that a very different set of 'striking traits' is apparent. The double or second self is rarely an exact replica. Often, only the face or head and torso are seen. The legs may be indistinct or out of step (one subject with an artificial limb reported that his double was identical to him, but for one detail: his limp). Although its expressions and movements mimic those of the seer, the double is usually translucent or lacking in colour. The only other elements common to the experience of autoscopy are that it is highly transient, lasting for seconds rather than minutes, and that the hallucination is predominantly visual, but almost always multisensory.

Epilepsy, organic lesions, acute intoxication, anaesthesia, trauma, near-death and chronic fatigue are just some of the contexts in which autoscopic hallucinations can occur. The emotional and intellectual responses that autoscopy gives rise to are equally varied. The following account is taken from an epileptic whose regular hallucinations were preceded by a 'distressing feeling of unreality':

> I always know when I am going to have this 'turn' . . . Everything seems so far away, so unimportant, so odd, and so unreal. I don't feel 'myself' anymore. I feel dazed and 'empty' in myself. My body is like an empty shell. Then, all at once, I see and feel how my 'shadow' or 'my other me' steps out of me, my earthly body. He makes two or three steps, then stops, and turns his head to me. I feel how my soul and my life leave my body and enter him. Soon *he* is the real me . . . Then he nods at me and begins to walk, and my body follows him like a shadow . . . He turns his face to me, as if saying: 'Come and get me'. In fact, I can hear him saying that, though really I hear it with my mind and not with my ears.

By way of contrast, an expert in visual perception who was a volunteer in LSD experiments had this slightly more comic experience:

> There were two of me walking down the corridor.
> The two people were not very accurately localised in space, but

74

the main one corresponded to the position I would have been had there only been one of me. The shadowy or more tenuous individual, the naughty one, was slightly to the left. We could talk to each other, exchanging verbal thoughts, but not talking aloud . . .

'Why not jump out of a window?' he said to me.

The invitation had a compulsive quality which was difficult to resist. But just as I was considering it, the main person answered for me, speaking with effortless strength.

'Of course not. Don't be such a bloody fool.'

Experimental research into body transformations under LSD has found that autoscopic hallucinations occur when consciousness recedes and the sense of the body is partially lost. This is also confirmed by reports of autoscopy and out-of-body experiences under surgical anaesthesia, where visions of the body also appear as a kind of 'compensation' for the lack of visceral sensation. The cold or numb feeling that often accompanies autoscopy, sometimes described as a type of paralysis, is more than likely a literal anaesthesia. While some neurologists have suggested that externalisation of the body image may take place because of a disconnection between the two brain hemispheres (a theory which Arthur Wigan proposed as a more general explanation of a number of anomalous states), Dr Peter Brugger, from University Hospital, Zurich, suggests that the double is better understood as 'a phantom of the entire body', that is as a 'feeling' that is reminiscent of the illusions of phantom body parts that are felt (and sometimes seen) by amputees.

This theory, which is by no means new, would at least help to explain why the double so often appears to be truncated or legless. When Wilder Penfield began to map the body schema in the 1940s, he found that the face and hands were massively over-represented on the surface of the cerebral cortex, at the expense of the lower body. When we lose sense of our bodies, the legs go first and the head last. Autoscopy appears to dramatise this diminishing sensibility directly.

Nerve-Storms

The Divine Seizure

In Paul Féval's 1844 novel *Les Mystères de Londres*, Doctor Moore subjects a young woman, who has been abducted and imprisoned in a padded cell in the basement of his home, to a series of grisly experiments. Tapping the growing fear that medical science, having once relied on the services of grave robbers and 'resurrectionists' to supply corpses for dissection, was now performing secret experiments on living subjects, Féval follows Dr Moore's attempts to induce and investigate epilepsy. The disease was well chosen. Few afflictions had given rise to so much medical opinion, to so many diverse treatments and to so much superstition. While powdered elk's foot, the dried placenta of a first-born child and the hearts and livers of frogs or moles remained popular folk treatments, epilepsy continued to inspire the same horror that induced the ancients to spit and shudder in its presence.

Known as the 'sacred disease' in classical times, epilepsy had long been linked to the divine and the supernatural. In one of the first medical treatises on the condition, Hippocrates is attributed with demonstrating that its divine provenance was bogus, used by 'conjurors, purificators, mountebanks and charlatans' as 'pretext of their own inability to afford any assistance'. Epilepsy was no more or less divine than any other disease, Hippocrates maintained. 'Its origin is hereditary, it occurs in those who are of a phlegmatic constitution, but does not attack the bilious'.

Both the causes and symptoms of epilepsy were rather more complex than Hippocrates could have ever imagined. Modern-day clinicians recognise at least a dozen different types of seizure – certain forms of epilepsy are linked to cerebral damage, but others are of uncertain cause. The effects that these seizures give rise to are physical (some female epileptics experience a 'sexual seizure' which is literally orgasmic), sensory and noetic. The most psychologically affecting and intriguing of epileptic seizures are invariably linked to damage in the temporal lobe.

Temporal lobe seizures typically begin with twitches on one side of the face, hand or foot, quickly spreading to other parts of the body. The symptoms that accompany these seizures vary according to the location and distribution of electrical discharge through the brain. (By observing the sequence of twitches and spasms in relation to the movement of discharge through the brain, John Hughlings Jackson was, in the 1870s, able to suggest the way in which the sensory fields were mapped in the brain.) In the 'dreamy states' that these seizures give rise to, the epileptic may be assailed by visions and half-memories, hear voices or music, feel a heightened sense of nostalgia or experience a sense of duality or divinity. These trance-like effects may themselves be presaged by an aura: visceral sensations, nausea, palpitations, hallucinations of smell or taste, or feelings of an invisible presence. The Russian novelist and epileptic Fyodor Dostoevsky experienced his aura as an expanded moment of oceanic intensity. Through the character of Prince Myshkin in *The Idiot* (1868), Dostoevsky described a magical halt in time, 'when his whole heart, and mind, and body seemed to wake up to vigour and light; when he became filled with joy and hope, and all his anxieties seemed to be swept away for ever'. Like Myshkin, Dostoevsky believed 'the feeling of intense beatitude in that crowded moment made the moment worth a lifetime'.

The disruptions and intensifications of self that temporal lobe epileptics sometimes experience during seizures can have a profound and, in some cases, lasting effect. Although the French neurologists Charcot and Marie had linked epilepsy and multiple personality in the mid-nineteenth century, and Jackson recognised the longer-term effects of epilepsy on the personality, it is only in the past thirty years that neurologists have spoken of the 'temporal lobe personality', or the so-called Dostoevsky syndrome. According to Norman Geschwind, one of the first neurologists to recognise the transformation of personality brought about by temporal lobe epilepsy, the condition may stir or intensify philosophical and religious preoccupations, providing a stimulus to creative activity. Besides Dostoevsky, who was convinced that his epilepsy had brought completeness to his life and writing, Van Gogh, Poe, Tennyson, Flaubert and Maupassant are just some of the celebrated epileptics whose lives are thought to have been variously blessed and blighted by their seizures.

If the degree to which most of these artists and writers found their life and work charged by epilepsy is uncertain, contemporary reports of temporal lobe epilepsy often describe seizures as a gateway to other worlds, producing significant changes in temperament and outlook. A case reported by V. S. Ramachandran in *Phantoms of the Brain* reveals how a spate of seizures was able to irrevocably alter the personality of one epileptic:

> He experienced a rapture besides which everything paled. In the rapture was clarity, an apprehension of the divine – no categories, no boundaries, just a Oneness with the Creator. All of this he recounted in elaborate detail and with great persistence . . . the next day Paul returned to my office carrying an enormous manuscript bound in an ornate green dust jacket – a project he had been working on for several months. It set out his views on philosophy, mysticism and religion; the nature of the trinity; the iconography of the Star of David; elaborate drawings depicting spiritual themes . . . 'There's one other thing I should mention,' he said. 'I have these amazing flashbacks . . . the other day, during a seizure, I could remember every little detail from a book I read many years ago. Line after line, page after page, word for word.'

For epileptics who experience seizures as states of expanded awareness or oceanic bliss, the sense of transport in time may be as compelling as the divine or mystical dimension. Whether visual or auditory, these 'convulsive memories' are always powerfully stirring. Wilder Penfield, the eminent neurologist who began to research temporal lobe epilepsy in the 1940s, considered these recollections 'a random reproduction of whatever composed the stream of consciousness during some interval of the patient's past life' – he was also able to artificially induce 'random' memories by stimulating the cortex. Penfield was nevertheless prepared to recognise the possibility that these transports were more than electrically dislodged detritus: certain memories might, he accepted, be awakened because they are more emotionally resonant than others.

Given that some sufferers of epilepsy find spiritual consolation in their seizures, was Hippocrates too hasty in denying the 'sacred disease'? Is there a natural affinity between epilepsy and religion? The Canadian neurologist Michael Persinger thinks so. His research suggests that electrical instability of the temporal lobe is intimately linked to the 'God Experience'. Persinger's thesis strikes a chord with various attempts to link shamanism and epilepsy, and gives renewed credibility to the medical claims once made for the prophet Mohammed and the Christian saints. But these connections are themselves doubtful. While the Byzantine historian Theophanes appears to have first diagnosed epilepsy in Mohammed in an attempt to tarnish his legend, epilepsy has never been a qualification for shamanic or prophetic office. And, although some Renaissance thinkers conceded the existence of epileptic prophets – fainting and epilepsy being thought to imitate rapture – their visions and prophecies were also regarded with suspicion.

The recent case of a young French epileptic who died after being repeatedly flogged and forced to drink salt water in order to exorcise her devils is a tragic reminder of the diabolic associations and horrific treatments more often connected to this affliction. As Dostoevsky noted, 'an epileptic fit fills many others with an absolute horror and unbearable terror, which has something mystical about it'.

Mechanical Boys

The term *autism* was first applied to a specific disorder of personality in children in the 1940s, when two Austrian-born clinicians, Leo Kanner and Hans Asperger, independently adopted the label after observing a number of children who preferred objects to people and who showed scant interest in others. These children were not schizophrenic; however, as Asperger noted, they shared one common denominator with psychotic patients: 'the shutting-off of relations between the self and the outside world'.

Fritz V, one of Asperger's very first reported cases of 'autistic psychopathy', was typical in his intransigence. Declared uneducable at the age of six, Fritz was a restless child who grabbed, tore and broke objects around him. His play was limited to jumping and hitting. Either aloof or aggressive in his interaction with other children, he showed no grasp of their thoughts or emotions. Fritz's 'strikingly odd' gaze immediately struck Asperger. With his eyes fastening fleetingly on his surroundings, he appeared strangely remote. His speech was slow and unmodulated, occasionally assuming a singsong quality. He rarely answered questions, but sometimes repeated them or simply exclaimed, 'I don't like to say that.' Observed on the ward, Fritz was by turns motionless and agitated. Without warning, he would hit another child or clear a table with a single swipe. At first, Asperger found it difficult to assess Fritz's intellectual abilities. Yet, according to his parents, Fritz had from an early age shown an extraordinary grasp of numbers and was able to handle fractions. Asperger was eventually able to confirm these claims. In this respect, Fritz was indeed precocious.

Unknown to each other, Asperger and Kanner described many of the same characteristics in autistic children. Both noted a number of deficiencies of speech – mutism, monotonous intonation, repetitive questioning and a tendency to reverse pronouns and to coin neologisms. Both observed the unnerving absence of eye contact. Both noted negative response to touch and sound. Both described certain repetitive bodily movements, the ritualised fixation with collecting, ordering or spinning mundane objects. And both were fascinated with the unusual talents that some autistic children demonstrated. Yet each had a rather different sense of the essential character of infantile autism. Having worked with children who were generally clumsier, but more linguistically advanced, Asperger believed that 'autistic psychopathy' was 'a disturbance of the lively relationship with the whole environment'. Kanner, on the other hand, emphasised those deficits that impaired the ability to form meaningful relationships.

Today's concept of autism is derived directly from Kanner's work. The classical syndrome which he described revolves around three core impairments, each of which is generally evident by the age of three. First, autism is a problem of social interaction. Alongside the poverty of verbal expression, there is an inability to signal one's focus of attention or to follow the gazes, gestures and prompts of others. Second, autism involves a failure of what cognitive psychologists have called 'mind-reading', the ability to attribute mental states to others. Third, most autistic children are unable to participate in symbolic play. A paper cup cannot become a hat. A belt cannot double as a snake. A box cannot serve as a house. Instead, such objects are hoarded, repetitively turned or placed in precise configurations. As the autistic child grows, the fascination with objects is often replaced by interest in television characters, maps, timetables, animals and 'collections'. 'Donald', one of the autistic children Kanner discussed in his original 1943 paper, was, for example, an obsessive collector of old copies of *Time* magazine. The listing and memorising of publication dates was one of his principal preoccupations.

Kanner had originally considered early infantile autism as an 'innate inability' to forge 'affective contact with people', but it became very quickly a 'pseudodiagnostic waste basket for a variety of unrelated conditions', most of which were assumed to have a psychogenic origin. In 1958, after two decades of work as a child psychiatrist, Kanner claimed that he had seen fewer than 150 cases of infantile autism. He estimated that only one in ten of the 'autistic' referrals to his clinic at Johns Hopkins University Hospital, a 'diagnostic clearing house' for much of North America, had been accurately diagnosed. The vast majority of these misdiagnoses were cases of childhood schizophrenia, which in Europe and America were often assumed to be synonymous with infantile autism. Kanner and a number of colleagues argued for the differential diagnosis of these two conditions, but the terms were often used loosely and interchangeably. The confusion of terminology was exacerbated by the increasing emphasis on autism (originally conceived, in 1911, as one of the principal symptoms of schizophrenia) as the defining feature of psychosis. Frieda Fromm-Reichmann, for instance, argued that all the symptoms of schizophrenia stemmed from the autistic withdrawal into fantasy, itself precipitated by a traumatic or deeply unsatisfying parental relationship.

That a psychodynamic interpretation should be applied to early infantile autism was perhaps inevitable. Bruno Bettelheim, founder of the Sonia Shankman Orthogenic School at the University of Chicago, proved one of the most dogged proponents of autism as a response to 'inadequate and overwhelming experience in early childhood'. Appearing immune to mounting claims for a neurological explanation, Bettelheim continued, throughout the 1960s, to promulgate the view that autism/schizophrenia (he used the terms randomly) was a maladaptive response to maternal deprivation. His case study of 'Joey: A "Mechanical Boy"', first published in *Scientific American* in 1959, provided him with powerful ammunition. Here, apparently, was a classic example of infantile autism successfully treated by therapeutic rehabilitation. More than this, Joey's autism was presented as a larger parable of 'emotional development in a mechanized society'.

When Joey entered Bettelheim's Orthogenic School at the age

of nine, he believed himself to be a machine. Switching himself on and off at will, he spent long periods of time silent and motionless. To get himself 'working', he would run through a series of gear changes, exploding into life while screaming 'Crash, crash'. In order to eat, he plugged imaginary wires into 'energy sources' that could power his ingestive system. He could only drink through a complex system of drinking straws which 'pumped' liquids into him. Next to his bed, he had constructed various devices (using cardboard, masking tape, light bulbs, radio tuners and other paraphernalia) that he required in order to sleep, breathe and defecate. Joey had even devised one machine, the 'criticizer', which prevented him from 'saying words which have unpleasant feelings'. Although Joey's preoccupations made it difficult for staff to engage with him, his speech was not, despite the odd neologism and grammatical reversal, impaired. Moreover, Bettelheim did not suggest that Joey was lacking in any aspects of non-vocal communication. In fact, Bettelheim's obvious fascination with Joey's delusory system appears to have blinded him to many facts that pointed against the diagnosis of autism.

To understand how Joey had become a human machine, Bettelheim conducted 'intensive interviews' with his parents and duly discovered that his automation had begun before his birth, when his mother had begun to deny his existence. For Bettelheim, Joey was nothing more than the product of a loveless upbringing. Deprived of maternal intimacy, fed on a rigid schedule, toilet-trained from an early age, he was diagnosed autistic at the age of four, by which time his obsession with machinery was well established. 'Joey had created these machines', observed Bettelheim, 'because it was too painful to be human.' Once Joey began to 'trust us enough to let himself become more infantile', he began to express his 'anal preoccupations'. Moving beyond his elaborate mechanical 'preventions', Joey seemed to begin, through his drawings and paintings, to search for a way to be reborn. At the age of twelve, he and his counsellors succeeded in this objective: Joey had forged real relationships with real people – 'he had ceased to be a mechanical boy and become a human child'.

Leaving aside the fact that Joey was probably schizophrenic – as his mother may well have been – Bettelheim placed an inordinately heavy burden on 'emotional refrigeration' as the principal cause of all childhood pathologies. With the publication of his 1964 book *Infantile Autism*, the psychologist Bernard Rimland effectively rescued autism from the psychogenic hypothesis. 'The appeal of the psychogenic concept [of autism]', wrote Rimland, pointing an accusing finger at Bettelheim's work, 'appears to preclude consideration of concealed organic defect. Somehow the adherents of the psychogenic hypothesis tend to overlook the possibility that the complex and little understood cerebrum could be structurally or chemically impaired.' Bettelheim resisted Rimland's claims in his 1967 book *The Empty Fortress*, which provided an even fuller account of Joey's treatment, but a sea change was already under way. Too many facts now pointed towards biology. Autism was six times as likely to affect male infants. Autistic parents were fifty times as likely to have autistic children. And the majority of siblings were unaffected. How could Bettelheim's psychogenic hypothesis explain these and other anomalies?

As neuroscience moved to explore how autism might be connected to defects in various brain areas, two minor break-throughs in the understanding of autism occurred. First, a number of autobiographies began to shed light on what happened to more able autistic children as they became adolescents and adults, revealing the extent to which intimacy and empathy with others could be achieved. Although these writings suggested that Bettelheim was misplaced in many of his views on the family background of autism, his attempt to read meaning into autistic behaviours appeared to be partly vindicated. For example, Donna Williams's autobiography *Nobody Nowhere* suggested that her own 'stereotypies' were never meaningless. 'These gestures', writes Williams, 'were and remain the most important language of my world.' In her engagement with objects, Williams describes trying to indirectly express things that were 'too important' to state or request. Her matching and pairing of objects was an attempt to demonstrate that 'relationships between one or more thing can exist'. However, it is difficult to read these insights as Williams's own. One characteristic of autistic individuals is, as Margaret Dewey notes, 'the tendency to belatedly convert other people's ideas into their own'.

Secondly, increasing clinical attention was paid to a subgroup of 'higher functioning' autists thought to be suffering from Asperger's syndrome. Despite some controversy over its diagnostic validity, it is generally accepted that this form of so-called 'mild autism', seen in both children and adults, involves only a handful of traits: speech which is pedantic or over-formal; poor non-verbal communication; clumsiness; absence of empathy and interests which are circumspect and all-engrossing. (Employing these criteria, a 1993 study of Swedish schoolchildren by Stephen Ehlers and Christopher Gillberg found Asperger's syndrome to be prevalent in approximately four in every thousand.) With these symptoms, it is easily possible for more capable autists to simply appear as odd, clumsy or gauche. The limitations that Asperger's syndrome imposes on individuals are, however, particularly telling when they are pressed to consider their emotional shortcomings. When asked how he felt after the death of his mother, one fifteen-year-old replied: 'Oh, I'm all right. You see, I have Asperger's syndrome, which makes me less vulnerable to the loss of loved ones than most people.'

The peculiar islands of creative talent or intellectual ability that subjects with Asperger's syndrome display can nevertheless easily overshadow their limited repertoire of social skills, allowing them to be perceived as simply 'gifted'. Some of the well-chronicled eccentricities of pop artist Andy Warhol are suggestive of Asperger's syndrome. Warhol was remote, unfeeling. Sex and death were for him abstractions that he was never able to deal with. In a catalogue to his first retrospective, Warhol wrote, 'I still care about people but it would be so much easier not to care. It's hard to care. I don't like to touch things. . . . That's why my work is so distant from myself . . . Machines have less problems. I'd like to be a machine.' Warhol's private life was filled with routine and idiosyncrasies. He only wore green underpants. He would never eat or dance at parties. He never attended funerals. He was fascinated with 'boring things', with celebrity, with Hollywood. And his speech was notoriously monosyllabic and inarticulate.

Like Wittgenstein, Bartók and Einstein – who have all been linked to Asperger's syndrome – it is possible that, in his art, Warhol at once channelled and transcended the 'strikingly odd' gaze of autism. What such a diagnosis might bring to the understanding of Warhol and his art is, of course, another matter.

A Literary Headache

After tumbling into Wonderland, via a rabbit hole that seemed to plunge her deep into the 'antipathies', Alice drinks a mysterious elixir that causes her to shrink to a height of ten inches. Unable to retrieve a golden key that is now high above her, she eats a small cake. Feeling 'curiouser and curiouser', she grows in stature, 'opening out like the largest telescope that ever was', before being ushered into a playhouse of paradox and absurdity.

Some eighty years after the publication of *Alice's Adventures in Wonderland*, Caro Lippman, a San Francisco ophthalmologist, noted that the hallucinations described by Charles Lutwidge Dodgson (aka Lewis Carroll) were typical of the aura that preceded the onset of a migraine. While some of Lippman's patients felt greatly diminished or inflated in size, others reported changes to specific parts of the body. One migraine sufferer, for example, reported that 'my head fell into a deep hole under the head of the bed – it was a very deep hole. I knew it wasn't true, but I was really worried as to my sanity.' Another patient described the strange asymmetry that overcame his body, the right and left sides feeling alternately twice as large as each other.

The symptomology of migraine was not studied methodically in Britain before the second half of the nineteenth century. While Tissot and Labbaraque had published major studies in France in the 1830s, it was not until 1865 (the year in which *Alice's Adventures in Wonderland* was first published) that Edward Liveing completed his seminal study *On Megrim, Sick-Headache and Some Allied Disorders*. Basing his study on sixty case studies taken from his own notes and other sources, Liveing identified the various symptoms and grades of seizure, from the 'simplest hemicranial pain, transient half-vision, or sick giddiness' to cases which involved 'a complex assemblage and wide range of sensorial disturbance'. Given that Dodgson's own library of 3000 or so books included a substantial section of medical titles, including W. H. Day's *Headaches: Their Nature, Causes and Treatment* (0000) and E. B. Shuldham's *Headaches: Their Causes and Treatment* (0000), he may well have been familiar with Liveing's work. If so, he would have found much that accorded with his own experience.

One of Liveing's more complex cases was 'H.T.', a young man who first consulted him as an outpatient at London's King's College Hospital in 1863. For five years, H.T. had experienced migraines that began with a 'dazzling appearance' and 'bright sparklings and colours' filling his field of vision. After fifteen minutes, these spectral visions were followed by a numbness that spread upwards from the right hand to the right side of the head and face, and on to other parts of the body. H.T. would then experience an inability to express himself. 'I can't tell you why, but it is utterly impossible to speak. If I were to try, I should say words quite different from those I intended or which would have no meaning, but my head is clear or only a little confused, and I know quite well what I wish to say.' After three-quarters of an hour, all of these symptoms would subside, and H.T. would experience an increasingly painful bilateral headache which would require him to lie down and sleep.

Liveing gave unusually detailed attention to the visual, somatic and affective aspects of the aura, the phase that so often anticipates the classical migraine. Oliver Sacks has gone as far as to suggest that 'nobody has given the aura its due, since Liveing'. The fact that it took so long for Alice's flight of fancy to be connected to 'the pathology of nerve-storms' – as Liveing subtitled his work – certainly suggests that the medical understanding of migraine has not been entirely cumulative. As with so many other illnesses, research into the causes and treatment has tended to obscure the lessons of case history.

The migraine aura, the phase that so often anticipates the classical migraine, occurs alongside a constriction of cerebral blood flow. Spreading across the cortex, this depression triggers a pattern of neural activity that fires visual disturbances and somatic hallucinations. The classic symptoms of migraine (pain spreading across one side of the temples, nausea and photophobia) are thought to be secondary effects of the initial depression of blood flow. This vascular theory of migraine was first proposed in the mid-seventeenth century, but it was not until the 1940s that John Graham and Harold Wolff confirmed the hypothesis by using intravenous injections of ergotamine tartrate to demonstrate that the intensity of migraine was related to the amplitude of temporal artery pulsation.

Before Hippocrates suggested that the symptoms of migraine were due to an imbalance of the humours, it was, like epilepsy, thought to have supernatural provenance. For five thousand years, the trepanning of a small hole into the skull was, across Europe, South America and the Pacific, a commonplace treatment for these demons in the head. While trepanation remained a recommended treatment until the seventeenth century, a host of remedies and elixirs were used. In the Mediterranean, olive oil in water was favoured. This treatment was probably more effective, and certainly more comfortable, than the one suggested by Erasmus Darwin, who recommended that migraine sufferers be spun in a centrifuge, allowing the blood to flow from head to feet.

Somewhere between two and five million people are estimated to suffer periodically from migraine in Britain. The vast majority of these suffer from the classical migraine that is often preceded by a visual aura. For the minority that suffers from more pronounced focal migraines, these visual symptoms are even more dramatic. Sometimes accompanied by Alice-type bodily hallucinations, particularly in relation to the head, hand and tongue, and difficulty in speaking, the visionary phenomena associated with focal migraines may overshadow or overlap with the headache itself. In all cases, the aura appears to be characterised by the appearance of white, flickering zigzags – Charles Dodgson's journals describe it as 'seeing moving fortifications' – which move towards the periphery of the visual field, leaving a scotoma, or blind spot. In focal migraines, geometrical shapes may swirl and pulsate, forming more graphic images of buildings or complete cityscapes. Auditory hallucinations have also been reported. One young migraine sufferer, for example, described hearing ambient sounds that fluctuated in intensity, as if coming from a radio the volume control of which was being constantly altered.

While medical science continues to pursue the causes of migraine (foodstuffs, genetic abnormalities, toxins, interrupted sleep patterns, etc.), there has been increasing interest in the ways in which migraine effects have insinuated themselves into art and literature. In *Hallucinations and Their Impact on Art*, E. M. R. Critchley suggests that 'Shakespeare, Dryden, Cervantes, Pope, Swift, Trollope, Chesterton, Kipling, Emerson [and others] have all utilised their own experiences of migraine in their writings'. (Darwin, Nietzsche and Freud might head an alternative list.) While Critchley goes on to point out the possible connections between migraine aura and op and kinetic art, rather more dubious diagnoses of migraine have been made retroactively using rather less convincing evidence.

Michel Ferrari, a neurologist from the University of Leiden, has claimed that, after 1937, the work of Picasso is replete with the same splittings and distortions found in drawings made by his own migraine patients. 'You suddenly see a change in style [in Picasso's work] . . . he starts to paint faces in two halves, with eyes out of line and a major distortion of parts of the face . . . the same classical vertical splitting as my migraine patients experience.' That not one of Picasso's biographers mentions him having suffered from migraines does not deter Ferrari from his speculations. He suggests that if Picasso suffered from migraine aura without headache there would be no 'official record'. The odds are poor. A 1996 study of the migraine aura reported in the journal *Brain* found that only seven in four thousand sufferers experience migraine without headache symptoms.

Even before the onset of the aura some migraine sufferers have an intimation of what is to come. This prodromal phase may involve alterations in perception and sensitivity to light, fluctuations in mood, or memory or speech problems. Liveing noted that fifteen of his sixty cases reported an impairment of speech – one patient 'spoke a mere jargon, in which a faint semblance of words of several languages was alone perceptible'. Freud, too, recognised the onset of his migraines by an inability to remember proper names and a tendency to make slips-of-the-tongue which formed portmanteau words. As tempting as it might be to imagine that this migrainous jumbling of words might have also provided Dodgson with the inspiration for 'Jabberwocky', the *Kubla Khan* of nonsense poetry, Dodgson's biographers agree that it was conceived as a parody of Anglo-Saxon.

Carnival of the Senses

The novels of Vladimir Nabokov are filled with characters who are able to *see* sounds, to *taste* colours, to perceive through a strange fusion of the senses. When describing these unusual faculties, Nabokov relied neither on research nor on imagination. The derangement of the senses that the French symbolists had tried to achieve in their poetry and prose was, for Nabokov, as it was for his mother, second nature. Letter sounds immediately formed themselves in his mind's eye: 'The long "a" of the English alphabet . . . has for me the tint of weathered wood, but a French "a" evokes polished ebony. The black group also includes . . . hard "g" (vulcanized rubber) and "r" a sooty rag being ripped.'

The coloured hearing that so enriched Nabokov's life and prose remains the most common type of synaesthesia, an entirely natural and involuntary form of cross-sensory perception estimated to occur in around one in 100,000 people. One of the first references to the phenomenon was made by English philosopher John Locke in 1699, when he wrote of a congenitally blind man who 'betrayed one day that he now understood what scarlet signified . . . it was like the sound of a trumpet'. In 1812, Dr G. T. L. Sachs delivered the first treatise on the subject of coloured hearing, outlining the sensations and associations he and his sister experienced. By this time, French and German mesmerists had also reported a 'transposition of the senses' during the trance state, with subjects demonstrating the ability to see and hear with their hands and stomach. Generally speaking, however, medicine remained ignorant of the extent to which all the senses could, under different circumstances, converge and unite.

The full range of sensory couplings that can be activated in

95

synaesthesia has to a large extent been revealed by pharma-cological research. Hashish, the Orient's fabled inspirer of dreams and fancies, was the first of the drugs to truly open the doors of perception. At the Club des Haschischins, co-founded by Moreau de Tours and Théophile Gautier in the 1840s, hashish became well known as a stirrer of visions that were gloriously shaken and unhinged. Writing of his experiences, Gautier described how he was able to miraculously perceive the 'sound of colours; green, red, blue and yellow'; how 'every object touched made a sound like a harmonica or aeolian harp'; how his body became a sponge to 'sounds, perfume and light', which he absorbed in 'streams of happiness'. Even Baudelaire, who would famously deride the 'sophisms of hashish', could not help but be impressed by the drug's enchanting capacity to expand the senses, to reveal analogies and correspondences.

While *fin-de-siècle* novelists (Huysmans), painters (Kandinsky) and composers (Schoenberg and Scriabin) championed syn-aesthesia as the acme of aesthetic experience, and as a gateway to a realm of mystical oneness, medical and clinical opinion was divided. Writing in 1889, the psychologist Alfred Binet observed that synaesthetes invariably showed a keenly developed aesthetic sensibility, being often professionally involved in the arts. Russian commentators such as Paul Sokolov, by contrast, characterised the synaesthete as a glorified idiot savant whose heightened imagi-nation masked an inability to think in abstract terms. These misgivings were to be later echoed by Aleksandr A. R. Luria in the 1920s. As much as synaesthesia heightened memory and visual abilities, Luria discovered that it impaired a range of quite simple cognitive and personal skills.

Two opposing theories sought to explain the causes of synaesthesia. The first and most simplistic argued that these anomalies of perception were essentially acts of mental asso-ciation. If, for example, a synaesthete felt his body swaying on smelling cod liver oil, the smell of the oil was thought to sub-consciously evoke the sea, which, in turn, recalled the characteristic rocking motion of a boat. Alternatively, a second theory proposed that synaesthesia was a vestige of a primitive mode of super-perception, in which the individual senses were not entirely differentiated.

This second theory has been resurrected and reworked by the American neurologist Richard E. Cytowic, who embarked on a comprehensive study of the psychology and physiology of synaesthesia in the late 1970s. Synaesthesia is, he suggests, linked to the limbic system of the left hemisphere, triggered by imbalances in the cortex which cause 'disconnections' that are experienced as mixed-up perceptions. Unlike migraine – which Cytowic regards as its physiological cousin – synaesthesia is an often pleasurable and sometimes ecstatic experience. These feelings suggest that the hippocampus, the 'emotional' centre of the temporal lobe, might also be involved. 'In synesthesia,' Cytowic writes, 'a brain process that is normally unconscious becomes bared to consciousness so that synesthetes know they are synesthetic while the rest of us do not.'

The assumption that synaesthesia has been slowly eradicated from consciousness, that it is an essentially primitive or infantile mode of perception, is clearly part of its enduring fascination. The historian Kevin T. Dann suggests that synaesthesia has attracted both literary and scientific interest 'because it seems to validate the belief in the primacy of human imagination, as well as to ratify the original wholeness, continuity, and interfusion of immediate experience'. Yet synaesthesia is not necessarily revelatory or joyous. Synaesthetes can suffer from a sense of too-muchness, of being overloaded or continually distracted by rogue sensations. These cases of 'maladaptive' synaesthesia may open a rather less romantic window on to our biological past.

Seeing Stars

Travelling along a tree-lined country lane to Marseilles, eyes squinting against the afternoon sun, the American painter and writer Brion Gysin was overwhelmed by an 'intensely bright pattern in supernatural colour'. He was swept 'out of time'. He was ushered into a 'world of infinite number'. Still reeling from this vision, recorded in his journal on 21 December 1958, Gysin wondered how the flicker of wintry sunshine through a leafy canopy could have inspired this cloudburst of spectral geometry.

On reading the scientific literature, Gysin found that biologists had stumbled across much the same phenomenon when examining the effects of stroboscopic light on brain rhythms. Exploring the possibility of using the technique in diagnosing epilepsy at the Burden Neurological Institute in the late 1940s, Grey Walter found that a small percentage of non-epileptic individuals were, when exposed to light flickering at somewhere between eight and twenty-five flashes per second, capable of experiencing visions and aura-like effects. Often referred to as 'light-dust' and 'ocular spectra' by early researchers, but now known as 'phosphenes', these images were composed of 'pulsating checks or mosaic . . . whirling spirals, whirlpools, explosions, Catherine wheels'. In some cases, these patterns of white, silver or coloured light – similar to those stimulated by migraine, fatigue, a blow to the head or pressure on the eyeball – developed into more complete dreamlike imagery. By fashioning a simple flicker machine of his own (a slatted cardboard cylinder on a turntable with a central light) Gysin was able to return to the inner landscape into which he had stumbled.

The first physiologist to study phosphenes purposefully was

Johanes Purkinje, a one-time monk whom Goethe encouraged to pursue medical and scientific research at the University of Prague. In 1819, Purkinje began his investigations by replicating Alessandro Volta's experiments with electrodes applied to the face. With his eyes closed, Purkinje observed stripes, arches and other 'galvanic light patterns'. Purkinje then turned his attention to digitalis, a much-used plant drug that was known to produce impaired and altered vision in higher doses. Unable to 'resist the temptation to look for a more exact explanation of the phenomenon', he consumed large doses over a four-day period, making sketches of the flickering geometrical forms that he continued to see well after the experiment had terminated. Purkinje thought the flickering visions induced by digitalis were due to the stimulation of cranial nerves. However, subsequent experiments with an aqueous extract of belladonna, applied directly to the eye, led him to conclude that similar stellate patterns were brought on by cycloplegia, paralysis of the muscles that adjust and focus the eye.

A century on, using more developed means of electrical stimulation, Max Knoll, co-inventor of the electron microscope, was able to unlock the basic grammar of phosphenes. Obtaining sketches from more than a thousand volunteers from diverse cultural backgrounds, Knoll discovered that fifteen elementary phosphene shapes – including sunbursts, diamonds, star shapes, concentric circles and checks – were stimulated by low-voltage, square waves of about 1 volt applied to the temples. Changes in the frequency of the electrical pulse affected the pattern. The widest spectrum of phosphenes was invariably observed by the mentally ill or by subjects who had been primed with a tiny dose of LSD. The particular mechanism involved in the generation of the phosphenes remained open to speculation. The fact that the same luminous visions could be generated by mechanical pressure on the eye suggested that the neural network of the retina might well be involved. Yet other electrical experiments pointed to the visual cortex and visual pathways, particularly in the case of phosphene patterns that were unaffected by a shifting gaze.

Here was a universal geometry. As anthropologists,

archaeologists and art historians would soon confirm, phosphenes were the ABC of the visionary and sacred arts. From African rock paintings to Tibetan mandalas, the same shapes had been etched, daubed, inscribed and painted. In the late 1960s, when the Austrian-born anthropologist Gerardo Reichel-Dolmatoff began his fieldwork among the Eastern Tukanoans, he found a pocket of the Colombian Amazon in which the very phosphenes Knoll had catalogued in his Munich laboratory covered everyday objects, clothes, tools and buildings. The Tukanoans witnessed these motifs during the first stages of a religious ceremony in which a potion known as *caapi* was drunk to facilitate travel beyond the 'Milky Way'. Reichel-Dolmatoff also discovered that the Tukanoans had coded around half of these into shorthand for teachings connected with mate selection, exogamy and fertility. Where the anthropologist saw shape and pattern, the Tukanoans read signs, warnings and exhortations. But these phosphene visions took the Tukanoans beyond the merely abstract and geometrical. The figurative images and natural scenes perceived by the Tukanoans in the second phase of intoxication were essentially interpretations of the complex and moving pattern of coloured phosphenes. As Reichel-Dolmatoff put it: 'the second phase is culturally conditioned and the visions consist of previously stored informations which are projected upon the screen produced by the drug.'

This process of transfiguration had already been observed by a number of medical experimenters. S. Weir Mitchell, one of the first Westerners to experiment with peyote, described how his closed-eye visions always began with the flicker of tiny points of light, like stars or fireflies. From this backdrop of silver starred light emerged scenes composed of 'definite objects':

> The stars sparkled and passed away. A white stone grew up to a huge height, and became a tall, richly finished Gothic tower of very elaborate and definite design, with many rather worn statues standing in doorways or on stone brackets. As I gazed every projecting angle, cornice, and even the face of the stones at their joinings were by degrees covered with what seemed to be huge

precious stones, but uncut, some being more like masses of transparent fruit. These were green, purple, red, and orange; never yellow and never blue. All seemed to possess an interior light, and to give the faintest idea of the perfectly satisfying intensity and purity of these gorgeous colour-fruits is quite beyond my power. All the colours I have beheld are dull as compared to these.

The visions induced by drugs such as peyote and *ayahuasca*, by flicker or by electrical stimulation, are rarely composed of memory images. Their style of composition is mechanical and anti-realistic. As Havelock Ellis remarked after his own experiments, the play of light '*suggested* pictures [that] were not really seen'. This inability to recall or reproduce natural forms is confirmed by the fact that the animals and beings witnessed in these visions rarely have a sense of scale or physical integrity. Théophile Gautier's account of his hashish fantasia, for example, evoked an array of 'goatsuckers, fiddle-faddlebeasts, budled goslings, unicorns, griffons, incubi, an entire menagerie of monstrous nightmares'. After taking *ayahuasca* in the early 1960s, the anthropologist Michael Harner reported seeing visions of dragonlike beings which combined pterodactyl-like wings and enormous whalelike bodies. This anti-realism extends to many types of hallucinations – objects or persons often appear to be enlarged, shrunken, multiplied and misshapen, or comprised of elements that are strangely disparate and incongruous. This is particularly true of the hallucinations associated with Charles Bonnet syndrome, a condition that probably accounts for more hallucinations than schizophrenia.

In 1769, the Swiss philosopher Charles Bonnet described how a cataract operation led his elderly grandfather, Charles Lullin, to perceive 'without external stimulus the images of men, women, birds, buildings that change in shape, size and place but which he never accepted as real'. Dominating the left side of his visual field, these visions occurred only when Lullin was standing or sitting. In conversation with the young Bonnet, Lullin would frequently interrupt his learned discourses to describe the progress of an unfolding vision. In later years, Bonnet himself experienced a number of fantastic objects which he recognised as illusory, but a long time would pass before physicians recognised that lucid visions of this kind were commonplace. In the 1930s, when Charles Bonnet syndrome (CBS) was first proposed as an umbrella term for hallucinations that occur with clear consciousness in the elderly, little was known about the cause or extent of the condition. It is only in the past decade that some advances have been made.

The imagery associated with CBS hallucinations can be simple or complex, static or animated, fleeting or lasting. Recent studies report a preponderance of faces (almost always strangers) and animals (one woman's hallucinations always featured a 'well-dressed monkey'). The formation of these images would appear to follow the same process of phosphene elaboration described by Reichel-Dolmatoff. The historian Hugh Trevor-Roper has recently described 'the little circular blobs of kaleidoscopic colour' and 'disorderly patterns of dark squares' which he saw in the first stages of CBS. While these patterns initially imposed themselves on objects and scenes that remained visible to him, the hallucinations progressed into a phantasmagoria of 'moving pictures which blocked reality', including bicycle and horse races, colonnaded Renaissance squares and 'a cemetery of dead machines'.

The fact that CBS hallucinations do not respond to anti-psychotic medication would appear to confirm that they are produced by physiological deterioration of the eye. However, geriatric psychiatrists have recently questioned the long-held assumption that CBS hallucinations are caused only by defects of the eye – glaucoma, macular degeneration, cataracts or diabetic retinopathy. Combinations of visual and cognitive impairments appear to provide the trigger to most CBS hallucinations. Isolation and bereavement have, moreover, been confirmed as significant causative factors. These findings have led Martin Cole of McGill University to propose that the syndrome might be better explained in terms of reduced sensory stimulation rather than fading sight per se. In either event, CBS hallucinations belong to a broad category of visual phenomena that appear to contradict the standard definition of a hallucination. Like the images stirred by flicker, illuminated by peyote and *ayahuasca*, these visions are not perceptions without a corresponding sensation. They are elaborations of the shifting geometry of phosphenes – the stuff that visions, and perhaps even dreams, are made of.

Pasts Imperfect

From Here to Oblivion

Psychologists have long been fascinated by the case of the Reverend Ansel Bourne, a New England preacher who, on 17 January 1887, withdrew $551 from a bank in Providence, Maine, and disappeared for two months. According to William James, who reported his investigations in his *Principles of Psychology*, Bourne, a man of 'firm and self-reliant disposition', had travelled by way of Boston, New York and Philadelphia before arriving in Norristown, near Philadelphia. There, he rented a small shop under the name of A. J. Brown. Stocking it with stationery, confectionery and fruit, he plied a 'quiet trade' for six weeks. Then, on the morning of 14 March, Bourne, not Brown, awoke to find himself in the back room of an unfamiliar shop, his memory of the last weeks a resounding blank.

Examining Bourne some three years after his misadventures, James used hypnosis to access 'Brown's memory' of the Norristown episode, but discovered no motives for his departure other than that 'there was trouble back there' and he 'wanted rest'. Like other physicians who had previously examined Bourne, James found no reason to question the veracity of this story. While he struggled to classify the amnesiac episode, suggesting that it might have been a 'spontaneous hypnotic trance' or a case of multiple personality, such cases were elsewhere not quite as unusual. The Bordeaux clinician Philippe Tissié had by this time published his *Les Aliénés voyageurs*, a comprehensive survey of recorded fugues and inexplicable wanderings. These cases, often involving conscripts and runaways, were the medical mysteries of their day. As with Bourne, their automatic travels were pieced together under hypnosis. If Bourne had travelled to Bordeaux or Paris rather than

Norristown, he would have been dubbed a *fugeur*, and his peregrinations would have been ascribed to hysteria or epilepsy.

More than a century on, 'sudden unexpected travel away from home or one's customary place of work, with inability to recall one's past' is the American Psychiatric Association's definition of a 'dissociative fugue'. Unlike the amnesiac travels of epileptics or drug users, the condition is thought to have a psychogenic origin, often connected to trauma or domestic conflict. Unlike Ansel Bourne, not all amnesiacs go on to assume a new identity. A fairly recent fugue case reported in the journal *Pennsylvania Medicine* describes how one woman, found unconscious in a bookshop, was unable to recall anything of herself. Under hypnosis, she gave the names of friends and acquaintances, but none of these people could identify her. The FBI and the police all failed to establish who she was. Discharged after two months, she guessed that she was fifty-eight, unmarried, childless, Christian and a legal secretary from somewhere in Illinois. For obvious reasons, such cases are a subject of endless curiosity for the popular press.

The fascination with piecing together amnesiac lives is not new. The mystery of Kaspar Hauser, the young German boy who was found wandering in Nuremberg in the 1820s, carrying letters indicating that he was abandoned, is a classic case. According to one observer, young Hauser was 'so entirely destitute of words and conceptions', 'so totally unacquainted with the most common objects and daily occurrences of nature . . . [that] one might feel one self driven to the alternative of believing him to be a citizen of another planet'. Although his development was seriously retarded, he was not mute, and his language skills developed quickly enough for him to inform investigators of the few facts he knew about himself. He told them he had been kept in a confined space, a cell or a dungeon. A man had brought him food twice a day. He had a wooden horse for company. Then, one day, he was taken by carriage into a world of people and houses, where he stumbled along, barely able to walk or communicate. This was all he knew.

As the story of Kaspar Hauser, the child with no past, made its rounds of the European newspapers and salons, various medics and aristocrats offered to help in his rehabilitation. Soon enough, a life was duly imagined for him. He was, some said, a kidnapped heir, the Crown Prince of Baden. Others had him down as an impostor. Either way, there were few substantiated facts. Eighty years after Hauser's death – in circumstances which compounded his mystery – the Scottish folklorist Andrew Lang suggested that neither explanation held true. Hauser was, he claimed, more likely to have been a compulsive wanderer – a *fugueur* before his time – who had suffered trauma and physical deprivation.

The year of 1887 proved a significant one in the medical history of amnesia. As Bourne travelled southwest, as Tissié published *Les Aliénés voyageurs*, a Russian physician, Sergei Korsakoff, published the first in a series of papers on a very different failure of memory. In treating a number of patients recovering from psychiatric illness associated with long-term alcoholism, Korsakoff noted that many were unable to acquire new memories. Events minutes past left no impression, although pre-illness memories were more stable. This amnesia had drastic knock-on effects. Patients showed little initiative, their intentions appearing to be forgotten before they were acted upon. Their thinking was generally repetitive and restricted to a small cluster of ideas.

In almost all cases of what is now called Korsakoff's syndrome, patients have no awareness of this deficit. A very small minority has nevertheless been observed with partial insight. 'When I watch closely, I know, but I soon forget,' remarked one patient. 'My brain feels like a sieve,' observed another. 'I forget everything. Even in my tiny room, I keep losing things. It all fades away.' When pressed to recollect the immediate past, Korsakoff patients may confabulate, drawing on past memories to fill in these recurrent blind spots. For example, when asked where he was and what he was doing yesterday evening, a Korsakoff patient might instead describe a night out some years ago. (These 'intrusory' memories are also found in Alzheimer's and following ECT and surgical treatments for epilepsy.) This confabulation is considered a form of self-defence against 'catastrophic reaction'.

In contrast to Korsakoff's syndrome, failures of recall due to cerebral damage are often accompanied by startling apathy, indifference and good humour. This is particularly true of lesions or injuries of the frontal lobes. In a portrait of one such case, Oliver Sacks describes how a young Hare Krishna devotee, 'Greg F', appeared to have discovered beatitude while suffering from a huge frontal tumour that claimed virtually all his recent memories, as well as his sight. Greg F lived in a dreamlike, timeless moment, a perpetual now, which was mistakenly taken as a sign of his spiritual ascent. Yet as profound as his inability to recall the recent past had become, it still managed to make an obscure and eerie impression on him. Sacks reports that, after his father died, Greg would invent reasons why he was no longer able to make his regular morning visits. In the night, he would wander his room, saying, 'I've lost something, I'm looking for something.' His searching was typical of the bereaved, but in Greg's case there was no grasp of his father's death. In some remote corner of his memory, the loss had perhaps been registered.

The impairments of memory found in Korsakoff's syndrome, cerebral tumours and other amnesiac syndromes have lent weight to various theories of memory and forgetfulness. It is generally accepted that amnesiacs suffer from a failure of storage (as opposed to retrieval or encoding) and that this failure is linked to the contextual aspect of remembering. In most instances, amnesia is thought to be a failure to recall the circumstances in which an event occurred or a fact was learnt. Experiments with Korsakoff patients have revealed that simple spoken statements can often be recalled after a few minutes, but not the context in which they were imparted. Almost a century ago, the Swiss psychologist Edouard Claparède confirmed this capacity for forming floating memories when, with a pin concealed in his hand, he shook hands with a Korsakoff patient. A few minutes later, when he offered his hand again, the patient refused. She did not remember being pricked, but observed, 'Pins are sometimes hidden in hands.' This phenomenon, known as 'source amnesia', is also a characteristic of post-hypnosis, during which subjects may recall impressively obscure facts and foreign phrases without having any conscious recollection of how they were learnt. But the reversibility of hypnotic amnesia – the ease with which most subjects will, on being given a prearranged cue, entirely recollect the learning process – marks it out as failure of retrieval.

Korsakoff syndrome belongs to a family of degenerative diseases of the nervous system which includes Alzheimer's, Parkinson's and Pick's diseases. All of these dementias usually manifest themselves in an inability to locate objects or recall proper names. Inevitably, these diseases lead to deficiencies in simple recall, to disorientation in time and space. The transformation of the whole person is, once again, dramatic. In his touching memoir of his wife, *Iris: A Memoir of Iris Murdoch* (1998), John Bayley describes the dramatic changes of personality that the writer and philosopher underwent as she went 'sailing into darkness'. Loss of bearings brought a need for constant reassurance. Tone of voice assumed new importance. Soon, Murdoch seemed to enter a second infancy. 'She never showed any interest in children before. Now she loves them, on television or in real life. It seems almost too appropriate. I tell her she is nearly four years old now – isn't that wonderful?'

Temps Perdu

The Ghost-Dance religion flourished when the tribes of the American southwest were dispossessed of their land and livelihood. From these upheavals there sprang a messianic cult that preached both the resurrection of the dead and the restoration of lost prosperity. In the first all-night ceremonies, Cheyenne and Arapaho dancers experienced visions in which they met and talked with the departed and once again saw the plains filled with buffalo, as they had been before the coming of the railroads. As the syncretic religion took hold in the 1880s, it was commonly held that the Second Coming of Jesus Christ would augur the return to an older and better way of life.

A ghost-dance of memory is liable to transport us all back to a lost Eden. Yet as powerful as the stirrings of nostalgia are in our conscious thoughts, our dreams and fantasies, it was only in the latter part of the nineteenth century that psychologists began to examine nostalgia as a natural form of *memory*. Before then, nostalgia was principally considered a malady of *displacement*, a disease of the exile who pined for a faraway homeland. When the Swiss physician Johannes Hofer conjoined the words *nostos* (a return to home) and *algia* (pain) in the seventeenth century, he had in mind a debilitating and sometimes fatal homesickness experienced by soldiers and emigrants. In a dissertation of 1678, Hofer wrote:

> The persons most susceptible to this disease are young people living in foreign lands, and among them especially those who at home live a very secluded life and have almost no social intercourse. When such individuals, even well-bred children, come among other peoples, they are unable to accustom themselves to

any foreign manners and way of life, nor to forget the maternal care received. They are apprehensive and find pleasure only in sweet thoughts of the fatherland until the foreign country becomes repugnant to them, or suffering various inconveniences they think night and day of returning to their native land and when prevented from doing so, they fall ill.

The German word for homesickness, *heimweh*, was evidently not appropriate to describe the condition Hofer had in mind. Through clinical observations that came to him secondhand, Hofer set out the course of the disease he called 'nostalgia'. Its first signs were, he claimed, heightened patriotism and an over-developed sense of personal injustice. As nostalgia took hold, the individual would succumb to a persistent melancholy, thinking constantly of home and family. Sleep would be usually fitful and appetite reduced. Palpitations and a potentially fatal fever would follow these symptoms. Despite Hofer's assertion that nostalgia was probably not exclusive to his landlocked, Alpine compatriots, this medicalisation was not evident in other European countries. To explain this narrow geographical provenance, one physician suggested that it might be due to changes in atmospheric pressure experienced when moving between country and city. More ingeniously, another suggested that it might be linked to damage of the inner ear, caused by persistent exposure to the ringing of cowbells!

By the middle of the nineteenth century, nostalgia began to take its place in the psychiatric literature. Aubert-Roche, for example, described the case of a young Frenchman, in the service of the Pasha of Egypt, who was assailed by a gloomy nostalgia. On taking the hashish that he was recommended, the young man 'experienced hallucinations more apt to increase than to lessen his sorrows. His eyes stared at the bare white walls of his room; he saw the house where he lived in the country, paths, the gardens, and his mother and his sister who strolled there and invited him to join them, reproaching him for his absence.'

Nostalgia nevertheless remained a preoccupation of military medicine, being principally diagnosed among foreign nationals serving in French, Austrian and other armies. While Highland Scots were observed to be particularly susceptible – especially on hearing the sound of bagpipes – Thomas Arnold proclaimed that the British 'know nothing of that passionate attachment that leads to this insanity'. French physicians serving in the armies of the First Republic and the Napoleonic Empire took nostalgia more seriously. They observed that conscripts from the most remote rural regions were easily nostalgia-stricken. The disease was, moreover, now observed in epidemic form, particularly after armies had incurred significant losses. While some soldiers were thought to feign nostalgia, malingerers were considered easy to root out, as they were usually averse to treatment.

While Hofer and other physicians had diagnosed cases of nostalgia in civilian life, it was not until the first half of the nineteenth century that it would be identified among sizeable numbers of migrant workers, particularly among young domestics who were isolated in the larger European cities. According to George Rosen, Paris physicians considered workers from Brittany particularly sensitive to nostalgia. As Rosen also points out, Balzac was the pre-eminent literary investigator of this new condition. 'The heroine of *Pierrette* suffers from nostalgia in the strict sense – that is, a continuing depression – after coming to Paris from Brittany, leading finally to death from consumption. Louis Lambert, the nostalgic youth, ultimately succumbs to schizophrenia. Then, in other stories and novels, Balzac extended the concept of nostalgia to cover frustrations not envisaged in medical accounts. Thus, Cousin Pons suffered Forman gastric nostalgia, and Claes in *La Recherche de l'absolu* develops *nostalgie scientifique*.'

The American Civil War saw a revival in the diagnosis of nostalgia, particularly among the legions of teenage conscripts. By the 1860s, however, few European psychiatrists continued to make reference to nostalgia, tending to regard it either as a symptom of melancholy or as a normative response to displacement and isolation. Only in Germany, in the context of forensic medicine, was the equivalent concept of *heimweh* still mobilised, in assessing the criminal responsibility of migrants who had committed arson or murder. These offences were explained in terms of an overbearing desire to return to their parental home. When Karl Jaspers presented his medical thesis on the subject of *heimweh* in 1909, he referred to around twenty cases, the last of which was reported in 1908. Four years later, when Jaspers published his *General Psychopathology*, *heimweh* was accorded little more than a sentence among reactive states such as 'prison-psychoses', 'battle-psychoses' and 'psychoses of isolation'.

Nostalgia was no longer the property of pathology. Moving beyond the clinical and military enclaves in which it had so long resided, the word 'nostalgic' could be readily applied to almost any aspect of nineteenth-century art and culture which looked backwards and borrowed from the past, or to any person given to such reminiscence. With Nietzsche complaining that an excess of historical remembrance was stifling creative potential, nostalgia was everywhere. Childhood, as once explored in Blake's 'Infant Sorrow' and Wordsworth's 'Intimations of Immortality' (which proclaims that 'Heaven lies about us in our infancy'), was now a central theme for writers as diverse as Dickens, Carroll and Ruskin. And in the fantasy worlds of incontinent nostalgics such as J. M. Barrie and Kenneth Grahame, childhood was imagined as an exalted state of innocence, a visionary Arcadia.

Psychology followed suit by examining the secret recesses of 'traumatic reminiscences' and 'infantile amnesia'. Hysteria, a disease once defined in terms of its physiological 'stigmata', was now re-imagined as a problem of recollection. While these memories were in most cases infantile memories that were repressed and inaccessible to normal recall, Freud and Breuer found that all the symptoms of hysteria quickly abated by awakening the original memory (often disguised beneath others) in its emotional entirety. Dispensing with hypnosis to stimulate recall, Freud employed the 'pressure procedure' on the hands and forehead, and it was from this 'small technical artifice' that he developed the talking cure, which sought to unravel and expose memory through associations.

As psychoanalysis developed its tools for the excavation of memory, Marcel Proust was engaged in his own *recherche*, exploring the mysteries and joys of nostalgia at its most aleatory. Proust's insight into the nature of nostalgia came to him on a winter's night in 1909, when he dipped a finger of toast into his tea and found that the faint scent of geraniums and apple blossoms took him back to his great-uncle's summer garden. This recollection was, for Proust, nothing less than 'a fragment of pure life preserved in its purity'. He had briefly returned to himself. Six months later, he decided that this epiphanic unfolding of time (famously reworked as the lime tea and madeleine scene in which Marcel feels himself transported back to Combray) would provide the key to his novel. As a telescope reveals stars that are invisible to the naked eye, he would wait for the tinkling of cutlery to recall the silent symphony of memory. This was his self-analysis.

Convinced that the intellect alone could not wrestle and revive the past, Proust began and ended his epic 'work of salvage' with memories that were unbidden transports rather than conscious recollections. 'From my point of view,' he explained, 'voluntary memory, which is above all a memory through intelligence and the eyes, gives us of the past only faces without truth; while, on the contrary, if a scent, a flavour, recaptured in quite different circumstances, brings us back almost in spite of ourselves, we find that it is a different past from what we believed we recalled through the pictures of voluntary memory.' Nostalgia, the disease of the exile, had travelled a long way.

The Strangely Familiar

'We have all some experience of a feeling that comes over us occasionally, of what we are saying and doing having been said and done before, in a remote time – of our having been surrounded dim ages ago, by the same faces, objects and circumstances – of our knowing perfectly well what will be said next, as if we suddenly remembered it!' When Dickens described this sensation of beguiling familiarity in *David Copperfield* in 1850, the experience of *déjà vu* was still to find its place and name among the memory disorders of *fin-de-siècle* psychology. The elusive and unaccountable sense of recollection had, however, already been the subject of conflicting interpretations. In what is possibly the first documented case of *déjà vu*, Pythagoras is said to have recognised a shield in Juno's temple in Argo, ascribing its familiarity to perhaps having himself worn it in a previous life, as Euphorbus, during the Trojan War – one of many incarnations attributed to him. Centuries later, Saint Augustine took issue with the Pythagorean belief in reincarnation, to claim that such intimations of a former life were 'untrue memories' influenced by malign spirits who sought to promulgate 'the false belief concerning the changes of the souls'.

In the mid-nineteenth century, new theories of *déjà vu* would be proposed and classical versions revived. In his 1844 book *The Duality of Mind*, Arthur Wigan advanced a purely physiological explanation prompted by his experiences at the funeral of Princess Charlotte in 1817. Wigan had slept poorly and eaten little when, after four hours of standing, he watched the coffin being lowered and sustained 'a *conviction*, that I had seen the whole scene before on some occasion'. Wigan proposed that tiredness might cause one brain hemisphere to be less alert than the other, causing a delay in the processing of information. This disjuncture, Wigan explained, would account for 'a sudden feeling, as if the scene we have just witnessed . . . had been present to our eyes on a former occasion'. The German physician Dr Jensen agreed, and it was from his account that continental thinkers turned to the double brain to explain this as yet unnamed anomaly of recollection:

> Just as two images take shape in the eyes, so do two perceptions in the hemispheres take shape, which however under normal circumstances mostly overlap, are almost wholly congruent and so are perceived as just single. What, though, when circumstances are not normal? When the two halves [of the brain] do not function in a congruent manner but like a squinting eye, there instead occurs incongruency between the functioning of the brain's two hemi-spheres. In cases of the eyes, there is a doubling of images – in case of the brain there would correspondingly be a doubling of perception. . . . We project double images outwards beside each other in space. Would it not be possible that we project double perceptions beside each other in space?

This idea of cerebral disruption was a central theme in late nineteenth-century medicine, providing an explanatory schema for epilepsy, insanity and a range of minor states of reverie and mental automatism. Finding support among influential thinkers such as Henry Maudsley, Wigan and Jensen's neurological speculations provided the dominant framework for understanding *déjà vu* in Britain until the very end of the century. In France, where the *bizarreries de la mémoire* occupied a more prominent place in the growth of psychological science, *déjà vu* (or *l'illusion de fausse reconnaissance*, as it was commonly referred to before the 1890s) was keenly debated in the pages of various journals, especially in the *Revue Philosophique*. Increasing emphasis was soon placed on the splitting of subconscious and conscious processes, yet the 'double-image' theory of *déjà vu* – lent weight by Théodule Ribot in his 1881 book *Les Maladies de la mémoire* – held sway for the best part of a decade. What it failed to address was why the first of the memory images should return to consciousness seeped in a tantalising sepia haze. And, more importantly, was *déjà vu* actually a deficit of memory?

The early literature on *déjà vu* discussed the phenomenon in both its transient and pathological forms. In 1896, when addressing the Société Medico-Psychologique, Arnaud, the first physician to suggest *l'illusion de déjà vu* as the standard terminology, described the case of 'Louis', a thirty-four-year-old army officer who was repeatedly subject to *déjà vu* after contracting malaria. On reading a newspaper, Louis recognised articles that he believed he had written. At his brother's wedding, he had the impression of having the previous year attended the same ceremony. When he was admitted to hospital in 1894, everything appeared to be repeating itself. He remembered the hospital, the staff, their words and gestures. The papers were always filled with old news. On being introduced to Dr Arnaud, he announced: 'You know me, doctor. You welcomed me last year, at the same time, and in the same room. You asked me the same questions, and I gave you the same answers.' There was, however, one vital difference between Louis's experiences of *déjà vu* and those recorded in transient form: Louis's 'memories' would never be located. In the more fleeting and more usual type of *déjà vu* there was simply an eerie, inchoate sense of the past.

Although Arnaud underestimated how common experiences of *déjà vu* were, he was one of the very first physicians to suggest that the underlying mechanism of *déjà vu* might be a projection of current experience back into the past, rather than an actual recollection. Not all psychologists, however, were convinced that the phenomenon deserved such attention. In his *Principles of Psychology*, William James gave the subject surprisingly short shrift. 'I must confess', he wrote, sounding a note of uncharacteristic scepticism, 'that the quality of mystery seems a little strained. I have over and over again in my own case succeeded in resolving the phenomenon into a case of memory, so indistinct that whilst some past circumstances are presented again, the others are not. The dissimilar portions of the past do not arise completely enough at first for the date to be identified. All we get is the present scene with a general suggestion of pastness about it.'

James's comments suggest that he, unlike Wigan, Jensen, Kraepelin and many of the early theorists, had no firsthand experience of genuine *déjà vu*. This was true of another eminent philosopher–psychologist, Henri Bergson, who conceded that he had attempted to 'induce experimentally the phenomenon in myself'. However, Bergson, writing twenty years after James, had examined enough reports to understand that *déjà vu* 'comes over a person quickly and as suddenly vanishes, leaving behind it an impression of a dream'.

In his 1908 paper on 'Memory of the Present and False Recognition', perhaps the last major study of the psychology of *déjà vu*, Bergson argued that its causation lay in 'a temporary enfeebling of a general attention to life'. Disagreeing with Pierre Janet, whose clinical work with psychaesthenic patients had led him to consider *déjà vu* a purely pathological state, Bergson found that it was not a disorder of memory, but a more profound confusion of past, present and future. It was as a suspension of future-directed thinking, as a defect of will, that *déjà vu* fascinated Bergson. By default, this strange experience appeared to reveal the 'life-impetus', the ceaseless striving towards action which was so central to Bergson's philosophy of the *élan vital*. Furthermore, Bergson speculated that *déjà vu* might have a psychological function: to prevent consciousness from lapsing into more profound states of temporal breakdown such as those witnessed in cases like that of Louis.

After 1910, relatively few papers on the subject of *déjà vu* were published. Freud's 1919 paper 'The Uncanny' discussed the phenomenon as the revival of infantile and quasi-primitive beliefs. Jung broadly followed suit, regarding *déjà vu* as the stirring of ancestral memories in what he considered the collective unconscious. But Arnaud, Janet and Bergson's resistance to the notion that *déjà vu* was a deficit of memory was partially vindicated in the 1940s, when two experimental psychologists, Banister and Zangwill, sought to create paramnesia (distorted memories) by showing hypnotised volunteers a series of pictures that they were induced to forget. When the pictures were later shown to volunteers, the sense of familiarity they reported did not express itself as *déjà vu*.

The latter-day history of *déjà vu* belongs to the laboratory and to neurological experimentation in particular. Not long after famous experiments at the Montreal Neurological Institute elicited *déjà vu* in epileptic patients through stimulation of the superior and lateral parts of the temporal lobes, experimenters at the University of California were able to produce similar results in non-diseased temporal lobes. These findings have given renewed credibility to the so-called 'double-access' hypothesis, which, following Wigan and Jensen, proposes that *déjà vu* is due to a delay in the normal transmission of images from the non-dominant to the dominant hemisphere. According to Robert Efron's 1963 paper in the journal *Brain*, a time lag of several hundred milliseconds (as opposed to the usual few thousandths) would cause the dominant hemisphere to receive the same information twice over, thereby causing the second impression to seem familiar.

Arnaud, Bergson and Janet would have all been rightly sceptical. To explain *déjà vu* in the language of hemispheric delay is, as Bergson might have put it, to 'know a symphony by the movements of the conductor directing the orchestra'.

Total Recall

In the 1920s, the editor of a Moscow newspaper sent a young journalist called Solomon Shereshevski to have his memory tested. This was no reprimand for late or shoddy copy. The editor was struck by the fact that, although Shereshevski never took notes of names, addresses and detailed instructions issued at morning briefings, he was able to repeat them all word for word. Keen to learn exactly how he had acquired his apparently infallible memory, Shereshevski's editor directed him to the laboratory of Aleksandr Luria, a psychologist who would distinguish himself as one of the most acute and humane observers of neurological disorders.

Luria quickly discovered that Shereshevski was able to reproduce, in given or reverse order, any list of numbers, words or meaningless syllables. Besides suggesting that 'his memory had no distinct limits', these experiments indicated that Shereshevski's recollections were recorded indelibly, filed away mysteriously, but always accessible for future reference. When asked to recall a series he had been asked to remember many years previously, Shereshevski would close his eyes, pause and replay his internal footage, adding incidental details of setting and circumstance.

Luria's account of his experiments and correspondence with Shereshevski over the course of some thirty years, *The Mind of a Mnemonist*, furnishes some intriguing insights into the basis of his 'total recall', a talent that he would eventually exploit as a professional memory artist. The secret of Shereshevski's prodigious memory was that he was able to *see* the information he was given. Words and numbers, for example, were immediately tabulated mentally so that he could recall them subsequently at will. To read these tables, he required absolute silence. If noise or speech interrupted him, 'puffs of steam' would obscure his mental imagery. These rogue blurrings alerted Luria to the possibility that synaesthesia, a fusion of sense modalities, might be implicated in his memory. Like other synaesthetes, Shereshevski not only heard sounds: he saw, tasted and felt them. 'I recognise a word not only by the images it evokes,' he confided to Luria, 'but by a whole complex of feelings that the image arouses . . . Usually I experience a word's taste and weight, and I don't have to make an effort to remember it – the word seems to recall itself.'

These sensory translations were vital to Shereshevski's memory, explaining how he could so easily convert and retrieve material. The very rare errors that Shereshevski made in recalling spoken information were in fact defects of perception and place-ment, and not memory as such. For example, when asked to remember a list that included the word 'pencil', Shereshevski would set off on an imaginary walk and place a pencil somewhere en route. When he inadvertently placed it against a fence and mentally retraced his steps, he failed to see the pencil among the wooden posts and hence failed to recall it.

Shereshevski's memory was, then, neither total nor natural. The feats of recollection that he undertook as a memory artist required him to develop and utilise long-standing mnemonic tech-niques to handle enormous amounts of information. These systems have a history that dates back to classical Greece. For example, Shereshevski's method of compiling inventories by taking mental walks and placing items en route is reminiscent of the locality system of memorisation that Frances Yates attributes to the classical poet Simonides in *The Art of Memory*. Orators following this topographical system would prepare their speeches by mentally dividing them and distributing the constituent parts in the rooms of a familiar building. Other long-standing mnemonic systems rely on techniques of visual association, and on acrostics and more complex codes that embed dates and numbers in verse and rhyme.

Unlike other prodigious memories studied by nineteenth-century psychology, Shereshevski's memory was not *eidetic*, that is, based on after-images which he visually retained. His memory was more mobile and spontaneous, allowing him to trawl far and deep. Yet his amazing capacity for recollection, Luria realised, also impacted on a personality that was essentially 'disorganized and rather dull witted'. Because faces were never exactly the same, he found them difficult to remember. Passages of literature read at normal speed made little sense. In fact, the impossibility of forgetting was as much a burden as a gift. Shereshevski had to teach himself to forget. His efforts were laboured and cack-handed. The closest he got was a kind of self-censorship, shutting down his internal archive before he had the opportunity to spy on its records.

Shereshevski's memory had other interesting knock-on effects, most of which would have been ignored by other psychologists. Being so image-led in his thinking, Shereshevski found it difficult to grasp homonyms and synonyms, and was more or less impervious to the poetic nuances of language. Even the language used to describe simple scientific propositions could produce 'images that tended to scatter memory'. All abstraction, particularly music, was elusive, betrayed by his incessant visualisation. Although this vivid imagination allowed him remarkable control of his bodily processes (Shereshevski could set his pulse racing by imagining himself running, raise the temperature of one hand by mentally placing it on a hot stove), Luria found that this 'magical' thinking was delusory and potentially treacherous. His imagination had become a surrogate form of action, a counterlife, allowing him to cut himself off from quotidian demands and obligations. Continually distracted by his thoughts, Shereshevski could mentally occupy two places at once, observing himself as a third person. In conversation, this led him to become long-winded and digressive, easily steered off-track. This dreamy absent-mindedness affected every aspect of his person. Stumbling from one profession to another – from musician to vaudeville actor, efficiency expert to herbalist and lawyer – Shereshevksi was perpetually distracted by the luminous brilliance of his memory and imagination.

The fact that other members of the Shereshevski family shared something of this exuberant talent for recollection led Luria and other psychologists involved in their study to suggest that it was genetically acquired. This conjecture is partially supported by research on autistic savants who have excelled as memory artists or calendar calculators. Increasingly understood as a biological condition, the vivid recall that autism gives rise to can be as prodigious as that of Shereshevski. In the case of the memory artist Stephen Wiltshire, who has excelled at producing detailed drawings of buildings and cityscapes from memory, the most ornate and complex of scenery can be fixed in his mind within a few seconds and, as with Shereshevski, permanently stored. Yet once again the term 'photographic' or 'total' recall may still be a misnomer. Wiltshire's use of mirror reversals and multiple per-spectives suggests that even these remarkably exact simulations are reconstructions rather than actual memory snapshots.

Psychologists who have studied other individuals with a capacity for summoning after-images, so-called *eidetikers*, have long realised that, as vivid and lasting as these memories are, they are never infallible. Many of the claims made for *eidetikers* have nevertheless been extravagant and romantic. The German psychologist Eric Jaensch, who studied eideticism between 1911 and 1930, claimed that most of the schoolchildren he had studied at his laboratory in Marburg were, to some degree, eidetic (B-types retained a graphic after-image of a given scene or object; T-types had less distinct after-images and could not summon and erase at will). This led Jaensch to propose that eideticism was a mode of perception shared by children and primitives. While Jaensch's claims for eideticism resonated with and lent credence to a raft of mystical theories of remembrance, including De Quincey's notion of mind as palimpsest, his findings have been rejected by almost all subsequent investigators. Eidetic recall, according to these more recent empirical studies, is at very best demonstrated, in weak form, by one in seven children. Never totally.

De La Trance

Dr Mesmer's Invisible Cure

Vienna, a city famed for its musical legacy, can claim to be the birthplace of some of the most radical ideas in modern medicine and science. Towards the end of the eighteenth century, as Mozart's symphonies and concertos filled the concert halls, the foundations of three important movements were, in part, laid there: magnetism, homeopathy and phrenology. Of these medical heterodoxies, magnetism was destined to be the most controversial and far reaching. As a scene from Mozart's *Così fan tutte* can confirm, magnetism's first champion, Franz Anton Mesmer, was, in the 1780s, the talk of most European cities. A century on, physicians and psychologists were still debating the nature and efficacy of Dr Mesmer's discovery.

Soon after publishing his doctoral dissertation on lunar and planetary influences on disease in 1766, Mesmer entered medical practice and began, through the use of steel magnets, to subject his patients to the therapeutic effects of 'a kind of artificial tide'. Initially believing that these devices healed through the ethereal power of 'animal magnetism', Mesmer became convinced that he could act as a conductor to this vital force. By staring into his patients' eyes, by pressing their thumbs and passing his hands over their limbs and torso, he was able to revive circulation, to recharge the nervous system and restore harmony to the body. These techniques probably owed much to the healing rites of exorcism, but Mesmer explained the idea of animal magnetism in a language that was as alien to the medieval church as it was to Enlightenment medicine.

Mesmer estimated that he belonged to a select minority of about one in ten people who could directly channel the powers of animal magnetism. With colleagues and former teachers unimpressed by his apparent discovery, Mesmer set out to publicise his findings and demonstrate his procedures. After travelling to Hungary, Switzerland and Bavaria, where he succeeded in gaining some converts, Mesmer returned to Vienna and, in January of 1777, began to treat Maria Theresia von Paradis, a teenage pianist who had been blind since the age of four. For Mesmer, this was an opportunity to stake his claims for a full scientific commission on animal magnetism. Paradis immediately responded to his 'passes' – her body trembled, her eyes hurt, her head was dizzy. In less than a month, her sight had returned imperfectly, but her playing deteriorated. Most of the physicians who witnessed Mesmer's magnetic cure (including a young Samuel Hahnemann, the future founder of homeopathy) were suitably impressed, but when Herr Paradis inexplicably turned on Mesmer, causing his daughter to relapse, his reputation was sullied by the ensuing controversy. Suspecting that the whole debacle had been contrived especially to damage him, Mesmer left Vienna for Paris.

Paris society was seduced by Mesmer and his magnetic cure. Provoking convulsions, tears, fits of laughter or sleep, he was able to claim notable successes in the cure of constipation, indigestion, hysterical blindness and paralysis. As word spread, Mesmer began to stage 'group sessions' around a *baquet*, a large wooden tub filled with magnetised water and iron filings. His circle of patients would sit around the *baquet* holding on to its protruding rods. With lighting and music from a glass harmonica intensifying the magnetic ambience, a lilac-cloaked Mesmer padded his way around the grand rooms of the Hôtel Bullion, boosting the flow of magnetic fluid with a theatrical wave of hand or wand. Besides curing an array of illnesses, the ensuing fits fired the imagination, leading patients to report lucid mental journeys and clairvoyance.

Under the auspices of the Society of Universal Harmony, magnetism quickly spread to the French provinces. Depriving more orthodox physicians of their previous monopoly on melancholics and hysterics, magnetism now cemented the reformist agenda that some of its more politically minded initiates, such as Jacques-Pierre Brissot, claimed for it. In 1784, two official committees were appointed to investigate this most alternative of medicines. Working in conjunction with the University of Paris Faculty of Medicine, the committee of the Royal Academy of Sciences reported that 'magnetism without the imagination can produce nothing'. Furthermore, it issued a 'serious warning' – 'that the touches and repeated stimulation of the imagination in the production of crisis may prove harmful . . . all public treatments of magnetism must in the long run have deplorable consequences'. The report of the Royal Society of Medicine was equally critical, but again the commissioners preferred to address only the theory of mesmerism, rather than its curative effects.

The magnetic cure nevertheless lived on, travelling to Europe and North America. As it crossed the Channel to Britain in the 1780s, animal magnetism was reworked by quacks such as James Graham, whose 'celestial bed' employed the same principle, but instead promised fertility and an angelic offspring to the married couples who could afford to spend £50 for one night's occupancy. When, in the 1830s, the medical community finally began to explore the psychosomatic potential of magnetism, its outward effects had already changed. Catalepsy and open-eyed trance replaced the convulsive fits that Mesmer and his contemporaries witnessed. More intriguingly, many patients now began to diagnose and prescribe for themselves and others.

Having witnessed these and other phenomena at first hand – in demonstrations given by Richard Chenevix and Baron Dupotet – John Elliotson embarked on a series of investigations that would lead to new scandal. Elliotson, Professor of Medicine at University College London, was a highly respected and well-connected physician. Convinced of mesmerism's therapeutic potential, Elliotson initially enlisted Dupotet to perform demonstrations at University College, but soon took sole charge. Two teenage sisters, Elizabeth and Jane O'Key, were among his first subjects. The sisters, who were both diagnosed as epileptics, became something of a pantomime double act. As Jane mimicked the actions of Elliotson, standing out of view, engaging objects in conversation and generally entertaining her audience with songs and jokes, Elizabeth would examine and diagnose other patients, report premonitions, speak in tongues and mock the clergy and aristocracy. Elliotson refused to censor these histrionics. When University College Hospital's medical council expelled the O'Key sisters and other magnetic patients, Elliotson resigned his chair in protest.

The mesmeric séance lost none of its fascination in the mid-nineteenth century. While audiences argued over whether subjects were faking, physicians remained unclear as to whether the trance state could be explained in terms of the magnetic forces that Mesmer had proposed or whether some other psychological or physiological explanation might be more appropriate. This was the question that Manchester surgeon James Braid set about investigating in the early 1840s. His observations of the *physical* appearance of trance subjects, combined with his experiments in induction, led him to propose that mesmerism was in fact a form of nervous sleep, *hypnos*, from which the term 'hypnotism' would be derived.

For Braid, nervous sleep was composed of two stages. The first 'subhypnotic state' was 'a state of mental concentration' in which patients were 'susceptible of being influenced and controlled entirely by the suggestion of others upon whom their attention is fixed'. While patients retained complete memory of actions undertaken during this period, the second stage of 'double consciousness', in which volition is further ceded, would only be recalled if the patient was again hypnotised. In this more profound state, the patient's body was completely insensible and could 'be pricked, or pinched, or maimed, without evincing the slightest symptom of pain or sensibility'. Braid's explanation of these phenomena was essentially physiological. The effects were, he maintained, produced by changes in respiration and blood circulation brought on by nervous sleep.

Although Braid is commonly considered mesmerism's first modern interrogator, he, like Elliotson, was in many ways a runaway convert. His 1843 book *Neurypnology, or the Rationale of Nervous Sleep* may have offered a new physiological explanation of the trance state – which he partially recapitulated, accepting the role of suggestion as a powerful and necessary agent – but it did not discount the extravagant claims made by many practitioners. Braid himself reported a catalogue of hypnotic cures for rheumatic disorders, headaches, epilepsy, spinal curvature and paralysis, and claimed that he had 'scarcely met with a single case of a congenitally deaf mute where I have not succeeded in making the patient hear to some degree'. Numerous experiments also led him to confirm 'how far phrenological manifestations could be developed during hypnotism'. Reporting the case of 'Mrs Col.', a respectable lady who apparently knew nothing of phrenology, Braid's endorsement was quite emphatic. 'In about three minutes after she was asleep,' wrote Braid, 'I placed two fingers over the point named veneration, instantly the aspect of her countenance changed; in a little she slowly, and solemnly, and majestically arose from her chair, advanced towards the table in the middle of the room, and softly sank on her knees, and exhibited such a picture of devout adoration as can never be forgotten.'

When Braid died in 1860, hypnotism was already being abandoned by the minority of physicians who had followed his example in adopting it as a surgical anaesthetic. Losing out to ether and chloroform, quicker and more efficient painkillers, hypnotism was in Britain reduced to role of public burlesque and scientific marvel. In France, however, there was a resurgence of interest, and Braid's work became an important reference for Eugène Azam and Paul Broca, who followed his procedures when hypnotising a number of surgical patients. The flurry of interest in 'Braidisme' was short lived, but with renowned figures such as Charcot, Forel and Janet undertaking experiments and observations, the hypnotic trance remained a bona fide field of medical inquiry.

After employing magnets to induce trance in his patients at the Salpêtrière, Charcot came to believe that *le grand hypnotisme* was peculiar to the hysterics and epileptics on whom he experimented. Moreover, Charcot, echoing Braid, observed that the symptoms of the somnambulistic trance could be physically manipulated. Rubbing patients' heads, for example, was thought to make them alert and susceptible to instructions. A bright light or sudden noise would, by contrast, freeze them in wide-eyed catalepsy, making them insensible to pain. The Nancy school of Liebault and Bernheim, who found that hypnosis did not require a neurotic or pathological personality, disputed all these claims. If properly induced, they claimed, the vast majority of people would succumb to an enhanced state of suggestibility, which Bernheim regarded as the keynote of the hypnotic trance. As for the symptoms displayed by Charcot's subjects, Bernheim thought these were due to a mimicking of other patients. Not one of the Nancy subjects who were hypnotised using only verbal suggestion showed these symptoms.

By 1890, when William James published the *Principles of Psychology*, the suggestion theory of hypnosis had triumphed over Charcot's physiological theory. The trance state was now thought to have 'no particular outward symptoms of its own'. Amnesia, paralysis, compliance, anaesthesia, hyperaesthesia and all the other effects that had been so far noted were, noted James, fashioned from the expectation of operator and subject. 'Thus it happens that one easily verifies on new subjects what one has already seen in old ones, or any desired symptom of which one may have heard or read.'

Freud, who had studied hypnosis under Charcot and Bernheim, and for many years employed it in his treatment of neurotic patients, had some early successes; however, as he turned to his own methods of analysis, he increasingly dismissed hypnosis as unscientific, akin to 'magic, incantations and hocus-pocus'. This about-turn had serious consequences for both its experimental and clinical uptake. It was not until the 1940s that hypnosis would make a significant return to the laboratory. After studies confirmed that Braid had been mistaken in regarding hypnosis as a form of sleep – breathing pattern, heart rate and EEG profile were all physiologically characteristic of wakefulness – researchers became largely preoccupied with measuring factors that accounted for the very marked variations in hypnotic susceptibility. Contrary to received wisdom, there is no significant relationship between gender and susceptibility. The optimum age for induction is between nine and ten, with susceptibility declining rapidly at around fifteen. Although mental disorder does not provide total immunity to hypnosis, neurotics and depressives are invariably the most difficult groups to hypnotise.

Of all the hypnotic effects studied in the laboratory in the past century, only two had not been recorded by the eighteenth- or nineteenth-century investigators – recovered memory and age regression. The enhancement of recall of recent and long-past events under hypnosis has been described in a multitude of experiments, but many investigators have also noted a corresponding lack of critical attention to the fidelity of the material that is being remembered. As John Kihlstrom writes, 'hypnosis is first and foremost a state of believed-in imaginings; in the absence of independent corroboration, there is no reason to think that any hypnotically refreshed recollection is an accurate representation of the historical past – and, in fact, every reason to doubt it.' For exactly the same reasons, the notion of age regression under hypnosis remains a misnomer. Hypnotic subjects do not regress to childhood, but they act *as if* they had.

Behavioural psychologists such as Theodor Barber have supported a role-enactment theory of hypnosis, which suggests that 'hypnotised' individuals by and large behave in ways that they think typical of hypnosis. Martin Orne's claim that the hypnotic state is precipitated by 'demand characteristics' of the situation, rather than any distinct trance state, is a powerful one. Orne demonstrated the power of expectation in various experiments. Unlike Barber, however, Orne did not discount a psychological component to the hypnotic state or 'trance logic'. He recognised that hypnosis allowed subjects to behave *as if* the instructions were true. For instance, the trance logic might allow a subject to imagine that a room is empty without colliding into all-too-solid furniture. This kind of 'selective inattention' underpins other hypnotic feats such as analgesia (inability to feel pain) and automatic writing, but does not necessarily provide a general theory of hypnosis. Attempts to understand hypnosis in terms of any single concept, from atavism to dissociation, goal enactment to goal-directed fantasy, have proved hopelessly reductive.

In its 200-year history, the techniques used to induce hypnosis have changed as much as the phenomena it produces. However, not all the effects that have been linked with hypnosis are genuine. The persistent belief that hypnosis can be used to bring a subject to reveal her most guarded secrets, or to produce absolute acquiescence, is absolutely unfounded. The CIA-funded work of experimental psychologists in the 1950s enjoyed little success in this regard. Yet this search to create a Manchurian candidate, a programmed assassin who would act out post-hypnotic suggestions without memory of the events, still colours the public perception of hypnosis as a form of mind control. Even amnesia, first reported by a subject of the Marquis de Puységur, a pupil of Mesmer, in 1784, is questionable as a result of hypnosis. As far back as the 1880s, the Nancy school demonstrated that a subject's apparent lack of memory could be easily breached, revealing fragments and sometimes complete knowledge of 'forgotten' events.

The manner in which hypnosis continues to be debunked nevertheless suggests that scientific scepticism has not necessarily evolved a great deal since the 1780s. Robert Park's recent book *Voodoo Science* (2000), for example, reminds us that French commissions were emphatic in denying Mesmer's claims. 'The commissioners,' Park writes, 'designed a series of ingenious tests in which subjects were deceived into thinking they were receiving Mesmer's cures when they were not, while others received the treatment but were led to believe they had not. The results established beyond any doubt that the effects of Mesmerism were due solely to the power of suggestion. The commission report, drafted by M. Bailly, an illustrious historian of astronomy, has never been surpassed for clarity and reason. It destroyed Mesmer's reputation . . .' While Park assumes that Mesmer was merely an ambitious quack, a more informed reading suggests that his fundamental mistake was to dress his discovery in metaphors – of magnetism and electricity – that would be investigated much too literally.

The Automatic Hand

The journals of Emmanuel Swedenborg record that the Swedish theologian and philosopher often felt his hand writing of its own accord, making statements of facts of which he had no actual knowledge, offering assertions with which he sometimes disagreed. These 'messages' were conveyed to Swedenborg in the 1740s, the decade in which he experienced his first waking visions. At this time, there was no standard term to describe such ghost writing. A full century passed before spiritualism gave birth to the idea of 'inspirational' and 'passive' writing. While angels and saints were initially the most prominent of the heavenly correspondents, mediums quickly found themselves playing the role of amanuensis to such celebrated personalities as Franklin, Jefferson and, most prolifically of all, Swedenborg himself.

For many years, the medical attitude to spiritualism as 'a direct and efficient cause of insanity' precluded serious investigation of any of its supposedly morbid manifestations. It was not until the 1880s that 'automatic writing' began to be examined in terms of its distinctive physiology and psychology, and that its therapeutic uses were explored. This research established that, when attention was properly diverted from the task of writing, the writing hand had a natural tendency to move. From this basic motor impulse, two types of automatic writing could develop. The most spontaneous, rather like that of Swedenborg, was usually rambling and repetitious. Truly automatic writing, for which individuals retained no memory, was more usually exhibited by individuals who had become habituated to what psychologists today call 'dual-tasking'.

The simplicity of inducing passive writing, combined with the fact that it could be undertaken without the assistance of a séance circle, ensured its popularity among the first generation of spiritualist dabblers. Besides pen and paper, passive writing required only the cultivation of a tranquil detachment that would allow the spirits to intervene and take control. These spirit messages provided comfort and guidance. They answered unvoiced questions. They permitted secret desires and dissatisfactions to be disclosed, with none of the responsibilities of authorship. They allowed the imagination to run riot with immunity. For all these reasons, passive writing would provide a refuge for the troubled, the grieving and the unfulfilled.

The English medium Florence Theobold first made contact with the spirit world via passive writing in the early 1860s. As with many of the most capable automatic writers, she was already intimate with hallucinations and other 'sensitive experiences' thanks to the 'hysterical affections' she endured as a child. The middle-class and Nonconformist circles which the Theobold family moved in were well disposed to the early spiritualist movement. Their family doctor, James Wilkinson, traversed some of the most important strands of spiritualism – he was a homeopath with an active interest in mesmerism and Swedenborgianism. Immediate neighbours of the Theobolds, William and Mary Howitt, had turned to spiritualism after the death of a child, and it was in their home that Florence first listened for the rapping spirits, fostering the hope that she, too, might develop a gift for mediumship. In 1863, after some years of fruitless experiment, illness and isolation finally ushered Florence's despatches from the Other Side.

On cultivating her talent for passive writing, 'Hundreds of pages of deep wisdom and of marvellous beauty were poured through my hands . . . and so rapidly was page after page written, that what was given in ten-minutes by the spirit writing, would take me an hour or more to copy'. Some of the first writerly spirits were the deceased children of her brother, Morell. Eventually, the whole family was won over by Florence's powers. Sitting two to three times a week, the Theobolds went on to receive lengthy communications from their deceased children, finding solace in their dazzling accounts of their spirit-births and news of their continued schooling. Although some spirit messages claimed to emanate from the likes of Napoleon and Queen Elizabeth, the Theobolds generally distrusted 'the free use of great names'. Florence urged the need for vigilance and discrimination when considering these dispatches. 'Do not believe everything you are told, for though the great unseen world contains many a wise and discerning spirit, it has also in it the accumulation of human folly, vanity, and error.'

It was through association with another female medium, Louisa Lowe, that passive writing became embroiled in a long-running debate concerning the relationship between spiritualism and insanity. Louisa Lowe turned to passive writing after witnessing her first séance in 1869. 'Soon, very soon,' she wrote, 'I became a fully-developed writing medium, of unusual power I believe; for we – that is, Passive Writing and I – dialogued together for hours at a time. I was very lonely, and this intercourse so fascinated me that for several days I did little else than enjoy it.' Lowe, a cousin of Charles Kingsley, was able, through her writings, to express her millenarian belief in the 'new and glorious day of progress' that was dawning. But much of her writings was pointed at her husband, the Reverend George Lowe, whom she suspected of adulterous liaisons. Her unhappy marriage to George Lowe, who repeatedly threatened and eventually succeeded in having her incarcerated, clearly provided impetus and direction to the free-flowing messages she 'received'.

In September 1870, shortly after one of her messages advised that she should live and work among like-minded people, Louisa left London for Exeter. Isolated, fearing that her husband might force her to return to the family home, she sought out the physician who had delivered her children, Dr Shapter. A few days after confiding in him, she was apprehended and taken to a large private asylum at Brislington, where she was diagnosed as suffering from 'mania and delusions'. Within six months, she was transferred to another private asylum, run by Henry Maudsley. After her release in 1871, Lowe launched herself into activism and litigation. Becoming honorary secretary of the Lunacy Law Reform Association, initiating legal proceedings against the Lunacy Commission, Lowe hoped to reform the legislation that had allowed her to be 'incarcerated and otherwise restrained as a lunatic for eighteen months, on the sole ground of claiming to be a passive or automatic writer'. Although she failed in this regard, Lowe was eventually able to influence the 1877 government select committee that investigated the lunacy laws, exposing a catalogue of medical violations of women spiritualists.

Passive writing was never a systematic release of censored or controversial beliefs. As Alex Owen makes clear in her study of late Victorian spiritualism, *The Darkened Room*, 'mind passivity' could give rise to nonsense, profanity, triviality and philosophising of the most bloated and indulgent kind. Many practitioners acknowledged that the rogue spirits could assume the guise of historical personages, or that fictitious personages might send them on a fool's errand. Spirit communications needed to be vigorously edited.

Significantly, it was a male medium, an Oxford graduate and clergyman, whose passive writings first elicited serious attention. William Stanton Moses began his second career as a passive writer when, in the early 1870s, he left his country parish to become a schoolmaster at London's University College School. Initially, the home circle he founded with friends was privy to a myriad of physical phenomena, from rappings and levitations to full-bodied materialisations. A year on, Moses became secretary to history's great and good, receiving passive sermons in keeping with the conservative Unitarian that he was. These writings soon appeared as weekly bulletins in the *Spiritualist*, the same newspaper that had supported Louisa Lowe's campaign against the lunacy laws. Preferring to bill himself as 'M. A. Oxon', Moses also chose to disguise the eminent sources of his Unitarian teachings: the Old Testament prophet Malachi became 'Imperator'; Plotinus assumed the name 'Prudens'; Saint Hippolytus was demoted to 'Rector'. These writings were enormously popular. Republished as *Spirit Teachings* (1883) and *More Spirit Teachings* (1928), Moses's work found a ready audience.

One aspect of these automatic writings that distinguished them from those of Florence Morell and Louisa Lowe was the degree of worldly information they appeared to receive from deceased persons not known to Moses. The best known of these, Abraham

Florentine, a recently deceased American, chose to communicate by table-tilting, but others took direct control of Moses's hand. After meeting with Moses, and consulting his notebooks, Edmund Gurney and Frederic Myers, would-be founders of the London Society for Psychical Research, returned convinced of his 'sanity' and 'probity'. Although they failed to trace the actual sources that might have, consciously or subconsciously, furnished Moses with information on the likes of Abraham Florentine – whose obituary notices were later shown to contain errors that Moses replicated – Gurney and Myers were astute enough to realise that neither trickery nor lunacy had a hand in automatic writing. After initially suggesting that automatic writing might be ascribed to the activity of the brain's right hemisphere ('right-brain writing' remains an appellation preferred by some of today's practitioners), Myers went on to provide a psychological explanation which pointed to the agency of a subliminal self – a buried storehouse of thought and sensation, feeling and memory – which becomes manifest in dreaming, hysteria and hypnosis.

Soon after co-founding the Society for Psychical Research in 1882, Gurney began a series of experiments that appeared to establish an important marker for automatic writing: impaired recall for the act or its content. In these experiments, subjects were hypnotised, their hands placed on a planchette (a heart-shaped table running on castors, with a pencil at its apex) and given tasks such as reading or mental arithmetic to occupy them:

> The planchette meanwhile was writing. In most of the cases where the writing did not prove to be the correct answer to the sum, the figures were sufficiently near the mark to make it apparent that an intelligent attempt had been made to work out the given problem. The paper and instrument were always concealed from the 'subject's' eyes, and he was never told what the movements of the planchette produced. As a rule, he was afterwards offered a sovereign to say what the writing was, but the reward was never earned. On rehypnotisation, he recalled the whole process – a clear indication that we have to do with secondary intelligence, not with unconscious cerebration.

Gurney described automatic writing as 'the production of words and intelligent sentences which the writer himself has afterwards to read in order to learn what they are'. The definition was rather narrow (it excluded the fragments and texts produced by Swedenborg, as well as passive writings composed by individuals who were cognisant of the act of writing, but unable to claim authorship), betraying Gurney's very specific interest in the possibility of creating simultaneous and entirely independent streams of consciousness. Gurney did indeed succeed in producing a significant degree of dissociation in one writing subject who was instructed to read the Humpty Dumpty passage in *Through the Looking Glass*. On being rehypnotised, the subject claimed no memory of Humpty Dumpty, but had a clear memory of struggling to write, but being unnerved by a nightmarish presence. This paralleled a case reported by William James. Testing for anaesthesia by pricking the hand of one young automatic writer, James found no indication of feeling. The hand, however, continued to write, asking, 'What did you do that for?'

Of all the automatisms observed by nineteenth-century science, automatic writing was, because of the higher functions it drew upon, the most alluring. If it had emerged in the first half of the century, automatic writing would have been examined in the context of somnambulism or double consciousness. In the 1880s, however, the notion of multiple personality was, as previously noted, taking shape, and hysteria continued to provide medicine with a privileged view of a secondary stream of consciousness at work. Early in his long and distinguished career, the French psychiatrist Pierre Janet found that a number of his hysterical patients could, through automatic writing, be led to recall events for which they had no conscious memory. Among the many cases Janet reported was that of a twenty-year-old woman who had wandered far from home, returning oblivious to her whereabouts or activities:

> Under distraction and while she was thinking of something else, I put her pencil into her right hand and she wrote me the following letter apparently without cognisance of what she was doing. – 'I

left home because mamma accuses me of having a lover and it is not true. I cannot live with her any longer. I sold my jewels to pay my railroad fare. I took such and such a train,' etc. In this letter she relates her entire *fugue* with precision although she continues to contend that she remembers nothing about it.

For Janet, automatic writing was at root derived from a lower, degenerative splitting of consciousness. Myers, who had reviewed Janet's research, disagreed. He proposed that the subliminal consciousness, as evinced by automatic writing, was natural and ubiquitous. Myers's views found a notable champion in William James, who pointed to combined activities involving some element of selective attention, such as walking and talking, reading aloud and thinking, as quotidian examples of *homo duplex*.

James had a long-standing interest in automatic writing. He had closely followed the activities of many American healers and mediums, amassing 'a whole drawer full' of automatic writings, including examples in mirror script and hieroglyphics. In 1885, he had carried out experiments at the Massachusetts Institute of Technology, making observations on the nature of anaesthesia (which he later found present in half of his subjects) and on the general psychology of automatic writing. Ten years on, James concluded the second of his Lowell lectures on exceptional mental states by suggesting that each member of the audience could verify the existence of the subliminal consciousness by experimenting with automatic writing. James was, nevertheless, acutely aware of the ways in which the subliminal consciousness exhibited in automatic writing could seek to pass itself off as another. A 'will to make believe', a 'curious external force impelling us to per-sonation', was not merely the baggage of spiritualism. Even the most sober and sceptical of experimenters could find that their writing *appeared* to emanate from another personality.

Most students of psychology recall that 1900 was the year in which Freud published his *Interpretation of Dreams*. Yet Freud's seminal work was, as Sonu Shamdasani points out in a recent essay, largely overshadowed by a Swiss psychologist's 400-page study of an amateur French medium. The psychologist was Théodore

Flournoy, and the subject of his book, *From India to the Planet Mars*, was Hélène Smith (real name, Catherine Muller), whom Flournoy had first met at a private séance in 1894. Flournoy had by this time spent some years on the look-out for a subject – a match for Mrs Piper or Eusapia Palladino – to study. He was immediately taken with Hélène's 'physical and mental vigor', features he had observed to be generally lacking in the most proficient mediums. Hélène was, in Flournoy's words, 'a beautiful young woman about thirty years of age, tall, vigorous, of a fresh, healthy complexion, with hair and eyes almost black, of an open and intelligent countenance, which at once invoked sympathy'. After attending her séances over a period of months, he found that she was much more besides. In a letter to William James, he described her extensive repertoire: 'she makes the table talk, – she hears voices, – she has visions, hallucinations, tactile and olfactory, – automatic writing . . . '

On becoming Flournoy's subject, Smith's automatic writing quickly evolved. One of her secondary personalities, 'Leopold', who had succeeded Victor Hugo in 1892, now uncovered two other former incarnations as the daughter of a fourteenth-century Arab sheikh and as Marie Antoinette. At first, the elaboration of these former lives relied heavily on dramatic re-enactment of a kind which 'the best actress, without doubt, could only attain at the price of great studies or a sojourn on the banks of the Gangees'. Then, in May of 1895, when Flournoy provided an entranced Hélène with paper and pencil, she wrote the name 'Simadini'. Now she began to produce colourful Oriental writings peppered with obscure details of geography and a smattering of Sanskrit, the origins of which Flournoy could not readily account for. After writing to various Orientalists, who all failed to recognise most of the localities and personages described by Hélène, Flournoy discovered a library copy of a history of India in which the province of Kanara, the fortress of Tchandraguiri and its founding sect, all of which featured in Hélène's writings, were mentioned. Although Flournoy could not furnish any positive proof that Smith had consulted this *General History of India*, the replication of certain key inaccuracies suggested that this book was the source of her past-life fantasy. As for her knowledge of Sanskrit, Fluornoy

'Round about the accredited and orderly facts of every science,' observed William James (1842–1910), 'there ever floats a sort of dust-cloud of exceptional observations, of observations minute and irregular and seldom met with, which it always proves more easy to ignore than attend.' James's pursuit of these marginal phenomena led to research into nitrous oxide, automatic writing, mediumship, hypnosis and hysterical automatisms.

The traditional costume of the Tungus shaman acts as a sacred armoury, providing protection from malign spirits that might impede his journey to the sky or underworld. The reindeer skin drum that this shaman holds is at once a map of the regions he will travel to and the 'horse' or 'stag' which speeds him on his ecstatic journey.

On 6 January 1976, Elaine Thomas and her two friends claimed to have been abducted by aliens while driving in Stanford, Kentucky. Under hypnosis, each of the three women – who had all suffered from burns and inflammation of the eyes – recalled the different physical examinations they endured aboard the alien craft. Thomas's sketch shows her placed within a glass cubicle, a scraping of skin being removed from her chest while her diminutive captors look on.

This engraving from Geiler von Kaysersberg's *Die Emeis* (1517) reflects the widespread medieval belief that, through the use of wolf-skins, salves, charms or magical incantations, humans could be transformed into wolves. Physical evidence of werewolfism was sometimes found in the phenomenon of 'sympathetic wounding'. Jean Bodin's *De la demonomanie des sorciers* (1580), for example, told how an arrow that pierced one wolf was some hours later discovered in the thigh of a man who had been asleep in bed.

The devil at the forearm of this possessed boy confirms its wickedness by fleeing as the bishop makes the sign of the cross. The 'spiritual remedies' favoured by late medieval exorcists included prayer and litany, communion and holy water, amulets and fumigation, and, in some cases, flagellation. During these rites, the exorcists would interrogate the demon, asking its name, when possession took place, and when it intended to vacate the body of the possessed.

'When worshipping the devil,' wrote the seventeenth-century friar Francesco-Maria Guazzo, 'the witches assume different postures. Sometimes they beg on bended knees; sometimes they fall down on their back; sometimes they kick their legs in the air.' The physical taxonomy of possession anticipates the attention that phreno-mesmerists would give to the poses adopted by entranced subjects in the 1840s, as well as the more fully realised iconography of hysteria that Charcot developed at the Salpêtrière.

The early career of the Soviet psychologist Aleksandr Romanovich Luria (1902–1977) included research on modes of non-literate cognition and the mental development of twins. At Moscow State University, he later undertook pioneering work on neurological disorders such as aphasia, and went on to produce two 'neurological novels' – *The Mind of a Mnemonist* (1968) and *The Man with a Shattered World* (1972) – which revived the nineteenth-century tradition of clinical writing.

MESMER'S TUB;

In around 1780, Franz Anton Mesmer (left foreground, attending to the seated lady) installed two *baquets* into the treatment rooms of the Hôtel Bullion. The larger of the two, seen above, enabled Mesmer to treat up to twenty patients at a time. Seated around the large wooden vat filled with 'magnetised' water, the circle of patients, connected by a single rope, hold on to the rods which jut through the wooden lid and await the tingles and twitches of healing 'fluid'. The *baquets* allowed Mesmer to popularise his magnetic treatment, but his detractors denounced his innovation as an occult corruption of the newly invented Leyden jar, which European physicians were now using therapeutically.

In the early 1740s, the theologian and scientist Emmanuel Swedenborg (1688–1772) underwent a religious crisis which, through a series of dreams, appeared to reveal the true nature of the spiritual world. After accepting this 'divine commission', Swedenborg experienced 'double thoughts', hallucinations, episodes of passive writing and, on one famous occasion in Gothenburg, in 1759, a vision of a fire taking place three hundred miles away in Stockholm. The latter incident was investigated by Immanuel Kant, who went on to collect eye-witness accounts to corroborate Swedenborg's feat of 'far-seeing'.

The recruitment drive undertaken by the Rev. Sun Myung Moon's Unification Church in the mid-1970s played a major part in revitalising the cold war mythology of mind control in the United States. To combat the dangers of religious brainwashing, the anti-cult coalition developed its own techniques of 'deprogramming' individuals who had been 'systematically denied their free-will'. By the end of the 1970s, the American Psychiatric Association identified coercive persuasion through 'brain washing, thought reform, and indoctrination' as a possible precursor to mental illness.

After being kidnapped by the Symbionese Liberation Army in February 1974, Patty Hearst changed her name to 'Tania' and embraced the revolutionary ethos of her terrorist captors. After her arrest, Hearst's original defence planned to present a case of 'involuntary intoxication, with amnesia'. A second defence team led by F. Lee Bailey instead argued that her allegiance to the SLA reflected the kind of pathological identification observed in the Stockholm syndrome.

Ezekiel received his prophetic calling with a vision of 'a huge cloud with fire flashing and shining around it, and in the middle of it … the likeness of four animals'. Contemporary ufologists have argued that the throne-chariot which Ezekiel witnessed was an early mode of alien transport.

The Japanese-born artist Yayoi Kusama began to produce her first 'dot paintings' in the early 1960s. 'My art,' she says, 'originates from hallucinations…. By translating hallucinations and fear of hallucinations into paintings, I have been trying to cure my disease [obsessional neurosis].'

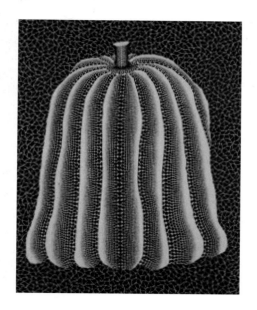

Alice's transformations in Wonderland echo the physical hallucinations that are sometimes experienced during the onset of focal migraine, which Charles Lutwidge Dodgson is known to have suffered.

7   11

quite dull and stupid for things to go on in the common way.
So she set to work, and very soon finished off the cake.
* * * * *
"Curiouser and curiouser!" cried Alice, (she was so surprised that she quite forgot how to speak good English,) "now I'm opening out like the largest telescope that ever was! Goodbye, feet!" (for when she looked down at her feet, they seemed almost out of sight, they were getting so far off) "oh, my poor little feet, I wonder who will put on your shoes and stockings for you now, dears ? I'm sure I can't! I shall be a great deal too far off to bother myself about you : you must manage the best way you can — but I must be kind to them", thought Alice, "or perhaps they won't walk the way I want to go ! Let me see : I'll give them a new pair of boots every Christmas".
And she went on planning to herself how she would manage it.

Frederic Myers (1843–1901), poet, classicist and co-founder of the London Society for Psychical Research, had his 'first personal experience of forces unknown to science' at a séance in November 1873. Ensuing investigations brought Myers into close contact with the most famous mediums of the period. Myers was also a close friend of William James, who supported his efforts 'to consider the phenomena of hallucination, automatism, double personality and mediumship as connected parts of one whole subject'.

Albert Dadas, the first diagnosed *fugeur*, travelled as far as Moscow, Constantinople and Algiers. These four photographs show him in his normal state (top, left and right), at the end of an episode of 'ambulatory automatism' (bottom left) and under hypnosis (bottom right).

concluded that the fragments contained in her automatic writing extended only as far as what could easily be acquired by reading the first few pages of a book of Sanskrit grammar. Hélène, of course, retained no memory of having read either.

Flournoy related the aspects of Hélène's automatic writings that discussed her former existence in terms of cryptomnesia, the awakening of forgotten memories. He was well aware that many of the quirks of her psychopathology – glossolalia, hallucinations and a natural talent for automatic writing, all of which she had experienced since childhood – had been systematised through her involvement with spiritualism. Embarked on a regime of self-improvement, this budding *salonnière* found that spiritualism positively encouraged her abandonment to a series of separate selves. The formation of discrete 'personalities' was, according to Fluornoy, due to 'the simple fact of her being occupied with spiritism and engaged in mediumistic experiments'.

Much of the written and spoken information that Hélène procured for her wide-eyed circle of sitters was anachronistic and derivative. (Flournoy himself overlooks a certain amount of probably unconscious plagiarism on her part. He fails to note that Victor Hugo, Hélène's first control, was himself an avid spiritist who received messages and that Leopold was the name of Hugo's own control.) There was nevertheless a genuine inventiveness in Hélène's writing. As Flournoy puckishly observed, 'The menu of the seances – if the expression is permissible – is always composed of one or two *plats de résistance*, carefully prepared in advance in the subliminal laboratories, and of various *hors d'oeuvres* left to the inspiration of the moment.' Nowhere was this *imagination créatrice* more evident than in the Martian language that Smith slowly fashioned after her first spirited visit to Mars.

Claims of interplanetary travel were not uncommon among mediums of this period. Mars was a popular destination, the question of its habitability having been much debated in both science and literature. Unlike the Hindu and Royalist adventures that had earlier preoccupied Hélène, the creation of an alien language could not rely on memory, however factitious. As much as her Martian alphabet of twenty-three letters twisted and contorted French phonetics, grammar and syntax, as much as it struggled to escape and hide its very obvious parentage, Flournoy rightly recognised this fabrication as 'an effort of imagination with which she must be credited'.

The publication of *From India to the Planet Mars* left Hélène Smith feeling bitterly betrayed. While some spiritualist publications welcomed Flournoy's work, even though it had effectively reduced mediumship to worldly psychology, Hélène resisted his interpretation, considering her messages to have only one possible provenance. The royalties that she insisted on did not lessen her sense of persecution. Almost ten years on, as she turned her automatic hand to religious painting, Hélène suspected that Flournoy 'continues to send me spies. To what end, I don't know.' In his own way, Flournoy was also haunted. He long searched for another Hélène, if only to better understand the way in which he might in fact have doctored her imagination.

Hélène Smith's Martian and Hindu writings remain one of the most elaborate sequences of automatic writing ever produced. Her spiritualist adventures in passive authorship are, however, part of a much wider, variegated tapestry. A full history of automatic writing would be obliged to move far beyond the confines of the séance. It would encompass psychotic writings that have been transcribed in the very form they are hallucinated. It would examine the unwilled compositions elicited during migraine and epilepsy, as well as the feverish dispatches produced in their hypergraphic aftermath. And it would give due attention to the various literary experiments in automatic prose and poetry undertaken by figures as diverse as Fernando Pessoa, André Breton, Gertrude Stein and James Merrill.

Equally importantly, the teeming maze of scrawls and scribbles that have filled every child's jotter, undergraduate's lecture notes and receptionist's notepad would find their rightful place in the automatic library. The unthinking doodle (which James did, to his credit, recognise as an 'undeveloped' form of mental automatism) might well prove to be less the marginalia of automatic writing than its principal text. Unfortunately, it has still to be seriously investigated by psychologists.

Mind Fog

'Brainwashing' entered the lexicon of mind control in the early 1950s, at the beginning of the Korean War, when CIA operator and journalist Edward Hunter coined the neologism to describe how sleep deprivation, isolation and other methods of psychological conversion were being used in the revolutionary programme of the Chinese Communist Party. In a stream of books and articles, Hunter repeatedly claimed that the Chinese thought reformers were able 'to put a man's mind into a fog so that he will mistake what is true for what is untrue, what is right for what is wrong, and come to believe that what did not happen actually had happened, until he ultimately becomes a robot for the communist manipulator'.

The false confessions and self-denunciations elicited from American POWs by communist captors gave particular credence to the efficacy of these brainwashing techniques. Shortly after Colonel Frank Shwable had been repatriated and repudiated the confessions he made to the Chinese communists regarding the use of biological weapons, Charles W. Mayo, a physician and government spokesman, issued this statement to the United Nations: 'the tortures . . . are subtler, more prolonged, and intended to be more terrible in effect. They are calculated to disintegrate the mind of an intelligent victim, to distort his sense of values, to a point where he will not simply cry out "I did it!" but will become a seemingly willing accomplice to the complete disintegration of his integrity and the production of an elaborate fiction.'

Raising public fears of the pernicious influence of 'totalism', the CIA found political capital for ongoing experiments with drugs, hypnosis and electroshock as tools of behaviour modification.

These claims that the Chinese and Russians had created new methods of thought reform were never established. When the CIA commissioned an independent study into communist brainwashing in 1953, doctors at Cornell University refuted the allegations that Marxism or Maoism had developed special techniques of brainwashing. A later study of 'ideological totalism' in China by Robert Jay Lifton concluded that techniques of 're-education', or conversion, were altogether more elementary. The conditions under which this took place relied on: the control of milieu, especially through limiting contact or communication; the promulgation of a 'higher' purpose or mission; the subordination of personal desire to the will of the collective; the use of confession as a form of initiation; and the assimilation of a new argot or shared language. There were, in short, no new means of inculcation.

As elementary as these methods of political indoctrination remained, the myth of brainwashing had already entered public consciousness. The belief that communism had spawned sinister and underhand means of inducing complete acquiescence was difficult to undo. Richard Condon's bestselling pulp novel *The Manchurian Candidate* (1959) popularised the notion that a communist-controlled assassin might be brainwashed and sent to kill the US president, and the conspiracy theory was given added credibility when J. F. Kennedy was assassinated by Lee Harvey Oswald, a suspected Russian spy. When the threat of communism began to recede, the fear of brainwashing was transferred in the United States to a new nemesis: the proliferation of religious sects. The dangers of ideological conversion were now a more pressing social problem. Initiation into the shadowy world of the religious cult was seen again to systematically rob the individual of all volition. Of all the religious groups, followers of the Lord of the Second Advent, Reverend Sun Myung Moon, were the most prolific proselytisers. The spectacle of the Moonies' mass marriage ceremonies was widely perceived as the apogee of brainwashing. Testimonies from ex-Moonies described the methods of personality and behaviour transformation that had been used to win over their hearts and minds. By way of direct response, the anti-cult coalition devised its own methods of anti-conversion, deprogramming, which at its worst perversely mirrored the very process of alleged initiation that it sought to undo.

Two experiments carried out in American universities in the 1970s revealed the extent to which drastic changes in behaviour could be quickly and easily produced without 'brainwashing'. A study undertaken by Stanley Milgram, a psychologist at Yale University, demonstrated that the majority of well-balanced student volunteers would, when 'authorised', administer what appeared to be painful electric shocks. Participating in what they believed to be an experiment assessing the effects of punishment on learning behaviour, every student volunteer obeyed orders to issue electric shocks of up to 300 volts to actors posing as 'learners', and 60 per cent went further still. An even more disturbing example of the ways in which volunteers would readily and unquestioningly assume given roles was demonstrated when a group of volunteers at Stanford University was randomly split into 'guards' and 'prisoners'. In a specially constructed mock-prison housed within the psychology department, Philip Zimbardo's role-playing experiment revealed profound changes in personality, with guards callously and arbitrarily deploying their authority over prisoners who became increasingly agitated and depressed. Fearing that the 'prisoners' might be physically or emotionally harmed, Zimbardo aborted the experiment after six days. The alterations in behaviour were far more dramatic than had been anticipated.

Like the truth drug, the recruitment pill and so many other experimental technologies of behaviour modification, brainwashing is a garbled mix of myth, magic and science. It owes more to fiction and legend than fact. The roots of this pseudo-technology in fact stretch back further than the Cold War. The CIA-endorsed myths of brainwashing echo the Persian legend of the Old Man of the Mountain, Hassan-I-Sabbah, who recruited his fanatical followers by drugging them with hashish and leading them into a hidden garden of unearthly splendours. Believing that they had glimpsed the afterlife, Sabbah's followers were willingly despatched on suicide missions. The mesmeric Svengali of George du Maurier's 1894 novel *Trilby* updated the assassin myth.

Modern-day reports of tourist druggings and 'hypnotic' robberies are filtered through the same folklore.

Yet in an entirely different context, the practice of 'brain-washing' or 'soul-cleansing' does have a legitimate and lasting history. In Dyak shamanism in Borneo, for example, the neophyte performs a symbolic cutting open of the head, a cerebral cleansing, to enable the would-be shaman to assume his new identity. Similarly, in the Iboga cult of the Bwiti, a secret society of the Gabon, the initiate must break all ties with his former self and family (whom he will no longer recognise). The fact that these acts are essential to the culture distinguishes them from the popular understanding of the term 'brainwashing'. In a modern context, brainwashing still provides a means of explaining and denigrating the adoption of beliefs and behaviours that are otherwise alien and incomprehensible.

The Big Sleep

Library of Dreams

The earliest known transcription of a series of dreams can be found in the *Epic of Gilgamesh*, the collection of Sumerian myths best known in a Babylonian version dating back to the seventh century BC. Gilgamesh, the king of Uruk, on the river Euphrates, has two dreams shortly after a council of elders calls on the sky goddess Anu to produce a rival to their reckless sovereign. In the first, an immense meteorite falls to Earth. When the people of Uruk gather round to pay homage to the meteorite, Gilgamesh embraces it; however, his mother, the goddess Rimat-Ninsun, urges him to compete with the immovable meteorite. In a second dream, the same drama is played out with an enormous axe, which Gilgamesh's mother once again presses him to do battle with. When Gilgamesh asks his mother what these dreams mean, she informs him that a man of great force and vitality will come to Uruk, and that he and Gilgamesh will be united in great deeds. The omen proves true. Embarking on his adventures with the brutish Enkidu, Gilgamesh goes on to have other dreams – of wrestling with a bull, of a thunderous storm that turns the plains to ash – and each of these is in turn interpreted for him.

The Babylonians and the Assyrians believed that dreams were prophetic and that the most disturbing dreams merited particular attention. When the library at Nineveh was excavated in the nineteenth century, British archaeologists discovered a vast quantity of other tablets alongside a handful relating to Gilgamesh. Among these tablets was the dream book of Ashurbanipal, the author of history's first dream guide. These cuneiform tablets explained, among other things, that to dream of flying at low altitude meant that 'ruin is ahead of you', but that to be cursed in a dream in fact boded rather well.

Oneiromancy, or dream interpretation, was practised by every early civilisation. Incorporating much from the neighbouring Assyrians, the Egyptians believed that the gods spoke to kings, priests and other worthies in dreams. The British Museum's Chester Beatty papyrus (c. 1350 BC) provides more than 200 interpretations of dream narratives. As a rule, the Egyptians favoured interpretation by opposites. Falling over augured prosperity. To dream of sleeping with one's mother suggested that one's family would remain loyal. On the other hand, to dream of losing one's teeth prophesied death at the hand of one's relatives. Not all dreams, however, were portents: the gods could also speak directly, offering advice and remedy.

These divine or 'true' dreams were sought through the practice of incubation. After rituals of purification, sacrifice or the consumption of hypnotic potions, individuals would sleep in remote spots in the hills or at an oracular shrine. The Greek centres of dream incubation were the oracle of Amphiaraus near Thebes, the oracle of Trophonius at Lebeadeia and, most famous of all, the oracle of Asclepius at Epidaurus, which assumed particular importance as a centre for medical incubation from the fifth century BC onwards. Those that came to sleep at the temple of Epidaurus, or at any one of the hundreds of Asclepian oracles, would hope that Asclepius, the son of Apollo, would appear to them in dream form, giving prescriptions and instructions for cure. Records of these dreams, as transcribed from votive tablets at Epidaurus, were published in the 1880s. Among the many inscriptions that testify to the apparently widespread cure by incubation is that of Aristagora of Troezen:

> She had a tapeworm in her belly, and she slept in the Temple of Asclepius at Troezen and saw a dream. It seemed to her that the sons of the god . . . cut off her head, but, being unable to put it back again, they sent a messenger to Asclepius asking him to come . . . When night approached, Aristagora saw a vision. It seemed to her that the god had come from Epidaurus and fastened her head onto

her neck. Then he cut open her belly, took the tapeworm out, and stitched her up again. And after that she became well.

Classical Greek views of dreaming were partly infused with Egyptian and Assyrian–Babylonian traditions. Although Greek myths abound with dream prophecies, the early philosophers denied the possibility of divination through dreams. Aristotle was particularly keen to purge dreaming of its supernatural associations. His theory of dreaming, outlined in three short essays, dismissed most prophetic dreams as mere coincidence. Aristotle did, though, concede two interesting exceptions. First, he notes that there are some presentiments that are in fact the very 'causes' of what they appear to anticipate, 'the starting-points of actions to be performed in the daytime'. This type of dream presentation, he suggests, 'befalls commonplace persons and not the most intelligent'. Secondly, he accepts that beginnings of 'diseases or other affections' can be sensed more acutely in a dream. '[D]reamers fancy they are affected by thunder and lightning,' observed Aristotle, 'when in fact there are only faint ringings in their ears . . . or that they are walking through fire, and feeling intense heat, when there is only a slight warmth affecting certain parts of the body'. This phenomenon, today called a 'prodromal dream', has been confirmed by a number of contemporary investigators. The American psychologist Harold Levitan has found that content of dreams can often 'diagnose' the onset of migraine, asthma and epilepsy. (The very opposite phenomenon, however, has also been observed. The body image of amputees, paralytics and other patients is only very slowly updated in dreams.)

Aristotle's observations led him to conclude that the skilful interpreter of dreams should look below the surface of the dream image to discern the internal motions of mind and body that generate such presentiments. However, as much as these thoughts are echoed by later philosophers such as Cicero, the prophetic view of dreams largely held sway and divination even found a legitimate role in medicine. Six centuries after Hippocrates, the father of modern medicine, made mention of the prodromal dream and its ability to illuminate the symptoms of incipient illness, Galen's treatise *Diagnosis from Dreams* linked specific dream imagery to humoral pathology: 'if someone dreams about a fire, he is troubled by yellow bile, if about smoke, fog, or deep shadow, by black bile . . . [but] snow, hail and ice [suggest] cold phlegm'.

From the first centuries of Christianity through to the birth of psychoanalysis, the definitive guide to dream interpretation was Artemidorus's *Oneirocritica*, from the second century AD. Artemidorus produced his systematic survey of dream symbolism after extensive travel. Collating many of the long-established dream interpretations found in both the Graeco-Roman and Arab world, he brought a new rigour to the soothsayer's work. First, two orders of dream, *somnium* and *insomnium*, were distinguished. While the *somnium* was pregnant with the future, the *insomnium* was merely a reflection of current health and preoccupations. To understand the *somnium*, Artemidorus argued that one must appreciate differences in culture and custom. Moreover, the interpreter of dreams should be aware of the background of the dreamer – his 'identity, occupation, birth, financial status, state of health'. Thus the dream and the dreamer needed to be understood simultaneously.

The reasons Artemidorus gives for needing this fuller picture anticipate Freud's ideas on the multivalency of dream symbolism. For Artemidorus, few dream events or objects have a fixed, intrinsic meaning. For example: 'The penis corresponds to one's parents . . . It resembles children . . . It signifies a wife or a mistress . . . It indicates brothers and all blood relatives . . . [It] is also a sign of wealth and posessions . . . It signifies secret plans . . . It indicates poverty, servitude, and bonds.' On the subject of dreams in which a man sleeps with his wife, Artemidorus equally admits many interpretations: 'The fact is that the mere act of intercourse by itself is not enough to show what is portended.' Depending on the type of 'embrace', the current health of the dreamer, his profession and other factors, the dream could be an intimation of future poverty, illness or the death of children, according to Artemidorus. Only in the case of 'a man who is involved in a law suit over land rights' does the dream bode well.

Published in Greek, French and Latin in the sixteenth century, the *Oneirocritica* eventually appeared in English in 1644. As affordable handbooks such as *The Golden Dreamer* and *The Old Egyptian Fortune-Teller's Last Legacy* became widely distributed, occultists returned to the dream as a source of privileged knowledge, using plant lore to stimulate dreams of the 'highest spiritual sphere'. The popularisation of ancient dream theory also had its opponents. Critical of the veneration of antiquity in all its forms, Sir Thomas Browne wrote of the ways in which 'we are confessedly deceived by the fictions and falsehoods of the dream'.

The Renaissance revival of the prophetic theory of dreaming had already reached its apogee. Girolamo Cardano, the Milanese doctor, mathematician and astrologer, had published the Renaissance's most important work on dream interpretation, *Synesiorum Somniorum Libri*, in 1562. Cardano had both a private and professional interest in championing dream interpretation. In his autobiographical writings, he repeatedly claimed to have been guided by his dreams. At the same time, he reinterpreted dreams recorded up to thirty years previously, finding (highly dubious) intimations of present events and circumstances. To claim a 'place for dreams in medicine', Cardano looked back to Artemidorus, Hippocrates and Galen, and also to Synesius of Cyrene, whose fifth-century *Discourse on Dreams* had recommended that everyone, whatever their station, should record all their dreams, 'whether trivial or important'. Endorsing Synesius, Cardano offered examples of how his medical duties had been greatly aided by dreams that assisted in diagnosis, alerted him to impediment and danger, and inspired him to make scholarly discovery.

Unlike Galen and Hippocrates, Cardano does not appear to have based his diagnoses on the dreams of his patients. Much to the disapproval of his contemporaries, it was always in relation to his own dreams that Cardano looked for diagnosis. Cardano's interest in dreams was, however, in many ways only incidentally medical. As much as he acknowledged the ways in which dreaming reflected the state of the body, dreams were for him the medium through which God instructed the soul. On many occasions, he was convinced of a divine influence at work in his nightly imaginings. When this gift deserted him in later life, he felt himself 'abandoned by some celestial power'.

Sixteenth-century thinkers were preoccupied not only with the supernatural aspects of the dream. Following Plato, who had recognised the workings of hidden desires in dreaming, the Swiss alchemist Paracelsus turned to the question of the *insomnium*. 'That which the dream shows is the shadow of such wisdom as existing in the man, even if during his waking state he knows nothing about it.' As Norman Mackenzie points out in *Dreams and Dreaming*, Freud was apparently unaware of Paracelsus's insight when he published the *Interpretation of Dreams* in 1900. Paracelsus's assertion could indeed have provided Freud's project with a rather more pointed epigraph than Virgil's *Flectere si nequeo superos, Acherota movebo* (If I cannot move heaven, I will stir up the underworld).

From the mid-nineteenth century onwards, as the idea of the unconscious took root, these insights into the *insomnium* begin to be widely embraced. For instance, William Hazlitt's essay 'On Dreams' maintains that there is 'a sort of profundity in sleep' which does have a prophetic function. When dreaming, Hazlitt observes, 'the voluntary power is suspended, and things come upon us as unexpected revelations, which we keep out of our thoughts at other times. We may be aware of a danger, that yet we do not chuse, while we have the full command of our faculties, to acknowledge to ourselves: the impending event will then appear to us as a dream, and we shall most likely find it verified afterwards'. Moreover, he notes that in dreams 'we may sometimes discover our tacit, and almost unconscious sentiments . . . We are not hypocrites in our sleep . . . in sleep we reveal the secret to ourselves'.

The Romantics placed huge stock in dreams both as a mirror of the dormant self, the unconscious, and as a source of creative inspiration. The idea that dreaming was a form of primitive picture language, accessible only in slumber, was proposed by a number of Romantic philosophers. Von Schubert's *Symbolism of Dreams* (1814) went further still, proposing that dreams were a universal language, 'a higher kind of algebra'. This philosophy of dreaming was, as Henri Ellenberger notes, quashed by the advent of positivist science and 'the notion that dreams were a meaningless by-product of automatic and unco-ordinating brain activity during sleep'. This view was certainly in the ascendant in the last decades of the nineteenth century. In 1878, the German physiologist Carl Binz, while pointing to the ways in which opium, hashish and other narcotics each yielded their own dream moods and scenarios, declared that dreaming was a mere function of brain chemistry. Binz was not alone in arguing for an organic interpretation of dreamwork, but the tide was set to turn.

It was only after abandoning his neurological research that Freud began to forge an approach to dreams and their 'metabolism of meaning'. To this end, Freud rejected flatly the notion that dreams were 'an expression of disintegrated cerebral activity, as the writers would have us believe'. Yet he also refused to accept that dreams were an open doorway to the true self, as Hazlitt and the Romantics proposed. *The Interpretation of Dreams* was a deeply autobiographical book, wrestled from a decade of self-analysis. By scrutinising his own dreams – especially those he had experienced after the death of his father – Freud proposed that wish fulfilment rather than true memory provided the key to unlocking dream content. 'When the work of interpretation has been completed, we perceive that a dream is a fulfilment of a wish.' As these motives were always repressed, however, the dream could only be seen in disguise. 'The dream content is, as it were, presented in hieroglyphics, whose symbols must be translated, one by one, into the language of the dream-thoughts.' To translate dreams back into this language one needed to consider the processes of condensation (the unconscious fusion of thought), displacement (the transference of an emotion to another person or object) and secondary revision (the filling-in of gaps).

Freud, always prone to classical allusion, imagined himself as the new Artemidorus. In the first chapter of *The Interpretation of Dreams*, he claimed that the 'technique which I am about to describe differs from that of the ancients in one essential point, namely, in that it imposes upon the dreamer himself the work of interpretation'. But this was clearly not to be the case. Through free association, psychoanalysis would allow the therapist to steal past the internal censor and spy on the latent meaning of the dream. Dreams were interpreted in spite of the dreamer, not by the dreamer. Freud's patients were sometimes at odds with the interpretations at which he arrived. For example, the Russian aristocrat known as the Wolf-Man, whose analysis is described in Freud's 'History of an Infantile Neurosis', remained absolutely unconvinced of Freud's explanation of the much-quoted dream of white wolves. It was all 'terribly far-fetched'.

Thirty years after the publication of *The Interpretation of Dreams*, Freud questioned the way in which psychoanalysts had tended blindly to accept his thinking on dreams, but maintained that his dream theory had been the turning point of psychoanalysis, transforming it into a 'psychology of the depths of human nature'. While Freud had become required reading in both Europe and America, the limitations of his unified dream theory were all too obvious. Wittgenstein spoke for many when he criticised Freud's attempts to find 'the *essence* of dreaming'. Instead, Wittgenstein (whose sister had been analysed by Freud) thought it 'probable that there are many sorts of dreams, and that there is no single line of explanation for all of them'.

A new biological perspective was now also beginning to emerge. The person largely responsible for this was Nathan Kleitman, a researcher from the University of Chicago, who, in the 1930s, began systematically to study the sleep cycle. After two decades of research, Kleitman, in conjunction with a graduate student, Eugene Aserinsky, made a vital breakthrough. Periods of rapid eye movement (REM) lasting up to half an hour were observed in sleeping subjects, and these were thought – rightly, as it transpired – to be associated with dreaming. From the study of EEG tracings on laboratory sleepers, Kleitman discovered that cycles of REM sleep were anticipated by changing brainwaves and increased pulse and respiration. To establish whether this phase of REM sleep was a true concomitant to dreaming, the Chicago researcher undertook a simple experiment. At the first burst of REM activity, volunteers were woken and asked to report what, if anything, they were dreaming. Twenty of the twenty-seven sleepers were able to provide graphic reports. From the control group of twenty-three subjects awakened from non-REM sleep, only four had any recollections. In these cases, it appeared that reports were either of earlier fragments of dreams or the imageless and undirected thinking of non-REM sleep.

William Dement and Howard Roffwarg were quickly able to confirm that patterns of eye movement during REM sleep were directly connected to the movement and action of dream imagery. Eye movement was now thought to be a form of internal scanning, a possibility first raised by G. T. Ladd, professor of mental and moral philosophy at Yale, in 1892. As the intensity of 'ocular motility' diminished, so, too, did the flickering details of the dream imagery. These findings opened the floodgates to dream research in laboratories across America and Europe. Moving beyond the behavioural and neurological examination of dreaming, inquiries now turned to the psychological necessity of dreaming.

The logical way to investigate the function of REM sleep was through dream deprivation. At Mount Sinai Hospital in New York, William Dement and Charles Fischer monitored sleeping volunteers and woke them whenever bursts of REM indicated that they were beginning to dream. What most interested Dement was the impact of dream deprivation on subsequent sleep. In a later experiment, he was able to confirm that deprivation led to a dramatic upturn in subsequent dreaming: REM rebound. Approximately twice as much dreaming occurred in one volunteer who had been deprived of dreaming sleep for five nights. Dement concluded that REM sleep served a definite psychological function: if REM pressure were allowed to build, 'the dream-REM process would erupt into the waking state'.

Dement's theory was in tune with nineteenth-century thinking on dreams and their supposed relationship to madness. Further experiments in sleep deprivation, however, suggested that cognitive and emotional disturbances were not in fact a necessary consequence of REM sleep deprivation. To begin with, Gerald Vogel's studies of dream deprivation in depressives provided evidence for the therapeutic effects of REM deprivation. Then, in the early 1980s, the Technion Sleep Laboratory in Israel reported the case of 'Y.H.', a war veteran who *never* dreamed but whose thinking and memory were exemplary. Up to this point, the absence of REM sleep had been presumed an impossibility by researchers of all persuasions.

The case of Y.H appeared in the neurological journals at a time when dreaming was coming to be increasingly theorised as a kind of 'neural dumping', a clearing-out of semantic memories acquired over the day. Graeme Mitchison and the Nobel Prize winner Sir Francis Crick argued, contra Freud, that we dream in order to forget. Alan Hobson, a psychiatrist and neurologist at Harvard Medical School, more thoroughly extended this critique of psychoanalysis, arguing that the distinction between the manifest and latent dream content should be overhauled. Hobson's activation-synthesis theory instead proposes a distinction between dream form and dream content. Formal aspects of dreaming (visual and motor hallucinations; the delusional acceptance of such hallucinatory experience as real; extremely bizarre spatial and temporal distortion; strong emotion; and finally, the failure to remember) are, Hobson claims, all linked to brain processes. To take one example, intense emotion in dreaming is linked to the action of the limbic system and the brain-stem startle networks. Activation of these emotions is thought to precede the content of the dream. The bizarreness of the dream is thus considered a consequence of primary translations of such processes, and not a defensive disguise. There is no inherent meaning in the dream.

The Freudian theory of dreaming has been the subject of further critiques and reassessments. The cognitive psychologist David Foulkes has, for instance, also argued that dreams have no intrinsic meaning and that they are produced through the random activation of short- and long-term memory. The Canadian psychologist Harry T. Hunt makes a more radical case for 'the multiplicity of dreams', arguing that not all can be reduced to the function of memory, random or otherwise. Yet the ghost of Freud need not be exorcised. 'The dream', observed Freud, 'has nothing to communicate to anyone else . . . and is for that reason totally uninteresting to other people.' If only more dream confessors had read their Freud.

The Night Shift

In Wilkie Collins's novel *The Moonstone* (1868), Franklin Blake is charged with delivering the eponymous Indian jewel to the Yorkshire home of his cousin Rachel Verinder. The diamond is presented to Rachel on the evening of her eighteenth birthday, and, by the following morning, it has disappeared. After Sergeant Cuff's inquiries draw a blank, Blake eventually discovers that he himself stole the moonstone, after being secretly dosed with opium. Under the guidance of Ezra Jennings, a downcast doctor suffering from a suitably mysterious affliction, Blake agrees to submit himself to an experiment. Given a large dose of opium in the Verinders' home, Blake is now observed as he repeats his somnambulant crime.

Collins claimed to have consulted medical texts as well as living authorities when writing about the 'physiological experiment' which was crucial to demonstrating Blake's unconscious theft of the moonstone. Through the character of Ezra Jennings, he was able to make reference to the work of William Carpenter and John Elliotson, who had both undertaken investigations into mesmerism and the borderlands between sleep and wakefulness. The convoluted twist on which the plot of *The Moonstone* turns was, at least in Collins's mind, based on scientific fact. 'I have', Collins wrote in relation to Blake's sleepwalking scene, 'altogether abandoned the novelist's privilege of supposing something that might have happened.'

The notion of a nocturnal self acting independently of its daytime watchman was not new to either fiction or medicine. When Shakespeare employed the device in describing the 'slumbr'y agitation' of Lady Macbeth, whose 'walking and other actual performances' belied her guilty secret, the phenomenon was being discussed by various scholars and physicians, including Horstius, Ab Heers and Paulo Zacchias (who thought that sleepwalkers acted out the internal motions of their dreams). Most of the early encyclopaedias included some discussion of somnambulism. The most cited case came from an Archbishop of Bordeaux, who described how a young ecclesiastic at the seminary he had once attended rose every night, composing sermons and music while still asleep. The archbishop stole into the young man's chambers on consecutive nights in order to establish whether he was truly asleep. On placing a sheet of pasteboard in front of his face, the archbishop found that the young man carried on writing.

For the Victorian readers of *The Moonstone*, the founding work of detective fiction, the sleepwalker, or somnambulist, was a familiar and newsworthy figure. To understand how somnambulism had continued to accrue a catalogue of outlandish exploits, it is important to remember that the term had, from the 1780s onwards, been used to describe the psychological state into which magnetised subjects were inducted. Artificial somnambulism, discovered by the Marquis de Puységur, at once confirmed and extended the repertoire of phenomena associated with natural somnambulism. Puységur's first somnambulist, a peasant by the name of Victor Race, was transformed into a powerful personality – his somnambulant self was able to both intuit the nature of his existing illness and diagnose the ailments of others. 'When he is magnetised,' observed Puységur, 'he is no longer a simple peasant who can barely answer a question; he is something I cannot describe.'

As magnetic somnambulism was more thoroughly explored, still greater powers of sentience emerged. According to C. A. F. Kluge, an early German theorist, three stages of magnetic somnambulism occupied the higher reaches of the magnetic trance. In the first, subjects were able to see with their eyes closed, through the pit of the stomach especially. People with knowledge of a second language now became unusually fluent. Powers of healing emerged next, with subjects developing acute vision of their inner bodies or a 'community of sensation' with the magnetiser or distant persons. Finally, in the highest realm of somnambulism, this facility for remote perception edged into precognition. These true somnambulists were also seen to display a heightened moral sensibility, with women being particularly sensitive to malevolent or indecent intention. And there was more . . .

Friedericke Hauffe, the uneducated daughter of a German gamekeeper from Weinsberg, became one of the most famous somnambulists of the early nineteenth century when she revealed a battery of dormant talents. When magnetised by the physician–poet Justinus Kerner – who had found her convulsive fever exacerbated by traditional remedies – all of her symptoms subsided. Asleep but 'more awake than anybody', she spoke in High German, making gnomic pronouncements on matters of theology, philosophy and cosmology. She foretold future events. She travelled the heavens. She prescribed her own medication. She spoke her own 'language' and invented a 'nerve tuner', a device to provide her with magnetic life support. These feats of somnambulism earned Hauffe the title of 'Seeress of Prevorst'. Her reputation led many notable thinkers to call on her to discuss her revelations. Shortly after her death in 1829, at the age of twenty-eight, Kerner recorded his observations and experiments with Hauffe in *Die Sieherin von Prevorst,* a book which proved enormously successful.

Experiments into these higher planes of magnetic somnam-bulism were soon offered as evidence of the afterworld. In an 1850 book, *The Celestial Telegraph: Secrets of the Life to Come Revealed through Magnetism,* Louis Alphonse Cahagnet, a cabinet-maker of Sweden-borgian persuasion, provided testimonies from eight 'ecstatic somnambulists' who had 'eighty perceptions of thirty-six deceased persons'. Having given up on hashish as a guide to the hereafter, Cahagnet intoned: 'I am about to prove to you that your relations, your friends, they await you with impatience; that you can, although on this globe, enter into communication with them, speak to them . . . or at least strive conscientiously to obtain the proofs you desire; by somnambulism you may have as many as you please.'

Cases of natural somnambulism in the mid-century were

reported alongside their magnetic and narcotic counterparts. Many of the reported cases of spontaneous somnambulism were, as Alan Gauld observes in *A History of Hypnotism* (1995), clearly instances of epilepsy, fugue and hysterical automatism. Somnambulism was an ill-defined and elastic concept. Almost any action undertaken without apparent awareness, and with lack of subsequent recall, was described as an instance of somnambulism.

With the demise of mesmerism, the somnambulist was slowly brought back down to terra firma. The supernatural powers described by Kerner and Cahagnet were all but rescinded by medical science. Where the medical literature discussed cases of natural or narcotic somnambulism, it was as a phenomenon of psychological rather than psychic import. Gould and Pyle's summary of somnambulism in their 1896 *Anomalies and Curiosities of Medicine* marvelled at the fact that 'anyone should when fast asleep perform a series of complicated actions which undoubtedly demand the assistance of the senses'. But the actual tasks associated with somnambulism were of no intrinsic interest. 'Often he [the somnambulist] will rise in the night, walk from room to room, go out into porticoes, and in some cases steep roofs, where he would not venture while awake. Frequently he will wander for hours through streets and fields, returning home to bed without knowledge of anything having transpired.'

Sleepwalking was being domesticated and deskilled. Somnambulists who translated from French and German, who composed sermons, who rode horseback and played billiards, belonged to a different era. The night shift was over. As medical interest in the 'nocturnal cerebration' switched to multiple personality and memory disorders, somnambulism became a subject for the forensic psychiatrist and the sleep specialist.

Sleepwalking continues to provide a criminal defence in cases of murder, rape and arson, but the validity of complex automatism – drunken or somnambulistic – has been seriously questioned. 'In a typical sleepwalking attack,' writes Roger Broughton, an expert on sleep disorders, 'the individual sits up quietly, generally an hour or two after falling asleep, gets out of bed and moves about in a confused and clumsy manner. Soon his behaviour becomes more co-ordinated and complex. He may avoid objects, dust tables, go to the bathroom, or utter phrases which are usually incomprehensible. It is difficult to attract his attention. If left alone he goes back to bed. And when he is awakened he has little if any recollection of his sleepwalking activities, and no recollection of dreaming.' Where the accused is known to have acted in a non-habitual manner, or performed actions never performed before, sleepwalking is regarded as unlikely.

Could a somnambulant Franklin Blake have really searched an unfamiliar bedroom? Did he act 'unconsciously and irresponsibly' under the influence of opium? Would he have repeated the very same act on two occasions? Given what sleep science has learnt about somnambulism, it would seem that Collins had indulged the 'novelist's right to imagine' more than he or his readers realised.

Lucid Dreaming

Dream research in the nineteenth century was never the sole preserve of the tenured scientist. In his 1867 book *Dreams and How to Guide Them*, the Marquis Léon Hervey de Saint-Denys claimed that the 'celebrated psychologists and physiologists have hardly shed a ray of light' on the mysteries of dreaming. Wilhelm Wundt and Hermann von Helmholtz, the two grandees of early physiological research into dreaming, had certainly neglected one aspect of our nocturnal psychology – the ability to be conscious of one's dreams as they occur, to be asleep and awake simultaneously. This was the subject in which Hervey, aristocrat, sinologist and all-round dilettante, became a little-known expert.

From the age of thirteen, the marquis kept a daily journal of his dreams. As he began to record images wrestled from behind his closed-eye world, the more he was able to recall and sustain memory of his dreams. After a short break, during which his obsession with dream reportage threatened to debilitate him, Hervey went on to record more than twenty years of dreams. Within months he had found that he had actually become aware of his dreams as they took place. Soon, he was able to wake at will, to record more interesting scenes, then focus in on particular aspects he wanted to investigate more closely. His ultimate goal, however, the ability to shape and direct the narrative of his dreams, proved only fitful and transient.

In his anonymously published book, Hervey referred to some of the many thousands of dreams he had recorded and included sketches of hypnagogic imagery (the largely geometric forms seen when falling asleep) that he had managed to fix in his memory. Hervey hoped to demonstrate the extent to which anyone could quite easily learn to dream consciously, *partially* directing the content of the dream and waking at will. He believed that conscious dreaming might be used to access the 'immense caves' of human memory, to stir the imagination and, not least of all, to open a scientific window on the verbal and visual trickery of the dream. His research enabled him to confirm that the vast majority of dream imagery was composed of memory snapshots. The absurdity of the dream was, he claimed, due to the random amal gamation of these recollections. Hervey did, nevertheless, recognise the role of the imagination. (To this end, Hervey describes a dream in which – note the shades of Oscar Wilde's *The Picture of Dorian Gray* – he looks into a mirror, seeing himself slowly turn into a decrepit old man.) The limits of the imagination were tested as he attempted to dream of his own death. On leaping from the top of a high tower, he suddenly found himself among the crowd of spectators who had witnessed him fall.

Hervey's work was never widely circulated. Alfred Maury, an archaeologist who had himself turned to self-experimentation, doubted that Hervey's experiences were actually dreams. Absence of volition was widely considered axiomatic of the dream state. As Maury put it, the 'dreamer is no more free than the madman or drunkard'. The English psychologist Havelock Ellis later proposed the same argument. Defiantly sceptical of the idea of conscious dreaming, Ellis announced that he did 'not believe that such a thing is really possible, though it has been borne witness to by many philosophers'.

Indeed it had. Aristotle's treatise *On Dreams* acknowledged the possibility of the sleeper being 'conscious of the sleeping state', although the lucid dream does not appear to have had a formal place in Athenian culture. Eight centuries on, Saint Augustine reported the dream of Gennadius of Carthage, in which a youth 'of remarkable appearance and commanding presence' convinced the sleeping physician of the reality of the afterlife – alerting him to the fact that he was lying in his bed, eyes closed, yet still perceiving. There are, however, only sporadic references to lucid dreaming through the Middle Ages. The Spanish Sufi Ibn El-Arabi, for instance, advised that the ability to control thoughts in a dream 'will produce great benefits for the individual'. It was not until the seventeenth century that a serious thinker, the philosopher Pierre Gassendi, reflected on a lucid dream on the basis of his own experience. A century later, in 1779, the philosopher Thomas Reid related how he was able to awake himself from nightmares by 'recollect[ing] that it was all a dream'.

The Victorians fared better. Frederic Myers had a modest strike rate, managing only three lucid dreams in 3000 attempts, but was nevertheless a keen advocate of auto-experiments. By contrast, the occult writer Oliver Fox clearly had something of a talent, stumbling into dream consciousness by accident at the age of sixteen. In his book *Astral Projection* (1939), Fox described how this, his first lucid dream, spurred him to further explorations:

> I dreamed that I was standing on the pavement outside my house . . . Now the pavement was not of the ordinary type, but consisted of small, bluish-grey rectangular stones, with their long sides at right angle to the white curb. I was about to enter the house when, on glancing casually at these stones, my attention became riveted by a strange phenomenon, so extraordinary that I could not believe my eyes – they had seemingly all changed position in the night, and the long sides were now parallel to the curb. Then the solution flashed upon me: though this glorious summer morning seemed as real as real could be, I was dreaming! With this realization of this fact, the quality of the dream changed in a manner very difficult to convey to one who has not had this experience. Instantly, the vividness of life increased a hundred-fold. Never had sea and sky and trees shone with such glamorous beauty; even the commonplace houses seemed alive and mystically beautiful. Never had I felt so absolutely well, so clear brained, so inexpressibly *free*!

Freud was seemingly unfamiliar with such dreams when he published *The Interpretation of Dreams*, which mentions his unsuccessful attempt to track down a copy of Hervey's work. In a later edition, Freud went on to acknowledge that 'some people' had experienced distinct awareness while dreaming and that Hervey 'claimed to have accelerated the course of his dreams just as he pleased, and could give them any direction he chose'. (The comment suggests that he had still not read Hervey.) By 1914, Freud had, however, met and corresponded with the Dutch psychiatrist, poet and novelist Fredrik van Eeden, who, like Hervey, had considerable experience of lucid dreaming.

Having studied and recorded his own dreams since 1896, van Eeden had his first glimpse of dream consciousness as he 'floated through a landscape of bare trees, knowing that it was April'. As with so many other lucid dreamers, it was the *defective* or *incongruous* elements in his dreams that served initially to stimulate awareness. Between 1898 and 1912, van Eeden kept a 'separate account' of these 'dreams, which I call *lucid dreams*'. He explained that in such dreams the dreamer 'reaches a state of perfect awareness, and is able to direct his attention and to attempt different acts of free volition'. The ensuing sensation of a double existence was 'most wonderful'. Van Eeden, like Fox, could not avoid the conclusion that there existed an astral body alongside the physical body.

A number of psychologists and writers now began to experiment with lucid dreaming. Mary Arnold Foster, a British psychologist, described her experiences in her 1921 book, *Studies in Dreaming*. The Russian philosopher P. D. Ouspensky and the French poet René Daumal used anaesthetics and 'various devices' in order to 'enter sleep in a waking state'. But despite his correspondence with van Eeden, Freud made no attempts to investigate the therapeutic potential of lucid dreaming or to consider its implications for his own model of psychic censorship.

As experimental psychology turned away from introspection, lucid dreaming edged its way back to the occluded fringes of science. The occasional researcher continued to ruminate on his dream experiences, but they were invariably unaware of previous reports and lacking in any conceptual shorthand. A. E. Brown's short paper on 'Dreams in Which the Dreamer Knows He Is Asleep', published in a 1936 edition of the *Journal of Abnormal Psychology*, is a telling example. Title and source tell us all we need to know about what had become of lucid dreams and where they would remain for some time.

It was not until the late 1960s, as the parapsychologist Celia Green published her book *Lucid Dreaming* and Charles Tart his seminal anthology of essays *Altered States of Consciousness*, that lucid dreaming discovered both an academic and a popular audience. Besides reprinting portions of van Eeden's 1913 essay, Tart's collection included an essay on lucid dreaming among the Senoi of Malaya by anthropologist Kilton Stewart. This latter essay was, as Tart recalls, enormously influential.

> [P]eople all over the world began work on inducing lucidity into their own dreams and forming dream groups to support each other, adapting the ideas about the Senoi to contemporary culture. Workshops became available teaching the method. Many people reported good results: they had lucid dreams where they had never had them before or the frequency of their lucid dreams increased markedly, and they gained more control over their dreams and found more guidance in them. 'Senoi Dream Worker' became a descriptive phrase for many dream workers' approaches.

These 'good results' were, however, all due to bogus anthropology. Stewart's essay had described how, while on an expedition through the central range of the Malay Peninsula in the 1930s, he was introduced to an isolated tribe of 'jungle folk, who employed methods of psychology and interpersonal interpretation so astonishing that they might have come from another planet'. 'Breakfast in the Senoi house', wrote Stewart, 'is like a dream clinic, with father and older brother listening to and analyzing the dreams of all children . . . The Senoi believes that any human being, with the aid of his fellows, can outface, master and actually utilize all beings and forces in the dream universe.' Stewart's observations would have been more accurate if written in the first person. The events he described were essentially a projection of his experiments with guided dreaming under hypnosis.

Stewart's influence in popularising lucid dreaming actually extended further than Tart suggests. In *Journey to Ixtlan* (1972), the third in Carlos Castaneda's bestselling series of books chronicling his initiation into the sorcery of the Mexican Yaqui Indians, lucid dreaming was presented in terms almost identical to Stewart's account of the Senoi dreaming. After Castaneda experiences a number of nightmares, Don Juan, his Yaqui mentor, advises him to tackle his dreams head on: to 'act deliberately', 'to manipulate them'. Even the techniques that Don Juan goes on to instruct Castaneda in, from gazing at his hands while dreaming to searching out a locale and making his own dream mood, are all lifted more or less verbatim from Stewart. For those intimate with Yaqui culture, these and many other details of Castaneda's work were simply absurd. As one expert remarked of Castaneda's work, it was 'the greatest hoax in anthropology since Piltdown man'.

Bogus anthropology was not, however, necessarily bad psychology. As far as the induction of lucid dreaming was concerned, Stewart and Castaneda were on to something. When Stephen LaBerge began to research the psychophysiology of lucid dreaming at Stanford University in the late 1970s, the New Age had fully embraced the 'empowering' and 'mind-expanding' potential of lucid dreaming. LaBerge and coworkers eventually linked lucid dreaming to the most active periods of REM sleep, in which muscular activity, eye movement and alpha activity were increased. By instructing laboratory participants to perform pre-arranged eye movements when they began to dream lucidly, LaBerge found that lucid dreaming corresponded with phasic REM, in which, in contrast to tonic REM, there are brief bursts of muscular activity. (This technique had been independently pursued by Keith Hearne, a PhD student at the University of Liverpool, whose principal subject, Alan Worsley, was an exceptionally gifted lucid dreamer.) LaBerge proposed that 'the high level of cognitive function involved in lucid dreaming requires a correspondingly high level of neuronal activity . . . Becoming lucid requires an adequate level of working memory to activate presleep intention to recognize that one is dreaming.'

These experiments thus confirmed that the British philosopher Noel Malcolm had been rather too hasty in proclaiming the statement 'I am asleep' a logical absurdity. (One reviewer from the journal *Science* nevertheless rejected LaBerge's first report on his experiments at Stanford in exactly these terms.) Having identified the underlying physiology of dream lucidity, however, laboratory investigations soon entered a cul-de-sac. With psychologists showing little interest in the subject, most research has of late been directed towards the use of lucid dreaming as a treatment for nightmares, anxiety, depression and grief. Transpersonal psychologists have, at the same time, claimed lucidity as a bona fide spiritual technology, a form of 'deep witnessing', comparable to various forms of meditation. '[O]nce you start to lucid dream,' promises Ken Wilber, 'an entirely new realm becomes available to you – namely, the subtle realm – and this is unmistakably reflected in your life, your writing, your theorizing, your spiritual practice.'

Forms of lucid dreaming certainly have a long-standing place in Tibetan dream yoga and Hindu dream-witnessing, in which the yogi attempts to meditate on the 'thatness of the dream state'. In New World shamanism, we also find the ability to wake oneself while dreaming serving a prophetic and curative function. These cultures did not, however, turn to lucid dreaming as a source of 'self-confidence'. The New Age proselytisers of lucid dreaming, LaBerge included, promise rather more than Hervey or any of his ancient precursors.

The Undercover Assassin

On the night of 18 June 1937, the French surrealist poet Paul
Eluard experienced a dreaming terror unlike any he had
experienced before. 'I dream that I am in bed,' he wrote in his
dream journal, 'and it is late. I am aching all over. I try to turn on
the light. I cannot, so I get up and grope my way in the darkness
towards my wife's room. In the corridor, I fall. Unable to get up, I
crawl slowly forward. I can hardly breathe. I have a terrible pain
in my chest.' Dreaming that he has woken, Eluard finds himself
unable to move. 'I try to call out to my wife, to make her hear me
as I call the word "pa-ra-lysed". In vain. In a horrifying moment I
realize that I am blind, dumb, paralysed, that I will never be able
to communicate anything of myself . . . Until it occurs to me to use
my fingertips to check whether I am really on the floor. I pinch the
sheets lightly, I am saved, I am in my bed.'

Awareness that one is asleep, pressure on the chest, rising panic
and feverish attempts to retrieve one's body are the keynotes of a
nocturnal drama that is by no means uncommon. 'The feeling is
terrible,' observed the poet Gerard Manley Hopkins, 'the nervous
and muscular instress seems to fall in and hang like a dead weight
on the chest. I cried on the holy name and by degrees recovered
myself as I thought to do.' Intriguingly, the same phenomenon has
been simultaneously experienced by identical twins. June and
Jennifer Gibbons, the subjects of Marjorie Wallace's book *The
Silent Twins* (1986), recorded how on more than one occasion each
'felt a great heavy breathing weight enveloping her as though a fat
man had lain on top of her, smothering her in the folds of his flesh'.

While the Gibbons twins dubbed their terrifying dream 'The
Beast', Hopkins described his as simply a nightmare. As used by

Hopkins, this was not a generic term for any type of horrifying dream. A 'night-mair', as it was more usually referred to before the seventeenth century, referred to a goblin, monster or incubus that was commonly thought to prey on the sleeper, squatting upon the chest or stomach. Although many medieval demonologists feared that the Antichrist would be born of this liaison, the incubus or nightmare was slowly claimed as a disease. King James I's *Daemonologie* of 1597, for example, admitted that a 'natural sickness' might 'explain the illusion of an unnatural burden or spirit, lying upon us, and holding us down'.

The dictionaries and encyclopaedias of the early eighteenth century extended this medical interpretation, giving more precise details of its nature and cause. In Ephraim Chambers's *Cyclopaedia* of 1728, for example, the incubus was described as 'a Disease consisting in an oppression of the breast, so very violent, that the Patient cannot speak, or even breathe. In this Disease the Senses are not quite lost, but drown'd and astonish'd, as is the Understanding and Imagination; so that the Patient seems to think some huge Weight thrown on him ready to strangle him. Children are very liable to this Distemper; so are fat people, and Men of much Study and Application of Mind.' Chambers refuted the notion that this disease might be the product of 'gross vapours filling the ventricles of the brain' and instead proposed that the nightmare was in all cases linked to 'some difficulty in Digestion'.

When Robert Macnish considered the nature of the nightmare in his 1830 book *The Philosophy of Sleep*, he endorsed Chambers's view that it was often linked to digestive problems (Macnish singled out cheese, cucumbers and almonds as particular culprits and warned that any ensuing nightmares might be aggravated into 'seven fold horror' by the reading of gothic novels), but provided a far more dramatic and picturesque account of its shifting terrors:

> Sometimes the sufferer is buried beneath overwhelming rocks, which crush him on all sides, but still leave him with a miserable consciousness of his situation. Sometimes, he is involved in the coils of a horrid, slimy monster, whose eyes have the phosphorescent glare of the sepulchre, and whose breath is as

poisonous as the marsh of Lerna [where the mythological Hydra was killed by Hercules]. Everything horrible, disgusting, or terrific in the physical or moral world, is brought before him in fearful array: he is hissed at by serpents, tortured by demons, stunned by the hollow voices and cold touch of apparitions. A mighty stone is laid upon his breast, and crushes him to the ground in helpless agony. . . . In every instance, there is a sense of oppression and helplessness . . . The individual never feels himself a free agent, on the contrary he is spellbound by some enchantment and remains an unresisting victim for malice to work its will upon. If pursued by any imminent danger, he can hardly drag one limb after another; if engaged in combat, his blows are ineffective; if involved in the fangs of any animal, or in the grasp of any enemy, extraction is impossible. He struggles, he pants, he toils, but it is all in vain: his muscles are rebels to the will, and refuse to obey its calls.

The terrors of the nineteenth-century nightmare correspond exactly with the experience of sleep paralysis, which also appears to underpin various beliefs concerning spiritual arrest and possession. Although most often reported at the onset of REM sleep, where it is accompanied by hypnagogic hallucinations, sleep paralysis may also be symptomatic of dissociated awakening in the tonic phase of REM sleep, as suggested by recent laboratory research. In both cases, inhibition of nerve impulses creates a state of muscle atonia which carries over into wakefulness, typically lasting for a minute or so. According to one estimate, about 15 per cent of the population can claim to have been subject to at least one attack.

The folklorist David J. Hufford first drew attention to the diverse folk afflictions which are derived from the experience of sleep paralysis in the early 1980s, after having studied attacks of the Old Hag in Newfoundland. The experience was in this province of Canada most commonly described in terms of being straddled by humans or animals while asleep, and it was often thought to have been precipitated by being 'agged' by a hostile neighbour. In northern Alaska, a night illness known as *uqamairineq* is similarly explained as the sleeper's soul being stolen by a spirit. And in the

Caribbean, attacks of *kokma* are believed to be perpetrated by the spirits of dead, unbaptised babies who attack sleepers, jumping on their chests and clutching their necks. In all these cases – and perhaps also in some cases of alien abduction which involve episodes of bodily restraint – the origins of a supernatural belief may be traced back to the 'coils of a horrid, slimy monster' called sleep paralysis.

Alien Infirmities

Running Wild

Derived from the Malay term for a frenzied and murderous assault, *amok* is an abbreviation of *gila mengamok* (running-amok insanity), which was first described by early British, Dutch and Portuguese travellers in southeast Asia. As a culture-bound form of violent rage, *amok* bears parallels with *pseudonite* in the Sahara, *cathard* in Polynesia and the berserk rage of the Vikings. Although the pre-colonial history of *amok* is obscure, it has been argued that its true origins are to be found in warfare and acts of religious fanaticism. From these beginnings, *amok* may have been sanctioned as a way of defending personal honour and restoring self-esteem.

The best documented cases of *amok* relate to the rural villages of nineteenth-century Malaya, where it was believed to be a form of spirit possession or soul loss brought about by broken taboo, witchcraft or evil spirits. According to folk belief, *amok* was the most pronounced and dangerous form of three forms of *gila* (insanity). As in the following report from 1891, the *pengamok* (person seized by *amok*) would vent his rage indiscriminately, attacking family, friends and neighbours in a series of assaults that might stretch over hours or days. While in this instance the *pengamok* claimed to have been possessed, before dying from wounds inflicted in self-defence by fellow villagers, other *pengamoks* showed no apparent recollection of events:

> Imam Mamat . . . had been at work fencing his lands all day, and at about 4 to 5 p.m. he entered the house of Bilal Abu [his brother-in-law] with a spear and a golak [bladed weapon] in his possession. On entering he took the hand of Bilal Abu and asked for pardon;

he then shook hands with his [own] wife Alang Resak and said the same thing, but immediately stabbed her in the abdomen with the golak. She immediately fell, and received two more superficial wounds . . . Bilal Abu rushed to the rescue, and received for his trouble a deep wound in the region of the heart and a superficial wound on the right side: he fell never to rise again. At this moment Ngah Intan, wife of Bilal Abu, followed by four of her children, rushed to the door and jumped out, her eldest son Kassim receiving a stab in the back as he jumped out. Imam Mamat jumped out [houses are on stilts] and, with two more spears picked up in the house, gave chase to Ngah Intan, who was followed by the three youngest children . . . One little girl, Si The, received two wounds in the back, not dangerous ones; a boy, Mumin, received a deep wound in the side . . . and the second little girl, Si Pateh, received a severe wound in the stomach, from which she died the next day. Having satisfied himself with the children, he followed up with the mother, catching her 100 yards off, and killed her on the spot by a stab in the abdomen . . . It appears that Imam then walked down stream 200 yards, and met a friend, Uda Majid, who was coming to stop him, but unarmed. Uda Majid saluted him respectfully, and asked him if he recognized him, and not to make a row; he replied 'Yes, but my spear does not know you,' and immediately stabbed him twice in the breast and stomach.

For much of the nineteenth century, Western explanations of *amok* were purely medical. Malaria, typhoid, syphilis and acute intoxication were some of the many physical causes suggested by Europeans. 'If excited by an overdose of hashish or opium,' wrote one German pharmacologist, 'a savage Moslem becomes an assassin, a Malay is seized by *amok* frenzy, whereas in the same situation, a scholarly, educated medical doctor carries out observations on himself.' This cultural stereotype of the Asiatic inevitably explained the frenzied madness of *amok* as much as any imputed disease or drug. In the 'peculiar temperament' of the Malays, another commentator observed a 'proneness to common disease of feeling resulting from a want of moral elasticity'. This left the mind of the Malay prey to the pain of 'grief', 'malignant gloom' and 'despair'. By the turn of the century, *amok* was being increasingly perceived as a transient insanity produced by 'spite, envy, or being affronted'.

The most recent Western studies of *amok* and *amok*-like violence in Malaysia and other parts of Southeast Asia have tended to focus either on the clinical profile of the *pengamok* or on the social structures and belief systems that tacitly sponsor his violence. Two very different pictures emerge from this different emphasis. From the clinical perspective, the psychological profile of the *pengamok* is invariably characterised by paranoiac sensitivity, a tendency to project blame and inability to express frustration. The particular pattern of behaviour that he engages in is seen as directly compatible with that of sudden mass murderers in North America and Europe. In both cases, a period of brooding introspection leads to protracted homicidal rage, followed by withdrawal or amnesia.

While the generality of *amok*-like behaviour is not disputed, anthropologists have, in contrast, noted that *amok* can only be regarded as a 'common pathway' when it is stripped down to its most basic essentials and robbed of context. *Amok*, they insist, is a cultural act. The rigid social hierarchy of Malay society, negative attitudes towards public expression of animosity, concepts of shame and the taboo against suicide – all are the stresses and strains that are specific to *amok* in its native form. As John E. Carr writes, '*Amok*, as it is it conceptualized by the Malay will be found prevalent only among people who share the Malay conceptualizations and norms. Behaviour similar to the *amok* phenomenon will be found in other cultures, but it will be conceptualized and valuated in other ways.'

The folk beliefs that once sanctioned classical *amok* as the ultimate veto are now overlaid by a medico-legal complex that extends into the most remote rural areas. The popular understanding of *amok* also reflects these changes. As one elderly lady informed the psychiatrist Joseph Westermeyer during his fieldwork in Laos in the early 1970s, 'You Americans do not go crazy and kill people like that because you speak your anger openly . . . We Lao are different. We seldom show anger, and when we do there is loss of face (*sea naa*). So the anger builds and can suddenly come out in killing.' If *amok* still functions as a last-ditch strategy of restitution, it is no doubt limited to the most rural and traditional pockets, where the notion of supernatural agency is still invoked. Yet even here the possibility of salvation has disappeared. The *pengamok* no longer retains the possibility of returning to the community he turns against. His violence is, like that of his Western counterparts, a farewell letter or suicide note composed in his victims' blood.

Northern Flights

While travelling across the western coast of Greenland in the 1890s, the Arctic explorer Robert A. Peary often observed the native Inuits in the throes of a peculiar type of seizure:

> The patient, usually a woman, begins to scream and to tear off and destroy her clothing. If on ship, she will walk up and down the deck, screaming and gesticulating . . . As the intensity of the attack increases she will sometimes leap over the rail, running perhaps half a mile. The attack may last a few minutes, an hour, or even more, and some sufferers become so wild that they would continue running about on the ice perfectly naked till they froze, if they were not forcibly brought back.

During twenty years of Arctic travel, Peary claimed that he had seen the seizure, known locally as *pibloktoq*, many times, but only once in a man and never in a child.

Although subsequent ethnologists and explorers did note some incidents among Inuit men, *pibloktoq*, or Arctic hysteria, as it would become known, was generally regarded as the female correlative of kayak fright (a paralytic seizure which afflicted younger and middle-aged hunters, who were periodically overcome by a frightening sense of their solitude). These later reports of Arctic hysteria expanded the range of behaviours associated with the condition to include glossolalia and animal imitations, attempts to walk on the ceiling, stylised and dancelike movements, and cherishing of found objects. During an attack of Arctic hysteria, Inuits were also seen to possess unnatural strength and stamina, enabling them to elude capture or restraint. Yet no harm to others was ever recorded.

Considered a natural illness among the polar Inuits, who neither feared nor attached stigma to such episodes, these 'bizarre tantrums' proved endlessly fascinating to Western observers. While Peary's lieutenant, Donald Macmillan, observed that the condition reminded him of 'a little child discouraged and unhappy because it imagines no one loves it or cares for it and therefore runs away', A. A. Brill, the psychoanalyst and translator of Freud, concluded that it was a primitive hysteria. Brill thought that, like the *grande hystérie* of Charcot's patients, whose attention-seeking theatricalities had been famously paraded at the Salpêtrière, it had its roots in grief, lovelessness or sexual problems.

Other researchers made much more of the social and ecological background to these seizures. Russian ethnologists thought that the 'cosmic milieu' of the Arctic was responsible for the nervous instability of the Arctic peoples. As the *locus classicus* of shamanism (the word 'shaman' is the Russified version of the Tungus *šaman*), the connections between this ur-religion and Arctic hysteria were much debated. A number of researchers maintained that arctic psychopathology and shamanism were intimately connected. Although some of the Inuits who took hysterical flight may have gone on to be apprenticed to shamans, who then instructed them in the art of possession, Arctic hysteria was by no means a sign of election. At best, the affliction may have provided an invitation to cure one's self: to master and take control of the spirit world.

While depression, epilepsy and calcium or vitamin deficiencies were elsewhere proposed as precipitating factors, the American anthropologist Seymour Parker claimed that Arctic hysteria and its attendant symptoms were all prevalent in societies that display three features. One, they were extroverted and emotionally spontaneous. Two, the female role was subject to deprivation and taboo. Three, there was a widespread belief in supernatural possession. These factors, Parker argued, all shaped the symptoms of Arctic hysteria. Although Parker did not suggest any direct parallels, the folk illnesses that best parallel Arctic hysteria are the *grisis siknis* of the Miskito Indians of Nicaragua and Honduras, and the 'wildman' behaviour of New Guinea. Like Arctic hysteria, these are well-recognised flight possessions that once had equally established counterresponses and interventions. Unlike the Western psychiatric syndromes such as intermittent explosive disorder, psychogenic amnesia or atypical dissociative disorder, in which individuals may also take flight, Arctic hysteria was in its own milieu recognised as a spiritual emergency that could, in exceptional circumstances, lead towards shamanic initiation.

When the psychiatrist Edward F. Foulks studied arctic hysteria in northern Alaska in the 1960s and 1970s, he found that almost all of the locals who took flight were influenced by their elders and alienated from, or suspicious of, their peers. Unable to find a way of life that was gratifying, they sought to escape, to hide from themselves and others. Neither pursued nor placated, the social contract that once underpinned Arctic hysteria had been undone by wholesale transformations in lifestyle and belief. Foulks's patients were the double victims of modernisation: railing against its effects in a language that was no longer understood. Like so many other exotic 'disorders' and 'afflictions', this 'bizarre tantrum' is now more or less confined to the annals of medical history. No longer providing a resolution to the conflicts and anxieties of Inuit life, arctic hysteria has been replaced by the familiar pathologies which modern medicine has come to under-write globally.

A Chinese Conundrum?

One of the most unusual afflictions listed in works of Chinese medicine and herbalism is a shrinkage or retraction of the penis that, if left to run its natural course, is thought to have fatal consequences. First recorded in northern China more than two thousand years ago, *shook yin* was first and foremost regarded as a symptom of sexual imbalance. According to the *Yellow Emperor's Inner Canon of Medicine*:

> When the pulse corresponding to the liver is slightly big there is numbness in the liver. The penis will shrink and there is a persistent cough which causes abdominal pain. Illness due to internal pathogenic factors causes impotence . . . illness due to cold causes retraction of the penis. In the case of the liver, grief moves the innermost self and causes harm to the mind resulting in madness, amnesia and lack of sperm. Without sperm, a person will not be well, and the manifestation is one of retraction of the genitals. Death usually occurs in autumn.

The Yellow Emperor's physician's view of *shook yin* runs through much of China's medical literature. Reflecting the theory of yin and yang, and the need for harmonious balance of all elements, the favoured treatment was a combination of heat-giving medicines to restore the depleted yang. Before the recommended yang-giving potion of bamboo, deer horn and other 'masculine' substances could be concocted, however, immediate assistance was required to prevent involution of the penis. This led to a state of heightened panic in which the sufferer would call on persons of the same sex – contact with the opposite sex being thought fatal at this stage – to vigorously massage the legs and genitals. Clamps and cords, chopsticks and pins would be used to prevent retraction.

Although the belief that retraction of the penis might prove fatal appears to be specific to China – especially on the southern coast, where it is linked to possession by the 'fox spirit' – *shook yin* does have equivalent afflictions in other Asian countries, being known as *koro* in the Indonesian archipelago, *rok joo* in Thailand and *jinginia* in India. Since the 1930s, when the first Western anthropologists were enthralled by the possibility of 'a living exemplar of Freud's castration complex', researchers of *koro* (the term most often used in medical and ethnological literature) have been preoccupied with a number of questions. Does the large-scale migration of the Chinese account for the diffusion of *koro* across Southeast Asia and India? Is *koro* really specific to these areas? Is genital retraction, in some cases, a 'real' medical condition? Addressing the latter question in the 1950s, the crosscultural psychiatrist George Devereux was one of the first commentators to suggest that not all cases of *koro* are psychosomatic. He pointed out that retraction of the penis, as well as muscle spasms and blurred vision, also occur in peritonitis and abdominal wall oedema, conditions that could indeed be life-threatening. Although penile contraction is also symptomatic of anxiety and depression, *koro*'s connections with sexual neurosis and acute hysteria have been most emphasised. A study of nineteen cases of *koro* in Hong Kong, undertaken by the British-born psychiatrist P. M. Yapp in the 1960s, found that almost all patients had a history of sexual conflict and maladjustment, with neurotic anxieties over sexual excess or deprivation, and fear of venereal diseases.

Collective cases of *koro* seem to be triggered by very different concerns. Just as large-scale outbreaks in China were concurrent with the Great Leap Forward in the late 1950s and Cultural Revolution of the late 1960s, recent *koro* epidemics in Singapore and Thailand have been fanned by social preoccupations. A total of 469 cases of *koro* were reported in Singapore in 1967. The epidemic, which spread principally but not exclusively through the Chinese community, was generated by a newspaper report that described a case of *koro* which developed after one individual had eaten meat from an animal inoculated with swine-fever vaccine. A subsequent report alleged that an inoculated pig had died with penile retraction, sparking fears that anyone who had eaten infected pork was at risk. The imaginary contagion was finally halted by a series of public health announcements via television and newspapers. In a comparable epidemic of *koro* in the provinces of northeast Thailand in 1982, contaminated mackerel, sardines, noodles and cigarettes were all held responsible for retraction of the genitals.

In her recent study of hysterical epidemics, *Hystories* (1997), Elaine Showalter asserts that: 'An Englishman can legitimately complain of headache or fatigue but not that his penis is retracting into his body.' Showalter is quite right: retraction or disappearance of the genitals has never become a recognised symptom of anxiety or distress in the West. Whatever other symptoms are suggested and mimicked in Western psychosomatic illnesses and mass epidemics, genital retraction is outside the standard hysterical remit. Yet the symptoms of *koro* as an individual and non-epidemic illness do appear outside its indigenous enclaves. There have been at least forty reports of *koro*-like disorders in Western cases of schizophrenia, brain damage and acute intoxication. The case of 'Koro in a Londoner', reported in the *Lancet*, described a thirty-three-year-old engineer who:

> . . . awakened at 3:00 a.m. with a feeling of impending doom and an awareness that his penis was shrinking into his body. He rapidly developed palpitations, sweating, nausea and other symptoms of a panic attack. The feeling that he was about to die was linked to the shrinking of his penis, which he sought to alleviate by pulling it . . . Over the following year, beginning at the same time of the morning, the patient experienced 12 to 15 attacks, though their intensity and duration decreased . . . He had no previous psychiatric history.

The fifty or so Western accounts of *koro* suggest that genital retraction might well be a relatively rare but nevertheless general symptom of depersonalisation. The insensibility that is felt in the genitals and legs is, for example, typical of schizophrenia and drug-induced psychosis, where the body image can slowly disintegrate. But epidemic *koro* cannot be classified as a 'mass hysteria', 'epidemic psychosis', a 'panic syndrome' or, worse still, as simply an 'exotic delusion'. The transmission of mass *koro* in China, Singapore, India and Thailand follows a pattern observed in numerous Western outbreaks of 'hysterical contagion'. A recent study by Sheuk-Tak Cheng from the City Polytechnic of Hong Kong found that *koro* principally affected poorly educated, adolescent males who subscribed to traditional beliefs about the depletion of sexual energies and, most importantly, that it occurred within communities experiencing economic hardship or uncertainty. Viewed from this perspective, the mystery of *koro* is not its strange and singular symptomology, but the way in which it enables communities to express and allay the shared anxieties that precipitate it.

Fits and Starts

It was with some anticipation that Dr George Beard left New York for Moosehead Lake, Maine, in the summer of 1880. For two years, Beard had conversed and corresponded with informants who assured him of the existence of the 'jumpers', or 'jumping Frenchmen', a handful of families in Maine, New Hampshire and Canada who suffered from the strangest of diseases. These jumpers were, quite simply, too easily taken aback. If one quickly pointed a finger at them, or called their name unexpectedly, they were a danger to themselves and others. They might strike out with whatever implement they were holding, almost cut their throats while shaving or scald themselves on a nearby stove. Even more curiously, when startled by a sudden noise or gesture, they would follow virtually any command, repeating the order as they did so. Told to jump a ravine or walk fire, they were helpless to resist.

Dr Beard found that the information he had received was 'more than true' in all but one respect – none of four families he visited was French. His experiments confirmed the dramatic seizures that so easily gripped the jumpers. Alarming them with an unexpected line from Homer or Virgil, Beard watched them jump and strike while repeating his words with staccato sharpness. As the condition was as taxing to the jumpers as it was dangerous to others, the families were happy to be attended to by Beard. He was, however, unable to offer practical assistance. The bromide of sodium he prescribed had no effect. The disease, he concluded, was hereditary and untreatable. Once a jumper, always a jumper. For reasons he did not elaborate on, Beard thought 'it was probably an evolution of tickling: the habit of tickling each other in the woods'.

The behaviour of the jumpers shared striking similarities with the *latahs* of Indonesia and Malaysia, and the *mali-malis* of the Philippines. When a *latah,* generally a middle-aged or older woman, is teased, tickled or startled, she may utter 'naughty talk', imitate the behaviour of those around her or undertake commands to dance, sing or mimic others. Nineteenth-century studies of *latah* (which in Malay means 'ticklish' or 'love madness') considered the phenomenon an indigenous form of hysteria or schizophrenia. Psychoanalytical interpretations suggested that *latah* was better considered a fright neurosis and that this instinctive behaviour was a defence through identification.

In other parts of the world, the act of being shocked or startled has been embroiled in other no less fascinating behaviours and beliefs. Various illnesses, misfortunes and fatalities have been ascribed to the impact of the startle reflex. The folk illness *susto,* found throughout Latin America, is locally considered an imbalance of bodily elements caused by any fearful experience causing the spirit to flee the body. When a Chinantec woman fell ill with *susto* two weeks after seeing her father almost swept away at a river crossing, a 'being of the water' was thought to have robbed the woman's strength and caused the fevers typical of the illness. To recover from *susto,* her spirit had to be recovered. In the Philippines, the fright illness known as *lanti* claims its infant and child victims more obliquely. A parent who is startled when seeing a snake, or while climbing a tree or visiting a cave, may feel the spiritual ties that bind him to his children jolted. The youngest child is thought to be most affected by the shock because he is weaker and more intimately connected.

Like the jumpers that Beard studied in the 1880s, a small minority of Westerners are also vulnerable to the most innocuous of stimuli. These 'hyperstartlers', as Ronald C. Simons calls them, find many aspects of their lives and personalities shaped by this over-developed reflex. Startled several times a day – sometimes to the point of harming themselves and others – they avoid certain social situations and are effectively impaired from entering certain professions. Like *latahs* they, too, may find themselves intentionally teased, caught in 'a chronic state of such readiness for startle', especially in institutions such as schools and army barracks. Hyperstartlers are not, however, amenable to suggestion, and they do not copy the behaviour of others.

Although *latah* is a highly elaborate and prolonged behaviour, Simons has argued that it is generated by the same startle response. His 1980 paper 'The Resolution of the Latah Paradox' fell somewhat short of what its title promised. His repeated attempts to understand *latah* as a local variant of a universal startle response have been rightly criticised for transforming a cultural idiom into a quirk of neurophysiology. The limitations of Simons's biomedical approach were blatant. How could the startle reflex explain why *latah* was a predominantly female phenomenon? How could it account for the different forms that it might take, from the mild cases characterised by verbal profanities to more elaborate performances? The debate nevertheless rumbled on, and *latah* retained its dubious place among the ragbag of the 'culture-bound syndromes'.

A missing piece of the ethnographic jigsaw emerged when Robert Bartholomew, a sociologist from James Cook University of North Queensland, had the opportunity of studying and gathering information from the extended Malaysian family into which he had married. Of 115 living and deceased family members, thirty-three were classified as 'mild' *latah* and three as 'severe'. One of the latter cases was 'Siti', an elderly aunt whom Bartholomew eventually had the opportunity to observe firsthand at a wedding:

. . . this timid, decrepit wizen-faced woman was intentionally startled by her elderly uncle, who walked near her and clapped his hands. She responded with a short vulgar phrase, stood up, lost all inhibition, and began following each of her teaser's commands and mimicking his every gesture. During the ensuing 10-minute episode, Siti was 'made to' cry like a baby, perform *silat* (Malay self-defence or martial arts), dance vigorously, and partially disrobe, all to the obvious amusement of the entire wedding party who crowded around her inside the bride's parents' home. . . . Throughout the episode, after some outrageous display she would apologize immediately and profusely for her vulgarity, then launch unhesitatingly into another series of behaviours, apologizing over thirty times during this particular paroxysm.

The repertoire was consistent with the sole paroxysm of *latah* described in the anthropological literature, but the context of this behaviour proved rather more exacting than presumed. Bartholomew was able to provoke a similar paroxysm in Siti at another crowded wedding reception – invariably the scene of the most florid *latah* attacks – yet later, in the presence of two relatives, he was only moderately successful. It was, it transpired, rare for any *latah* to perform extensively outside large social occasions. More importantly, the 'teasers' were usually close relatives who would handle the 'victims' responsibly.

These ground rules point to a highly ritualised theatre that has been too long draped in the language of pathology. The anthropological evidence suggests that *latah* is in reality an idiom through which marginality and distress express themselves. Its function is, at root, that of the carnivalesque – catharsis. Through mimicry and ribaldry the *latah* casts off the prohibitions and taboos of everyday life, and, while complying with the demands of others, the *latah* briefly enjoys the attention and privileges of the court jester.

The Beast Within

From Nebuchadnezzar's transformation into an ox in the Old Testament to Lucius's equine adventures in Apuleius's *The Golden Ass*, tales of shape-shifting describe a menagerie of animal guises. The wolf has a special place in this human bestiary. Travelling by way of Roman mythology and Norse saga, the man-wolf has roamed and stalked its way through European folklore, fable and fantasy. Ovid's *Metamorphoses*, for example, tells the story of Lycaon, the tyrannical and bloodthirsty king of Arcadia, who, when visited by Jupiter, was forced to flee into the countryside, where:

> he uttered howling noises, and his attempts to speak were all in vain. His clothes changed into bristling hairs, his arms to legs, and he became a wolf. His own savage nature showed in his rabid jaws, and he now directed against the flocks his innate lust for killing. He had a mania, even yet, for shedding blood. But though he was a wolf, he retained some traces of his original shape . . . and he preserved the same picture of ferocity.

Delusions of metamorphosis into wolves and dogs are still reported occasionally in today's medical literature. Known to the Greeks as *lycanthropy* and the Romans as *insania lupina*, the wolfish transformation has a particularly long and substantial history. The Alexandrian physician Paulus Aegineta described lycanthropic patients whose legs were ulcerated from travelling on all fours, who wandered cemeteries at night and howled till daybreak. Attributing these symptoms to brain damage, humoral excess or drugs, he recommended bloodletting, a restricted diet and opium to prevent night wandering.

From the end of the sixteenth century, lycanthropy, as described in classical medicine, was increasingly deemed a supernatural atrocity. Believing that witches had the power to assume all animal forms, European demonology variously gave birth to the werewolf in Britain, the *loup-garou* in France, *lupomanaro* in Italy, and *wahr-wolfee* in Germany. It was, however, only in regions infested with real wolves that their mythical counterparts were charged with rape, murder, cannibalism and other crimes. The coincidental sighting of a wolf and human in the same vicinity seems to have been sometimes considered sufficient evidence for shape-shifting.

In Britain, where no prosecutions took place, opinion as to the reality of the werewolf was divided. Although demonological treatises and trial proceedings from the Continent circulated in the sixteenth and seventeenth centuries, giving credence to the phenomenon, Reginald Scot's *Discourse of Witchcraft* (1584) and Robert Burton's *Anatomy of Melancholy* (1621) saw werewolfism as nothing more than age-old lycanthropy, a melancholic delusion in which Satan had no part. Yet these occult and medical interpretations were not necessarily opposed. Physicians and demonologists alike suspected that Satan might, at the very least, delude humans into thinking that they were wolves, either by confusing the humours or providing them with magical ointments. Thus, while Della Porta's *Magia Naturalis* argued that lycanthropy was a result of potions made from henbane, belladonna and other plant hallucinogens, this did not rule out the possibility of demonic collusion.

While many persons accused of werewolfism during the witch mania of the late Middle Ages were victims of scapegoating (in terror-stricken communities besieged by human and economic loss), some were, no doubt, mentally disturbed. The notorious Peter Strubbe, who confessed to incest, murder and eating human flesh at his trial in 1589, is said to have been discovered in 'wolfish likeness' outside the town of Bedbur, Germany, where numerous women and children had been killed and mutilated. Evidence of his supposed twenty-five-year career in sorcery was scanty. Attempts to substantiate Strubbe's claims to have been empowered to transform himself into a wolf through the use of a girdle given to him by the devil were, unsurprisingly, unsubstantiated, but his fate was already sealed.

In the case of Jean Grenier, the young French werewolf tried in 1603, the court concluded that despite Grenier's admissions (like Strubbe, Grenier claimed to have powers of self-transformation and confessed to having been given a magical salve and wolfskin by a man on horseback, who introduced himself as the 'Master of the Forest') of shape-shifting, he was grossly deluded. Consequently, Grenier was sentenced to life imprisonment in a Bordeaux monastery, where, on arrival, he is reported to have '[run] frantically about the cloister and garden on all fours, and finding a heap of bloody and raw offal, fell upon it and devoured it'.

Recent speculation on the diseases and conditions that might explain the savage behaviour or appearance of individuals tried for werewolfism or suffering from lycanthropy – a distinction which some demonologists recognised – has given rise to a number of theories. Rabies, for example, may explain how real wolves came to attack humans, the heightened fear they inspired and the feral behaviour of infected individuals. Its transmission across Europe in the fifteenth and sixteenth century coincides with rising belief in werewolves. Its symptoms include hyperactivity and violent spasms, photophobia and increased salivation, with periods of irritation and mania punctuated by lucidity and alertness. Paralysis of the throat muscles might also cause loss of voice, giving rise to animal-like 'grunts' and 'howling'.

Autism has also been linked to werewolfism and more recent cases of feral children thought to have been raised by wolves or monkeys. In the 1940s, when anthropologists and sociologists still lent credence to cases of feral children such as the wolf-children of Midnapore, the child psychologist Bruno Bettelheim argued that these were more likely abandoned autistic children. Their apparently savage behaviour, he argued, was a consequence of their autism and not their animal upbringing. From experience, Bettelheim was aware that the development of autistic children was dramatically arrested. Bettelheim observed that autistic children were, besides being acutely remote and linguistically impaired, prone to violent temper tantrums during which they might bite adult carers. They would, furthermore, often retreat into dens and seek out raw food. These characteristics accorded with those of feral children and werewolves such as Jean Grenier.

The extent to which solanaceous plants played a part in werewolfism is, despite the commentaries of Aegineta and Della Porta, and the confessions of werewolves who referred to using unguents and salves, little known. There is no reliable evidence of the ritual use of these drugs, and no vestiges of any purported tradition have survived. Some historians have nevertheless been willing to accept that the witches and werewolves of the Middle Ages were magical fraternities who employed plants from the solanaceous family of psychoactive drugs, found throughout Europe. More intrepid researchers who have self-experimented with these drugs have attested to both the powerful feral and the flight-inducing effects of these substances. As with the disease-based interpretation of werewolfism, however, this pharmacological interpretation is effectively ahistorical. Demonology may have interpreted some illnesses as werewolfism, but the uneven distribution of cases of werewolfism across medieval Europe suggests that more powerful, social factors were at work.

While werewolfism died a death in the seventeenth century, lycanthropy has survived to find a place among today's psychiatric syndromes. Viewed by clinicians as a disorder of depersonalisation, the conditions with which it has been most recently connected include schizophrenia, manic psychosis, hysteria, psychotic depression and brain injury. The following case of lycanthropy, reported some years ago in the *American Journal of Psychiatry*, is typical in reporting the transformation in both physical and psychological terms. In this instance, the patient attributed his recurrent episodes to having been bitten by a rabid dog:

> When I'm emotionally upset I feel as if I'm turning into something else; my fingers go numb, as if I have pins and needles in the middle of my hand; I can no longer control myself . . . I get the

feeling I'm becoming a wolf. I look at myself in the mirror and I witness my transformation. It's no longer my face; it changes completely. I stare, my pupils dilate, and I feel as if hairs are growing all over my body, as if my teeth are getting longer . . . I feel as if my skin is no longer mine.

While the symptoms of lycanthropy are redolent of various folk possessions including the Japanese *kitsune-tsuki* – the victims of which, generally women, are exorcised of foxes or other animals that have occupied their bodies – werewolfism is a more complex and questionable phenomenon. Historians and anthropologists are still debating whether the werewolfism of the medieval witches was a bona fide magical tradition or simply the projection of 'persecuting society'. The historian Carlo Ginzburg has, for one, argued that werewolfism does have a real history in parts of southern and eastern Europe, and that these ecstatic and ceremonial rituals correspond to the more ancient complex of the zoomorphic shamanism, which assumed various animal guises when entering the spirit world. Refracted through the prism of demonology, the vestiges of zoomorphy may in some pockets of Europe been transformed and debased into the notion of were-wolfism. Elsewhere, it was the unearthly progeny of demonology.

E is for Ergot

On Thursday, 16 August 1951, Roche Briand's bakery on the Grande Rue in the French village of Pont-Saint-Esprit sold no more nor less than the usual amount of bread. The following day, the local doctor, Dr Gabbai, returned from his annual vacation to find his waiting rooms unusually full. Two other doctors in the village were equally overwhelmed. All the patients reported nausea, vomiting, abdominal cramps, cold chills and difficulties in breathing. Soon, others arrived and described rather different sensations, including giddiness and convulsive fits. By the weekend, 230 people were affected. When Gabbai met his two colleagues, all their information pointed to Briand's bakery as the source of the food poisoning.

Botulism, salmonella or staphylococcal poisoning could not, however, account for the strange feelings of detachment that Marcel Delacquis had experienced when riding his bicycle-cum-heavenly chariot into a blazing rainbow of colour. Not one of these would explain why M. Mison, like many others, had run out into his yard, screaming that he was on fire. Inability to sleep, feelings of elation and goodwill, irrational fears, compulsion, hallucinations and unusual fixations could certainly not be ascribed to any of these common forms of food poisoning. When laboratory tests failed to shed any light on the phantom illness, the villagers devised their own theories, implicating arsenic, hashish and other agents. Uncertainty as to the nature of the mystery affliction caused panic, which in turn made many of the symptoms experienced by victims of *le pain maudit* infectious. Family, friends and neighbours who had not eaten the bread shared their surges of panic and elation and, in some cases, the physical symptoms too.

On Monday, 20 August, the mysterious poison claimed its first life and threw dozens into profound psychotic episodes. An armed villager barricaded himself into his house, protecting himself from an invisible assailant. An eleven-year-old-boy attacked his mother. The local mechanic single-handedly demolished his bedroom, believing that he was a circus strongman performing for a packed audience. Six days after the sale of *le pain maudit*, a malady that had been largely confined to people's homes went public. Scuffles broke out. People ran through the streets screaming that they were burning, that they had snakes in their stomachs or that their heads had been turned into copper. Some claimed that they were already dead. Meanwhile, the local mechanic continued his circus antics with a highwire act on the cables of the temporary suspension bridge that spanned the Rhône. As ambulances began shuttle runs to the local hospital Hôtel-Dieu, which had never before dealt with an influx of psychotics, Joseph Puche, a former pilot, jumped from the second floor of the hospital, but did not ascend the Provençal skies as he had expected. By the end of August, four had died. Two weeks later, doctors were attending to new symptoms – gangrene, haemorrhages and skin rashes.

These symptoms would eventually be traced back to ergot, the sclerotium of the fungus *Claviceps purpurea*, the spores of which infest spring grasses to produce black spurlike growths. Throughout the Middle Ages, outbreaks of ergot poisoning had been common in much of Europe, particularly in regions which relied on rye as the principal grain. When consumed in infected bread, ergot caused two types of non-contagious disease. In its most lethal form, ergot produced a condition that was commonly known as St Anthony's Fire, or the Holy or Infernal Fire, which caused the blood vessels to contract and the extremities to tingle and burn before becoming gangrenous. Blackened limbs, genitals or other bodily parts would literally drop from the bodies of its most badly affected victims. The first outbreak of this type of ergotism may have occurred in Greece as far back as 436 BC, but a more certain epidemic was reported in AD 857 in Duisburg, Germany. In what is thought to have been one of the worst epidemics of ergotism, the disease is said to have finally halted when the remains of Saint

Martial were exhumed and shown to the people. Elsewhere, the Virgin Mary and a number of saints were invoked to offer cures. By the twelfth century, Saint Anthony began to assume special importance in combating the disease. Pilgrimage to Dauphine, France – where the saint's remains had been moved in 1070 – resulted in many miracle cures.

A convulsive form of ergotism, the symptoms of which included cramps, itching, hallucinations and delirium, occurred mainly in Germany, Holland and Belgium, where it may have played a very minor role in the dancing mania that was widespread throughout the Protestant countries in the fifteenth and sixteenth century. Reports of the dancing mania in Germany and the Low Countries describe how groups of peasants, artisans and children would gather spontaneously to dance furiously for hours on end. Screaming, shouting and writhing, these frenetic dancers would periodically fall to the ground, gasping for breath, before finding themselves again energised by the music. Feverish and wild eyed, many of the dancers witnessed celestial visions.

Although other diseases may have also played their part, the effects of convulsive ergotism could have been one factor in medieval outbreaks of St Vitus's dance. (Ergotism's connection to cases of alleged demonic possession is less well founded.) Between 1581 and 1889, there were, according to one estimate, sixty epidemics of convulsive ergotism in Europe, approximately half of these in Germany and the rest elsewhere in northern and eastern Europe. By the early twentieth century, the threat of ergot poisoning was effectively eradicated through automation of the grain-milling process. Yet the spectre of ergotism was not so easily consigned to history.

The source of the infected grain in *le pain maudit* in Pont-Saint-Esprit was eventually traced back to the *moulin* of a certain M. Maillet, which fell well short of modern standards of washing and grinding grain. Attempts to trace the actual toxin were, however, protracted and ultimately inconclusive. The fact that the region had experienced a particularly wet summer lent credence to the ergot theory supported by most physicians. The police and the authorities who managed the lengthy investigation, however, were reluctant to accept that ergot, a substance that toxicologists then knew very little about, was the true source of the poisoning. Tiny traces of mercury and ergot were found in flour samples and in the victims' bodies. While ergot was thousands of times more potent than the mercury, the latter was seized upon, despite the fact that it could not account for most of the symptoms.

From what is now known about the psychopharmacology of ergot, and its laboratory cousin LSD, there can be little doubt that Pont-Saint-Esprit had fallen victim to a thoroughly medieval madness. All the effects of ergot, from the compulsion to jump from windows to the strange pungent smell emitted by its victims, were soon observed in laboratory studies of LSD. Albert Hofmann, a young Swiss chemist who had overseen ergot research at Sandoz Pharmaceuticals in Basle, could personally vouch for many of these effects. In 1943, after accidentally ingesting a minuscule amount of a newly crystallised batch of ergot-derived LSD-25, he found himself in 'a dreamlike state', 'being affected by a remarkable restlessness combined with a slight dizziness'. During his first planned experiment with a dose of 0.25 milligrams, he took an unplanned bicycle ride into 'an uninterrupted stream of fantastic images of extraordinary plasticity and vividness'. On returning home, he seemed to temporarily depart his body. His thinking was by turns lucid and confused. He felt an inexplicable urge to laugh. Objects became grotesque. His neighbour appeared to him as a 'malevolent, insidious witch with a coloured mask'.

Hofmann was one of many foreign researchers to arrive in Pont-Saint-Esprit in the summer of 1951. No one knew more about ergot and its derivatives. Meeting with academics and doctors, he assured them that light traces of ergot discovered in forensic tests would indeed account for the outbreak. Ergot, unlike mercury, would be quickly expelled from the body. The facts supporting the mercury were feeble, particularly if the 'contagious' aspects of the outbreak were considered. Mercury, a substance that principally affects the liver and kidneys, could not explain the delirium that scores of villagers had experienced.

In the wake of the poisoning at Pont-Saint-Esprit, research into the visionary effects of LSD moved on apace. As the pharmacology and psychology of LSD were unpacked, renewed attention was given to ergot as a catalyst of medieval possession and classical religious experience. While convulsive ergotism was suggested as the cause of cases of diabolic possession at Salem in 1692, rather more convincing evidence emerged to link ergot with the sacred drink of the Greeks, *kykeon*. An aqueous extract of ergot-infested barley was, according to Hofmann and his co-researchers, consumed in the Eleusinian mystery cult, whose initiates, Plato and Socrates included, are said to have witnessed flaming visions of Persephone. M. Delacquis, who had been compelled to write poetry and songs throughout his *euphorie béate* at Pont-Saint-Esprit, would probably not have been surprised.

Cannibalism: Its Uses and Abuses

In 1976, the Nobel Prize for medicine or physiology was awarded to Dr Carleton Gajdusek, in recognition of two decades of research on the epidemiology of *kuru*, a slow-virus native to the Fore population on the Eastern Highlands of Papua New Guinea. Having established that the cause of this disease – of which the vast majority of victims were adult women – was not solely genetic, Gajdusek's work took an about-turn in the mid-1960s, impelling him towards social and environmental factors that might account for its origins and transmission. Having excluded a number of leads, Gajdusek returned to a theory that he had previously dismissed and that he now returned to with some trepidation – cannibalism.

Although Gajdusek had no firsthand evidence implicating *kuru* victims in cannibalistic funerary rites, anthropological studies of *kuru* were now also beginning to consider the practice as the source of the virus. Since the cannibalistic mourning rites of the remote villages had been outlawed by the Australian government in the 1950s, the disease had certainly begun to decline. Following this hypothesis, Gajdusek's laboratory work supported the theory that transmission could occur via infected brain tissue. With many questions remaining unresolved, he came to believe firmly that the Fore's consumption of diseased flesh (rather than mere contact with it) explained the genesis and transmission of *kuru*. In a summary of his research for a popular magazine, Gajdusek graphically condensed his thesis into two illustrations. One showed a dying *kuru* victim. The other captured the Fore in the act of cannibalism, its caption explaining how they prepared and feasted on human meat. The mystery of *kuru* was apparently solved.

Gajdusek's theory was quickly dealt a double blow. While medical opinion gave increasing credence to the possibility that the virus could be acquired through the bloodstream, Gajdusek's claims about Fore cannibalism were shot down in an anthropological polemic. In *The Man-eating Myth* (1979), William Arens argued that the *kuru* debate demonstrated the extent to which normal standards of academic research were jettisoned when the question of cannibalism was broached. Just as the religious and pre-modern accounts of cannibalism among the 'dark savages' were of dubious provenance, not one single anthropologist had ever witnessed cannibalism in *kuru*-stricken New Guinea – or for that matter in east Africa, the Matto Grasso or the Amazon basin, regions still considered the centres of cannibalism. That Gajdusek could attach his own flesh-eating by-line to a photograph of the Fore feasting on a pig rather demonstrated Arens's point.

From Hans Staden's *True History and Description of a Country of Savages* (1557) to the fieldwork of many distinguished anthropologists, cannibalism was, Arens argued, contrived from wilful fantasy and uncorroborated hearsay. Without dismissing the possibility that customary cannibalism may have had a sporadic history, he was emphatic in asserting that no evidence existed to suggest that cannibalism was ever 'a prevalent cultural feature' in any part of the world. The question to be asked of cannibalism, wrote Arens, is not why people eat human flesh, 'but why one group invariably assumes others do'.

Anthropologists on the trail of real-life cannibalism had certainly demonstrated a good deal of naiveté. When undertaking fieldwork among the Urubu Indians of Brazil in the early 1950s, Francis Huxley (nephew to Aldous) was naturally keen to inquire into the cannibalistic traditions of a region that was notorious for its head-hunting. The Urubu were aware of, and aggrieved by, their reputation. Huxley's questions met with silent disdain. However, the wily anthropologist had brought with him a book – 'a favourite wherever he went' – to move the conversation forwards. Hercule Florence's account of a journey through the Brazilian jungle in the 1820s contained illustrations of neighbouring tribes that, as Huxley gently reminded the Urubu, used to eat people. This aide-mémoire brought angry demands to have it burnt, but it also provoked claims that a subgroup, the Capiwans, had eaten the Urubu's forefathers. The cannibal tale that Huxley went on to record in his book *Affable Savages* was presented as a historical fact, not as a perennial story of the cannibalistic other.

Many of Arens's anthropological colleagues acknowledged the paucity of ethnographic evidence for cannibalism, but most nevertheless believed that endophagy (the consumption of deceased relatives and tribal members) and exophagy (the consumption of outsider enemies) had both been established cultural practices in various regions. The popular interpretation of these practices suggested that cannibalism was a symbolic ritual through which divine powers were transmitted and renewed, through which relations with the dead were preserved, or health and vitality achieved. With materialist anthropologists arguing that cannibalism was in reality no more than a last-ditch response to protein shortages (particularly among the Aztecs, who, according to Marvin Harris, had 'a state-sponsored system aimed at the production and distribution of . . . human flesh'), the lively debate looked set to sidestep the questions Arens had raised. How did accusations of cannibalism arise? What function might they serve? When Lou Marano, another equally sceptical anthropologist, began to research the so-called '*windigo* psychosis' of the Ojibwa and Cree Indians in North America, some unexpected answers emerged.

Windigo was first identified as a culture-bound illness in the 1920s, when a missionary, Father Saindon, described the case of an Ojibwa woman who feared that she might be driven to kill strangers, as they all appeared to her as wild and dangerous animals. Saindon was informed that her illness was known locally (west of Lake Superior) as *windigo* and that it had been commonplace in the previous century. 'The Indians [had once] stood in great fear of potent attack by this malady, such fear that in the last stages of the malady they thought it necessary to kill the patient [because of their maddening desire for human flesh].' The publication of Saindon's report unleashed a torrent of conjecture and interpretation, often from anthropologists who had no direct knowledge of the Ojibwa or Cree tribes. John M. Cooper, the first to apply the term 'psychosis' to *windigo*, did not allow the facts – or lack of them – to prevent him from imagining the scenarios in which it might have occurred:

> Cannibalism was resorted to by the Cree only in cases where actual starvation threatened. Driven to desperation by prolonged famine and often suffering from mental breakdown as a result thereof, the Cree would sometimes eat the bodies of those who had perished, or, more rarely, would even kill the living and partake of the flesh. This solution, however, of the conflict between hunger and rigid tribal taboo often left, as its aftermath, an 'unnatural' craving for human flesh, or a psychosis that took the form of such a craving. More rarely such a psychosis developed in men or women who had not themselves passed through famine experience.

Modern anthropology quickly succumbed to the belief that the victims of the *windigo* psychosis would, after passing through the first stages of depression, be consumed by their insatiable cravings for flesh. While there was in fact no direct evidence of such an illness, around seventy cases of *windigo*, drawn from police reports, missionary notes and ethnographic fieldwork, were eventually catalogued. An 1871 letter from a Methodist missionary, Egerton Young, described how a fifteen-year-old Cree boy had, according to his family, 'in his ravings kept asking for flesh to eat'. After the boy allegedly attacked his father, the boy was deliberately strangled and his body burnt. 'Poor boy,' lamented Young, 'he was only a lunatic, and perhaps a few months in an asylum would have restored reason to its throne.'

On reviewing the available evidence, it was obvious to Marano that only a handful of cases of *windigo* were anything other than rumour or hearsay. There was not a single eyewitness testimony. The sole case of murder-cannibalism had occurred under starvation conditions, without ensuing pathological compulsion. There was, furthermore, no evidence to suggest that the victims of *windigo* who had been murdered were guilty of the purported crimes. As far as Marano was concerned, 'all executed "*windigo* victims*"* met their deaths at the hands of their fellow Indians for reasons unrelated to the threat of their committing cannibalism'.

Marano's fieldwork confirmed that *windigo* was a far more flexible category of mental illness than previous commentators had assumed. If the cannibal theme had once been central to *windigo*, it would have reflected the burden and danger that the mentally ill constituted in a semi-nomadic society under the constant threat of starvation. Not discounting the possibility that some *windigo* victims might have been genuinely suspected of cannibalism, the belief complex provided 'rationalization for homicide' – the moral licence to kill, not eat.

Return of the Zombi

In 1979, the *Journal of the Tennessee Medical Association* announced that the 'Walking zombie syndrome' – a condition in which depression and withdrawal led individuals to unconsciously believe that they were dead – was on the increase. Illness, coma, high fever, operations performed under partial anaesthesia, and bereavement were, it claimed, just some of the situations through which a 'death suggestion' could be unwittingly assimilated. Fortunately, there was, according to the hypnotherapists who 'discovered' the condition, one simple and effective cure: age regression. By returning patients to the event which triggered the 'death suggestion', the 'symptoms of death' could, it was claimed, be at once relived and remedied. Although most physicians remained unaware of the diagnosis or treatment, the pseudo-illness continued to claim factitious casualties. By the late 1980s, the United States had apparently overtaken Haiti as the zombi capital of the world. According to one estimate, there were 'thousands of walking zombies on the streets of every city'.

Beyond a small body of American medical hypnotists, few people have subscribed to this myth of the urban zombi. In Haiti, by contrast, Article 246 of the penal code continues to recognise zombification as a criminal offence equivalent to murder. This legislature reflects a widespread Haitian belief that *bokos*, voodoo sorcerers, are able to resurrect innocent victims from the grave and, while in a comatose state, claim them as slaves. To this day, hundred of zombis – outwardly recognised by their fixed stares, limited speech and clumsy gait – are identified each year. For the family members who are reunited with their deceased, there are at least three explanations for the zombi's release from servitude.

First, the bottle containing the zombi's consciousness, the zombi astral, may have been broken. Second, the *boko* master may have died. Third, beneficent spirits may have intervened to release the zombi from his diabolic toil.

For more than seventy years, American and European anthropologists have been on the heels of the zombi. While most fieldworkers have concluded that this subhuman archetype belongs only to the realm of folklore, some have sought a rational explanation behind the apparent resurrection of the dead. In 1938, after visiting what she believed to be a zombi in a Haitian hospital, the American anthropologist Zora Hurston concluded that 'semblance of death' was initially 'induced by some drug known to a few'. An antidote then revived the victim: while 'destroying part of the brain which governs speech and will-power', it left him 'able to move and act but unable to formulate thought or resist instruction'. While the old penal code had indeed outlawed the use of 'substances' for these purposes, Haiti's intelligentsia was sceptical. Hurston was berated for having peddled half-baked evidence, for betraying the reality of peasant customs. She had not verified the identity of her 'zombi' or provided any indication, let alone sample, of the mysterious poisons that could have produced this state of pseudo-death.

In 1982, after three decades of research into the elusive zombi drug, Nathan Kline, a pharmacologist and expert in tranquillisers, claimed to have at last found a clear-cut case of zombification. The man in question, Clairvius Narcisse, had appeared a year earlier in the marketplace in the village of Morbien. He introduced himself to his 'sister' using a boyhood nickname. He claimed that his 'brother' had made him into a zombi, and that, after two years of work on a sugar plantation, his master had died and he had spent eighteen years wandering the countryside, fearing reprisal. Staff at the Psychiatric Institute in Port-au-Prince questioned Narcisse. His response to a series of detailed questions, conceived by staff and family, convinced psychiatrists that Narcisse was, as his family and neighbours believed, a genuine zombi.

Enter Wade Davis, a young botanist from Harvard University, employed by Kline to investigate the composition of the drug used in the zombification of Narcisse. After succeeding in collecting samples of differing zombi powders from various *bokos* – but failing in his attempt to commission the creation of a zombi – Davis claimed to have finally solved the mystery. A *boko* victim was, he claimed, administered powders that contain powerful neurotoxins, the most significant of which were derived from three varieties of puffer fish (containing the deadly nerve toxin tetrodoxin) and two species of the potent hallucinogenic datura plant (the so-called zombi cucumber), which might act as an 'antidote to zombi poison', inducing a state of 'psychotic delirium' during which the zombi is led to his workplace. The process of zombification was, he concluded, a rare but real instance of pseudodeath:

> From ethnopharmacological investigation, we know that the poison acts to lower dramatically the metabolic rate of the victim almost to the point of death. Pronounced dead by attending physicians who check only for superficial signs of heart beat and respiration, and therefore considered physically dead by the family members and critically by the zombi maker himself, the victim is in fact buried alive. Undoubtedly, in many cases the victim does die either from the poison itself, or by suffocation in the coffin. The widespread belief in the veracity of physical zombis in Haiti, however, is based on those instances where the victim receives the correct dosage of the poison, wakes up in the coffin and is dragged out of the grave by the zombi maker . . . The victim, affected by the drug, traumatised by the set and setting of the graveyard and immediately beaten by the zombi maker's assistants, is bound and led before a cross to be baptised with a new zombi name. After the baptism, he or she is made to eat a paste containing a strong dose of a potent psychoactive drug (*Datura stramonium*) which brings on an induced state of psychosis. During the course of intoxication, the zombi is carried off to be sold as a slave labourer.

Davis's exhumation of the zombi myth met with substantial interest. In the same way that newspaper reports from the 1930s and 1940s inspired Jacques Tourneur's classic horror film *I Walked with a Zombie,* Davis's bestselling book *The Serpent and the Rainbow* (1985) went on to provide the basis of Wes Craven's film of the same name. But the clinical evidence to back Davis's claims was not forthcoming. Independent investigators found that Davis's samples of 'zombi poison' contained insignificant traces of tetrodoxin. As the pharmacologist C. Y. Kao wrote: 'it can be concluded that the widely circulated claim in the lay press to the effect that tetrodoxin is the causal agent in the initial zombification process is without foundation.'

With the demise of this magico-chemical theory of zombification, psychological and sociological explanations have returned to the fore. Three recent cases examined by the British psychiatrist Roland Littlewood were respectively diagnosed as catatonic schizophrenia, organic brain syndrome and learning disability. With DNA fingerprinting able to confirm that these 'zombis' were in fact unrelated to the family members who claimed them, it is the rationale behind their adoption that remains the real mystery. Why do families claim these forlorn individuals as their own? Do they truly believe that their sons and daughters, brothers and sisters, have returned from the dead? Littlewood is surely right to suggest that the process might best be regarded as 'an institutionalised restitution of the destitute mentally ill'. Behind the supernatural smokescreen, zombification is essentially one culture's version of care in the community.

The Alchemy of Emotion

Fear is the Key

'How often do our involuntary movements reveal our secret thinking and betray us to those about us!' wrote Michel de Montaigne in his *Essays* (1580). Three centuries later, spurred on by his observation of the ways in which the body can 'reveal the thoughts and intentions of others more than do words', Charles Darwin embarked on the first comprehensive study of this treacherous body language, *The Expression of the Emotions in Man and Animals* (1872). Of all the emotions studied by Darwin, fear was the most articulate. In all primates, 'the heart beats wildly or may fail to act . . . there is a deathlike pallor; the breathing is laboured, the wings of the nostrils are widely dilated . . . All the muscles of the body are relaxed. Utter prostration soon follows, and the mental powers fail'. Darwin saw the same expressions of fear in different cultures and ethnic groups, as well as in the congenitally blind, who had not had the opportunity to learn the lexicon of facial and bodily signs.

If Darwin overstated the expressive aspect of fear (observations from physical anthropologists suggest that the nonverbal communication of fear is more labile and open to misinterpretation than Darwin appreciated), his general thesis stands. The biological basis of the fear system is strikingly similar in humans and other animals. The fear response – withdrawal, immobility, defensive aggression or submission – is biologically hardwired; however, across the animal species, it is adapted to different needs and provoked by different stimuli.

When the psychologist G. Stanley Hall conducted his classic survey at the turn of the twentieth century, an inventory of no fewer than 6456 fears was described by 700 people he interviewed.

To account for such variation, J. B. Watson, founder of the American school of behaviourism, argued that the fear response was conditioned by prolonged or sudden exposure to stimuli whose *associations* were negative. In an experiment devised to demonstrate the associative affect that any object could acquire, Watson and Rosalie Rayner conditioned an eleven-month-old baby, 'Little Albert', to fear a white rat. Triggering a loud clanging noise (one of a limited range of 'unconditioned stimuli' thought intrinsically capable of eliciting fear) whenever Albert reached for the rat, Albert began to show 'signs of fear' after five soundings, crying whenever the rat came near him. When Albert was tested four months later, Watson claimed that his fear of the rat had extended to other furry animals, to sealskin and to cotton wool.

Watson's understanding of fear as a conditioned response was intended as a direct rebuttal of Freud, whose theory of neurosis and phobia as displacements of unresolved sexual conflict was first laid out in his case study of Little Hans. In this landmark essay, Freud interpreted the fears that Hans developed after seeing a horse fall in the street as expressions of a castration complex, a symptom of his frustrated desire for his mother. While psychoanalysis sought 'to enable the patient to obtain a conscious grasp of his unconscious fears', behaviourism had little time for such convoluted exegesis. In the same paper reporting the procedure used on Little Albert, Watson and Rayner lambasted the Freudian approach. Psychoanalysis, they wrote, 'will show that Albert at three years of age attempted to play with the pubic hair of his mother and was scolded violently for it'. The treatments behaviourism developed for phobia were altogether more pragmatic, focused on purging the symptoms of fear rather than unravelling its nebulous causes.

Both Freud and Watson have been accused of misrepresentation. While Freud relied on selective information supplied by Hans's father (a devotee of psychoanalysis), the extent to which Albert was conditioned to fear the rat has been questioned. When one experimenter replicated Watson's technique (using a wooden toy instead of a rat) none of the fifteen children displayed any fear towards it, suggesting that fear was rather less open to conditioning than the behaviourists assumed. Despite the differences between Freud and Watson, however, both agreed on one important point: human fears were shaped by experience. Neither was prepared to regard any fear as innate.

All psychological surveys list fears relating to the dark, snakes and strangers as far and away the most prevalent. Psychologists are today more prepared to accept the possibility that some fears are innate. The fact that most infants are thought to become fearful of strangers at between eight and ten months is often used to support this case. But more persuasive evidence for the biological transmission of specific fears comes from twin studies. Identical twins that have been separated at birth seem far more likely to share the same fears than fraternal twins reared in the same family environment.

The neuroscientist Joseph LeDoux suggests that the extent to which humans and animals are able to feel fear is at least as likely to be biologically driven as it is conditioned by experience. 'Not everyone exposed to a traumatic event develops a phobia,' writes LeDoux. 'Some people's brains because of their genetic make-up or past experience must be predisposed . . . In these people, the amygdala [the brain's almond-shaped 'arousal centre' that controls the autonomic aspects of the fear response and prompts release of adrenaline and other hormones into the bloodstream] may be supersensitive to some classes of prepared stimulus or the amygdala may have other alterations that make fear conditioning especially potent.' In his recent book *The Feeling of What Happens*, neurologist Antonio Damasio cites the case of a young patient, 'S', whose amygdala was calcified by a rare congenital disease known as Urbach-Wiethe syndrome. While S's intellectual abilities were largely unaffected by the condition, her manner was 'excessively and inappropriately forthcoming'. This demeanour eventually revealed itself as a by-product of her inability to register fear or anger. Tests administered by one of Damasio's colleagues confirmed that she was unable to identify, mimic or represent expressions of alarm and fright. Like patients who have had their amygdalas surgically removed, she, quite literally, knew no fear.

Further evidence of the biological basis of the fear response comes from sleep research. A small minority of individuals are susceptible to an affliction known as night terror, which was for a long time mistakenly considered as an acute type of nightmare. Night terror in fact occurs in between stages three and four of the sleep cycle, which is non-dreaming sleep. The screaming, flailing panic it gives rise to is due to an anomalous triggering of an 'arousal response', which sets the heart rate sprinting to up to 170 beats per minute.

Although childhood fears may sometimes persist into adulthood, fears generally become less tangible and more diffuse with age. Phobias are the exception to this rule. All the major types of phobia (social, animal, insect, illness and agoraphobia) produce severe attacks of panic and convoluted avoidance strategies, but they are all generally responsive to treatment. Desensitisation (relaxation combined with active imagination) and flooding (prolonged exposure to the source of anxiety) have all proved successful in varying degrees. By contrast, diffuse or 'existential' fears are more resistant to intervention. This is true of both psychotic delusions and paranoia. As the clinical psychologist Louis Sass notes in relation to schizophrenic paranoias, 'these are not primarily concerned with the *content* of reality – with issues *within* the world that would be likely to evoke heightened fears or feelings of persecution . . . but of a profound transformation in the co-ordinates of experience itself'. The schizophrenic's panic is inner-directed. It is an ontological crisis of self-sovereignty, a struggle to retain bodily integrity and psychic capital, described in these words by one of Sass's patients:

These thoughts go on and on. I'm going over the border. My real self is away down – it used to be just at my throat, but now it's gone further down. I'm losing myself. It's getting deeper and deeper. I want to tell you things, but I'm scared. My head's full of thoughts, fears, hates, jealousies. My head can't grip them: I can't hold on to them. I'm behind the bridge of my nose – I mean, my con-sciousness is there . . . I don't know whether I have these thoughts or not.

By subjecting himself to intense physical pain or danger, it is possible for the schizophrenic to 'scare some life into himself'. This empowering use of fear is echoed in many magical rites. In the vision quest of the Native American tradition, for example, rituals of initiation – which were widespread in the Pre-Columbian era – would sometimes culminate in the Night of Fear. After a period of fasting and self-mutilation, the vision seeker might dig his own grave and lie waiting to be reborn, to experience the Oneness of Great Spirit. But it is not only in the context of mental illness or spiritual inspiration that we find fear acting as a catalyst to opposite emotions. Examples of the way in which panic and distress can inspire passion or devotion can, as we shall now see, also be found far closer to home.

A Tale from the Vault

Shortly after ten o'clock on an August morning in 1973, the Sveriges Kreditbank in Stockholm was filled with blasts of machine-gun fire. As shards of glass, plasterdust and paper rained on the floor, Jan-Erik Olsson, a thirty-two-year-old prison escapee, announced to bank employees and customers that 'the party has just begun'. Taking four employees hostage, Olsson demanded that his friend and cellmate be released from prison and allowed to join him. Over the next five days, while the four workers shared a large carpeted vault with their captors, an unexpected alliance was forged. When the captors made demands for money and safe passage for all, the hostages supported them. When negotiations between police and captors broke down, the hostages shared their frustration. In a telephone conversation with the Swedish prime minister, one hostage insisted, 'The robbers are protecting us from the police.'

When the siege finally ended, the psychiatrists who debriefed the hostages were surprised to discover that, despite suffering nightmares concerning their captors' re-escape from prison, not one of them expressed any animosity towards them. All of the hostages in fact felt a deep bond with their captors. Indeed the youngest of the hostages, Kristin Ehnmark, had become romantically attached to Olsson. What had begun as a crime-thriller had turned into the most unusual of love stories.

Dubbed the Stockholm syndrome by FBI Special Agent Conrad Hassell, the same phenomenon was soon observed elsewhere. After the hijacking of a Chicago-based Boeing 727 in September 1976, some of the victims went on to form a defence fund for their Croatian captors, even though the bomb they had left behind had killed one police officer and injured others. Describing the immediate aftermath, one victim reported: 'I recognised that they had put me through hell, and had caused my parents and fiancée a great deal of trauma. Yet, I was alive. I was alive. After it was all over, and we were safe and they were in handcuffs, I walked over to them and kissed each of them and said, "Thank you for giving me my life back." '

A series of very different events that same year brought the Stockholm syndrome to wider media and public attention. Two years previously, in February 1974, the Symbionese Liberation Army (SLA) had kidnapped Patty Hearst, the granddaughter of publishing tycoon William Randolph Hearst. While keeping her in a closet for two months, Hearst's captors made demands for a free-food programme for the California poor and for the publication of revolutionary literature. Hearst went on to become a member of the SLA, assuming the name 'Tania' and adopting her captors' revolutionary ethos. Eighteen months and one shoot-out later, Hearst was eventually arrested in San Francisco. In a taped recording played at her trial, she admonished her parents' 'efforts to supposedly secure my release. The [food] giveaway was a sham . . . You were playing games, stalling for time, which the FBI was using in their attempts to assassinate me and the SLA elements which guarded me'. Hearst's defence lawyers claimed that all her actions were typical of victims of the Stockholm syndrome.

To explain such sentiments, psychiatrists turned to the phenomenon of 'identification with the aggressor', which Anna Freud described in her 1936 book *The Ego and Mechanisms of Defence*. In the face of mental or physical abuse, Freud suggested that fear might prompt a victim to identify with the 'enemy' figure. She gave various examples of how, through 'impersonating the aggressor, assuming his attributes or imitating his aggression, the child transforms himself from the person threatened into the person making the threat'. The concept of identification with the aggressor was not, however, Anna Freud's. Moreover, her examples of children mimicking and introjecting the minor 'aggressions' of teachers, dentists and analysts were a world removed from the abuses that the term had originally sought to understand. First formulated by her father's one-time collaborator Sándor Ferenczi, the idea of identification with the aggressor ran against the grain of some of the most central tenets of psychoanalysis.

At some point in the early 1930s, Ferenczi's experience with neurotic patients convinced him that the Oedipus complex might be 'the result of real acts on the part of adults, namely violent passions directed toward the child, who then develops a fixation, not from desire but from fear'. This heresy led him to be abandoned by colleagues and denied the courtesy of reference or footnote wherever his terminology was invoked.

Sigmund Freud, Ferenczi's long-time mentor, had also once believed in the reality of the sexual abuses sustained by his patients. The paper in which he first defended the actuality of these experiences in 1896, 'The Aetiology of Hysteria', alienated the young Freud from the German-speaking medical community. Within a few years, Freud abandoned this euphemistically titled seduction theory and moved instead to examine the role of fantasy rather than real trauma in hysterical illnesses. From this switch of emphasis, which Jeffrey Masson has investigated in *The Assault on Truth* (1984), psychoanalysis was born. From then onwards, the patient's dream life would take precedence over real life.

More than thirty years on, Ferenczi would return to the original seduction theory. In a paper delivered to the International Psychoanalytical Congress in 1932, Ferenczi insisted that children fell 'victim to "real rape" much more frequently than suspected. Either parents themselves seek substitution for their lack of satisfaction in this pathological manner, or else twisted persons such as relatives (uncles, aunts, grandparents), tutors, servants, abuse the innocence and ignorance of children'. Children's need for love and intimacy was, Ferenczi insisted, being widely exploited. Through identification with the aggressor, the child introjected the parent's guilt, often becoming emotionally and intellectually precocious. 'Fear of the uninhibited . . . turns the child into a psychiatrist, as it were. In order to do so and protect himself from dangers from people without self-control, he must first know how to identify himself completely with them.'

Ferenczi's insights into the process of identification with the aggressor have thrown some light on the kind of twisted bond that compels hostages to cling to their captors. Yet the passage of this concept from the literature of child abuse to commentaries on international terrorism is in itself noteworthy. The recent histories of moral panics relating to drugs, paedophilia and satanic abuse all follow the same trajectory: away from the less palatable violence and abuse that take place within families. Maybe it is not just psychoanalysis that prefers its demons undomesticated?

A Secret Called Shame

The collapse of the Japanese economy at the end of the 1980s had a profound impact on the lives of Tokyo's middle classes. While the stigma of joblessness drove many to suicide, a sizeable number of the newly unemployed instead entered into an elaborate masquerade. Revealing their redundancy to few, they continued to rise at the usual time, to dress for work, to ride the rush hour subway. After hours spent in libraries or public gardens, these ghost workers returned home to their families and the illusion of an evening's leisure.

Anthropologists have long recognised the centrality of shame in Asiatic cultures. The strange double life that Tokyo's salarymen were prepared to undertake to save face is difficult to imagine in other industrialised societies. In most modern societies, where norms are increasingly internalised rather than externally policed or sanctioned, guilt comes to replace shame. Guilt is a form of self-castigation; shame is a reaction to other people's criticism, real or imagined. More than fifty years ago, Ruth Benedict endorsed this distinction in her study of Japanese culture *The Chrysanthemum and the Sword* (1947). 'The early Puritans who settled in the United States', wrote Benedict, 'tried to base their whole morality on guilt and all psychiatrists know what trouble contemporary Americans have with their conscience. But shame is . . . less extremely felt than in earlier generations . . . we do not expect shame to do the heavy work of morality.' The distinction, previously endorsed by Freud, suggested that guilt was a grown-up version of a primitive or infantile sentiment.

Over the past thirty years or so, however, shame has been reclaimed as a primary emotion. Now accorded a role in depression, anxiety, addiction, sexual disorders and so-called shame-based disorders, its relationship to guilt has become increasingly blurred. Many psychoanalysts now accept that both emotions are often found in tandem, one often masking the other. The history of shame, the ways in which it has circumscribed the socially permissible, has also been more closely examined. According to the historian Norbert Elias, the propriety that shame encourages in regard to one's body, to the expression of emotion, or to one's appearance, was alien to Europe before the eighteenth century. This was the era in which shame was first mobilised in the name of manners, decorum and deference. Elias claims that the anticipation of shame was vital to the 'civilizing process', but that it remained an undercover emotion, often leading people to behave in ways they were little aware of.

The rediscovery of shame as a vital emotion in the fields of psychology and psychoanalysis begins with the work of Helen B. Lewis, who, in the late 1960s, methodically examined the expression of emotion in the course of the therapy session. Echoing Elias's observation that shame had become a secret or hidden emotion, Lewis found that the expression of shame, although apparent in virtually every therapeutic encounter, was never manifested straightforwardly. Unacknowledged shame appeared to inform much of the language and the manner with which patients described rejection and inferiority, indignity and transgression. This in turn led Lewis to re-examine Freud's case studies, where she also found shame to be repeatedly mute or in hiding. 'Difficulties in identifying one's own experience as shame have so often been observed', observed Lewis, 'that they suggest some intrinsic connection between shame and the mechanism of denial . . . while shame is occurring the person himself is unable to communicate.'

Lewis identified three reasons why shame was so difficult for patients to identify. First, feelings of shame could be absorbed or masked by guilt. Second, denial could obscure the shame effect, so that while the shamed person was aware of the emotion and the rationale for its occurrence it might only register as a 'wince', 'jolt' or 'blow'. Third, because shame is a painful experience from which most of us prefer to hide – if only we 'could die', 'disappear', or 'crawl into a hole' – it is particularly affecting, especially when accompanied by sweating, blushing and other autonomic responses.

The expression 'losing face' perfectly encapsulates the physical and psychological aspects of shame. The sense of one's deficiencies leads the head to bow, the gaze to be averted, communication to cease. From New Guinea to New York, the physical expression of shame is the same: body language conveys the sense of being paralysed by indignity. And because the signs of shame can be so easily read, especially on the face, the body becomes a liability for the shamed. How do others perceive it? What should be done with it? The shamed, the shy and the embarrassed all feel, in varying degrees, that others are in some way able to see through them, to enter their thoughts and register their failings. For this reason, the avoidance of eye contact is common to all forms of shame. Blushing, however, is rather less easily explained. In his study of this 'most peculiar and most human of all expressions', Darwin observed: 'It is not the simple act of reflecting on our own appearance, but the thinking of what others think of us, which excites a blush.' Both praise and admonishment, or the prospects of either, are triggers to the reddening flush of the face, neck and chest.

Clinical research into the experience of shame has, as noted, led therapists and psychiatrists to revise their understanding and approach to a number of psychological illnesses. Depression has been particularly connected to failure and familial humiliation. Gershen Kaufman, a psychologist at Michigan State University, has suggested that the commonly held view of depression as anger-directed 'misses the central and prior role of conjoined shame and distress . . . the depressive episode is a condition in which shame and distress have become sufficiently prolonged as to be experienced as a continuing mood'. Phobic syndromes such as claustrophobia and agoraphobia are thought, in some instances, to be avoidance strategies that protect individuals from the shame of being exposed. In such cases, the suffocating symptoms that accompany anxiety states might relate more to the psychological effects of shame rather than fear.

While the significance of shame has been less explored in relation to psychosis and breakdown, the emotion does also appear to throw some light on the genesis and continuing experience of delusions and hallucinations. In the case of Daniel Paul Schreber, the famous German schizophrenic whose memoirs have already been referred to, his entire childhood was a systematic exercise in degradation at the hands of his punitive physician father. Schreber's breakdown manifested itself through the delusion that God was willing his transformation into a woman, so that he could repopulate a devastated world. The voices continually spoke to him, asking, 'Are you not shamed?'

De Amore

It is a sickness. It is a drug. It is blind. It is the wisdom of the fool, the folly of the wise. It is two souls, but with a single thought. It is a religion whose church canonises all lovers . . . The family of conceits and tropes through which the sentiment of love expresses itself is, according to Dennis de Rougemont's *Love in the Western World*, directly descended from the medieval rhetoric of passionate or courtly love. 'The West', he writes, 'is distinct from other cultures not only in its invention of passionate love in the twelfth century and the secular elaboration of conjugal love, but by its confusion of the notion of eros, agape, sexuality, passion. Classical Greek used at least sixteen different terms to designate love in all its forms; eros for physical love, agape for altruistic love, philia for tender or erotic feelings, etc.'

De Rougemont's attempt to historicise love, arguing through literary citation that certain emotions arise at precise junctures, has found no shortage of critics. What, after all, could be more natural, more instinctive, than love? Surely, the capacity to love requires neither schooling nor encouragement? Yet de Rougemont's thesis also found notable supporters. After initial scepticism, Jean-Paul Sartre suggested that passionate love is not an essential trait, and that its evolution is 'not the effect of some internal mechanism but . . . of historical and social factors'. Others have also argued that love, although universal, has undergone dramatic distortions in different historical and social contexts. Controversially, it has been suggested that the classical world provides no evidence of a single instance of passionate love that was not considered pathological.

Most anthropologists believe that romantic love exists in every society, but not in the same way. The Tahitians and other peoples of the south Pacific are, for example, reputed to have had little concept of the dizzied, enraptured heights of love that their Western visitors brought with them. It is only in societies that are highly individualistic, where there is sufficient distance and difference between people, that this kind of love is conceivable. Such findings suggest that romantic love might well be, as de Rougemont proposes, a modern invention with a medieval patent.

But it is not just romantic love that appears to have its variations. The psychiatrist Takeo Doi cites the Japanese noun *amae* (derived from the verb *amaeru*, meaning 'to depend and presume upon another's benevolence') as a revealing example of the cultural lability of love. Doi suggests that the sentiment of *amae*, used generally to designate a child's attitude to its parents, reflects a basic psychological difference between the mentality of the Japanese and the West. Doi does not claim that this emotion is absolutely exclusive or alien to English-speaking countries (he concedes something akin to it may be 'sparingly' evident in religious milieus), yet he does nevertheless makes special claims for the 'Japaneseness' of *amaeru*.

Evolutionary psychologists do not take these claims too seriously. Just as Gertrude Stein proclaimed that a rose is a rose in perpetuity, this branch of psychology claims that love, like other basic human emotions, is everywhere and forever the same. Unfortunately, the evolutionary model restricts itself to the outward functions of love, its tangible consequences rather than its psychological vagaries. The language of 'mate selection', 'exclusivity' and 'sexual fitness' is here employed to suggest that acts of love existed before the linguistic category of love was invented to describe these acts. In his recent book *Emotion*, Dylan Evans, for example, dismisses the idea that romantic love has a medieval heritage as 'among the front-running candidates for the most ridiculous idea of the twentieth century.' Instead Evans suggests that love and all the emotions are only partially plastic:

> . . . romantic love is played out slightly differently in different cultures. In the West it is marked by special features not found

elsewhere. These include the idea that romantic love should take you by surprise, the idea that it should be the basis for a lifelong commitment, and the idea that it is the supreme form of self-fulfilment. So, while romantic love is a universal theme, it is a theme that admits some minor variations.

But has the song of love always been the same? The sheet lyrics that de Rougemont points to certainly confront us with more than 'minor variations'. Antiquity does indeed, as de Rougemont claims, seem to harbour different sentiments of love. In Plato's *Symposium*, we are presented with an emotion that takes us beyond the realm of physical desire, which takes as its ultimate object truth and beauty. Here love is noetic, it grants a special form of comprehension. Yet elsewhere Plato conflates love with illness rather than philosophy, identifying love as a frenzy, a possession that spreads from body to spirit. At its best, this possession may be divine, so that the lover 'lives as if in heaven', yet even this sentiment little chimes with our modern-day concept of romantic love.

The letters of Abelard and Héloïse, the most famous of the early romantic lovers, are composed in a language that has much in common with the raptures and passions of Christian mysticism. In his sermon on the Song of Songs, Saint Bernard, the most swooning of the twelfth-century mystics, writes: 'Of all the movements of the soul, of all its feelings and affections, it is love alone by which the creature responds to its creator, though in less than equal measure.' Saint Bernard recognises degrees of love – for one's self, one's neighbours, one's family – but pure love belongs 'only to those who are joined in marriage' to God. In this spiritual wedlock, all other affections, all carnal desires, must be renounced. The romance of Tristram and Iseult thus finds the lovers' passions permanently thwarted and tormented, and it is this 'exquisite anguish' which defines their love. They are in love with love and all its obstacles. Romantic love can never be truly consummated. The kiss, the gaze, the caress are its modus operandi. These provide for the kind of intimate and mystical union that is to be found in Dante's love for Beatrice, in

Shakespeare's Dark Lady sonnets, and in John Donne's meta-physical love poems.

'The adoption of certain linguistic conventions', writes de Rougemont, 'naturally involves and fosters the rise of latent feelings most apt to be expressed in this way. That is the sense in which it may be said, following La Rouchefoucauld, that people would never fall in love had they never heard of love.' Through myth, literature and pop culture, love is, de Rougemont main-tains, encouraged, rubber-stamped and ultimately transformed. De Rougemont cannot be dismissed as a naive cultural materialist. 'In the absence of this rhetoric,' he accepts, 'the emotions would no doubt still exist, but accidentally, lacking recognition, and they would be treated as unmentionable and contraband peculiarities.'

In the late nineteenth century, a number of European thinkers began to take a look at love in exactly these terms. Freud's war on neurosis was nothing less than an attempt to understand the ways in which the capacity for sexual love could be damned from within. Freud was not alone in attempting to rescue the sexual *instincts* from their social impediments. Paulo Mantegazza – whose *Physiology of Love* had, according to Freud, caused Dora to become 'over-excited' – also sought to liberate the innate drives. Mantegazza was, however, essentially a sexual hygienist. Through copious reference to the sexual proclivities of the animal world, Mantegazza asserted that most races exhibit a 'radical polygamy, dissimulated under a show front of monogamy'. 'Physiologically,' he insisted, 'monogamy is in no way requested by the normal condition of human life.' Unsurprisingly, this scientific endorsement of the sexual drives did anything but liberate the possibilities of romantic love. Without impediment, passion could never reach the heights described by the twelfth-century troubadours. Without its secret liaisons, its whispered promises, how could romantic love ever be the same?

With the discovery of neurons and neurotransmitters, it eventually became possible to investigate the alchemy of love in more literal terms than the troubadours intended. Since the 1970s, the full spectrum of feelings associated with being in love, from euphoria to abjection, have been examined in terms of the mood-altering effects of brain chemicals. While testosterone has now become a by-word for the male libido, fluctuations in the hormone estradiol have more recently been connected to increased sexual drive in women. Similarly, dopamine and serotonin are thought to act as sexual stimulant and inhibitor, respectively. The problem that much research in this field of psychopharmacology encounters is that love and passion are in chemical terms virtually indistinguishable from states of happiness, wellbeing or transcendence. Experimentation with cannabis, LSD and psilocybin do, nonetheless, suggest that sentiments akin to love can be induced chemically. Time and again, the rapture of intoxication presents itself as a swooning dissipation of the self.

Eileen Garrett, a British medium who took an active interest in LSD research in the 1950s, claimed that feelings of love and empathy elicited by LSD were a valuable aid to her work. 'True telepathic communication could only be achieved through emotional transmission and reception,' she wrote. Other paranormal studies appear to confirm that telepathy is experientially a kind of far-minded love, sympathy at distance. Even Freud – whose scepticism on occult matters brought about his famous break with Jung – eventually accepted the existence of 'thought-transferences' as the perception of the other's unconscious wishes. These observations disposed Freud to find parallels between hypnosis and love in its least physical and most romantic form:

> From being in love to hypnosis is evidently only a short step. The respects in which the two agree are obvious. There is the same humble subjection, the same compliance, the same absence of criticism, toward the hypnotist as the loved object . . . no one could doubt that the hypnotist has stepped into the place of the ego ideal. It is only that everything is even clearer and more intense in hypnosis, so that it would be more to the point to explain being in love by means of hypnosis than the other way round . . . The hypnotic relation is the unlimited devotion of someone in love, but with the sexual satisfaction excluded.

Like its modern-day tropes, the age-old association of love and illness is more than a metaphor. Lovesickness, according to classical observers, had many forms. While sleeplessness, sighing, sobbing, dry throat and hollow eyes were some of its lesser symptoms, it could climax in a full-blown delirium that confirmed Virgil's pronouncement that 'Reason is overcome and sway'd by passion'. The Renaissance increasingly treated such excesses as a disease. Marsilio Ficino's 1484 treatise *De Amore* observed that 'the anxious care which vulgar lovers are vexed day and night is a certain species of madness. As long as love lasts, they are afflicted . . . by the burning of black bile, and then they rush into frenzies and fire'. In his 1609 treatise *Of Lovesickness, or Erotic Melancholy*, the most substantial compendium of the period, the Paris physician Jacques Ferrand takes most of his references from Arabic sources such as Avicenna. Relying on these authorities, Ferrand asserts that the diagnosis of lovesickness can be made by observing its tired, deep-set eyes, its babbling speech, irregular breathing and pulse. These symptoms were found 'not only in those already afflicted but also in those inclined to passionate love'.

With more than forty dissertations on lovesickness appearing in Europe before 1750, the disease travelled far beyond its Mediterranean and Arab home. By the early nineteenth century, when 'erotic monomania' took its place in the classification of mental illness, the symptoms remained essentially those described by Ferrand. According to Esquirol, 'the look of this class of patients is dejected; their complexion becomes paler; their features change; sleep and appetite are lost . . . These patients are ordinarily exceedingly loquacious'.

In the age of modern psychiatry, love continues to insinuate itself into various pathologies. In erotic fixations, sexual addictions and personality disorders, the passions are distorted or excessive. In schizophrenia and the affective psychoses, the emotions are often impeded to the point that empathy and meaningful contact with others is fraught with difficulty. The highs of mania are an exception. As Kay Redfield Jamison notes of her own highs, in her memoir *An Unquiet Mind*, 'shyness goes, the right words and gesture are suddenly there, the power to captivate others a felt certainty. Sensuality is pervasive and the desire to seduce and be seduced irresistible.'

In Search of the Sublime

Finding himself among an 'accidental party of travellers' while touring north Wales, Samuel Taylor Coleridge stopped to gaze at 'a cataract of great height, breadth, and impetuosity, the summit of which appeared to blend with the sky and clouds'. On proclaiming this spectacle sublime 'in the very strictest sense', Coleridge recalled that one of the ladies replied: 'Yes! And it is not only sublime, but beautiful and absolutely pretty.' Like one of Jane Austen's newly monied additions to the chattering classes, this effusive traveller betrayed her ignorance of aesthetic philosophy. If, like Coleridge, she had read Kant's *Observations on the Feeling of the Beautiful and Sublime* or Edmund Burke's *Philosophical Enquiry into the Origin of our Ideas of the Sublime and Beautiful,* she would never have conflated the simple charm of the beautiful with the momentous, awe-filled pleasures of the sublime.

Kant's essay of 1767 had attempted to erect a firm and unassailable boundary between objects that were beautiful and sublime. In this respect, Kant followed Burke and many other commentators who had discoursed upon the subject in the wake of Nicolas Boileau, who had revived interest in the late Roman writing of Longinus in the 1670s. Gardens, the sea, trees, birds, streams, houses and women were, according to Kant, beautiful. The night sky, St Peter's in Rome, a snow-covered mountain, these were all, by contrast, filled with the stark grandeur of the sublime. 'The sublime *moves*, the beautiful *charms*. The mien of a man who is undergoing the full feeling of the sublime is earnest, sometimes rigid and astonished . . . the lively sensation of the beautiful proclaims itself through shining cheerfulness, in the eyes, through smiling features, and often through audible mirth.' Kant's essay, a triumph of empiricism over psychology, influenced a flurry of eighteenth-century commentators who attempted to slavishly catalogue the formal qualities of the sublime. By 1790, Coleridge's 'Illustrious Sage of Konigsberg' had, however, revised his theory of the sublime. Kant's *Third Critique* argued that the sublime was not synonymous with the object that occasioned it. The emotional impact of the sublime was also extended, giving new emphasis to the sense of fear and pain which attended it.

The fascination with this dread sublime had already reached its acme with the Gothic, which, abandoning neo-classicism, looked to the medieval to find Burke's 'images of Trouble, and Terror, and Darkness'. Loitering in ruins and graveyards, exposing itself to chilling elements, the Gothic explored the supernatural aspect of sublime astonishment. James Usher's monograph *Clio: Or a Discourse on Taste* (1767) was, for example, unrestrained in championing the pursuit of beauty in the madness of rapture. For Usher, the sublime was more mystical and intuitive than others had allowed. At the heart of the sublime was a 'religious passion, attended with less tumult, but more constancy than the other passions'.

The sublime in many ways secularised and extended emotions that had been primarily religious and feminine. The psychological state most equivalent to the sublime in the Middle Ages was, as Usher suggests, rapture. Derived from the verb *rapire* (meaning 'to ravish or seize'), rapture was also a legal term for sexual violence against a woman. In its religious sense, rapture accessed the pain of Christ's passion. The enraptured, such as Vana of Orvieto or Claire of Rimini, all burned with divine love. That their bodies became rigid and insensible was theological proof of true inspiration. But in the fifteenth century, these outward signs of rapture, a pre-eminently feminine state, became markers of demonic possession. As rapture was to medieval mysticism, the sublime was to Enlightenment aesthetics. While the former found itself at odds with the classical theology, the sublime, with its aesthetic of excess and self-obliteration, was the dark underbelly of Enlightenment rationalism.

In the Gothic romance, and the novels of Mrs Radcliffe in

particular, the wilds became a cathedral of swooning and tremulous emotion. Emily, the heroine of *Udolpho*, takes to the woods and mountains, 'where the silence and grandeur of solitude impressed a scared awe upon her heart, and lifted her thoughts to the GOD OF HEAVEN AND EARTH'. As Samuel Monk points out in his classic monograph *The Sublime*: 'For a volume and a half she [Emily] is put through her paces as a lover of scenery . . . No heroines were ever such puppets as are Mrs Radcliffe's; they exist to be harrowed by the incidents of melodramatic plot . . . Supernatural terror alone can overcome their rage for the terrific in nature.'

Coleridge's lady traveller would undoubtedly have been familiar with the work of Mrs Radcliffe, but William Gilpin's more sober essays on picturesque travel would have provided her with a more practical guide to enjoying the newly discovered countryside. Unlike other travel writers who used the term 'picturesque' to bridge the concepts of the sublime and beautiful, Gilpin had little time for high-minded philosophy. Instead he offered his readers a straightforward, didactic guide to natural scenes that 'co-incide with the rules of beauty, and composition'. All but ignoring the sublime emotion in which Mrs Radcliffe wallowed, Gilpin writes with a painter's eye for composition. When finding landscape that met with his approval, he was apt to remark: 'This whole scene and its accompaniments are not only grand, but picturesquely beautiful in the highest degree'. The language exactly echoes the lady traveller in north Wales. Coleridge's derision appears to have been aimed squarely at Gilpin.

At the very end of the nineteenth century, Romanticism was about to discover a *via regis* into the sublime's psychological interior. The chemist Humphry Davy co-opted a number of eminent figures, including Coleridge, to provide testimony to the 'sensations similar to no other' that he had experienced courtesy of his experiments with nitrous oxide at the Bristol Pneumatic Institute. Their attempts to give expression to these vertiginous yet elusive feelings led to analogies with dreaming, drunkenness, walking and mountaineering. Among the many adjectives used to describe the effects of the gas, the word 'sublime' was foremost.

Yet if these experiments opened up a new window on to the sublime, it remained, in contrast to the rapture of medieval times, a decidedly masculine emotion. In the conclusion to his *Researches Chemical and Philosophical* (1800), Davy includes a handful of reports that address the question of whether 'nitrous oxide was capable of producing hysterical and nervous affections in delicate and irritable constitutions'. More than one 'delicate lady' fell into a trance of which they could give no account. But while others experienced flights of exhilarating and high spirits, presumably akin to those described by Mrs Radcliffe, they were not called on to provide testimony. Once again, this was no place for lady travellers.

Culture Shocks

Since the first European explorers and traders described their travels in the Orient, the psychological effects of exposure to other cultures have been endlessly attested. In Herodotus's *Histories*, the oldest surviving account of Western travel in the East, the itinerant Greek scholar documented the practices and beliefs of the lands through which he passed. Writing at a time when the boundaries of Europe were unknown, Herodotus's preoccupations were primarily with health and religious rites. He declared the Libyans 'the healthiest people in the world', found Egypt to be a land that was 'religious to excess', and observed that the Scythians had a hatred of all foreign customs, especially those of the Greeks. Yet Herodotus himself was rarely fearful or repulsed by the peoples or customs he met with. Even the cannibalistic practices of the Issedones and nomadic Scythians roused little response in him.

Europe's first confrontation with the indigenous peoples of the Americas was an altogether more affecting and ambivalent experience. These 'savage' cultures at once offered a vision of unsullied paradise and primitive anarchy. On his first journey to the West Indies, Columbus found the natives of Hispaniola to be 'so guileless and so generous with all they possess, that no one would believe it'. As lacking as they were in so many respects, their apparent innocence could not help but seduce Columbus. On his return from a second voyage, however, Columbus and his crew were attacked by the once peaceable Caribs, and a relief expedition found human remains displayed in the villages. 'It plainly appeared', Herrera later wrote in his *General History* (1601), 'that the Devil was entirely possessed of these people.' Far from being 'a people in their original simplicity', these primitives were now perceived as cannibals, sodomites and concubines, representative of everything that was anathema to European Church and State.

As colonialism articulated its civilising mission, the Enlightenment found in the New World a dystopian spectre of lawless society. In his *Leviathan* (1651), Hobbes argued that the state of natural lust in which the savages of the Americas lived was a vindication for absolute government. As fearful and repulsed as the Enlightenment philosophers were by this vision of primitive society – even Rousseau was circumspect in his estimation of the Noble Savage – not one of its critics had actually set foot in the savage societies they described. The tableau vivant of savage life they constructed was almost entirely imaginary and self-serving. Steeped in prejudice and misunderstanding, it was far removed from the actual descriptions offered by the first traders who found the American natives to be by turns 'malicious' and 'ingenious', 'inconstant' and 'cautious'. For these first American frontiersmen, the primitive was more complex and less comprehensible.

Yet the New World continued to enchant and seduce. When Captain James Cook arrived in the South Seas at the end of the 1760s, Tahiti was seen as 'the truest picture of Arcadia', the beauty of its peoples 'defy[ing] the imitation of the chisel of Phidias'. A second voyage in 1774 returned with a living specimen, Omai, who, after being presented to King George III and Queen Charlotte, proved an endless source of fascination to the literary and philosophical circles to which he was introduced. For the Romantics, Byron especially, Polynesia still provided a readymade Utopia populated by 'naked knights of savage chivalry'. Disease, commerce, Christianity and other European imports would, however, soon corrupt this bacchanalian idyll. By the time Gauguin left France for Tahiti in the early 1890s: 'It was all over – nothing but civilized people left'.

The Enlightenment and Romantic fascination with the New World was in stark contrast to the suspicion which had attended the discovery of other continents and cultures. When Marco Polo first travelled to China and described this fully fledged counter-civilisation, with its own alphabet, arts, medicine and science, his accounts met with disbelief. China shocked Europe in ways that the New World could not. When accounts of Chinese life, history and customs became accessible in the seventeenth and eighteenth centuries, the literary imagination was deeply affected. While Coleridge conjured his vision of Kubla Khan, De Quincey developed, solely from his reading, an almost pathological dread of China and all things Chinese. During the worst phase of his addiction to opium, De Quincey was haunted by China in his dreams:

> I have been every night . . . transported into Asiatic scenes. I know not whether others share in my feelings on this point; but I have often thought that if I were compelled to forego England, and to live in China, and among Chinese manners and modes of life and scenery, I should go mad. No man can pretend that the wild, barbarous, and capricious superstitions of Africa, or of Savage tribes elsewhere, affect him in the way that he is affected by the ancient, monumental, cruel and elaborate religions of Indostan, &c. The mere antiquity of Asiatic things . . . overpowers the sense of youth in the individual. In China, over and above what it has in common with the rest of Southern Asia, I am terrified by the modes of life, by the manners, and the barriers of utter abhorrence . . . I would sooner live with lunatics, or brutes.

Contemporaries of De Quincey, such as Chateaubriand, Flaubert and de Nerval, reacted to the Orient, especially Egypt, very differently. Unfettered liberty, hedonism and, above all, mystery were all to be indulged here. The 'secret terror' that Chateaubriand felt on his travels through the Holy Land was not remotely akin to that of De Quincey. The thrill of the exotic served only to energise and vivify the creativity of Chateaubriand and other travellers in the Orient.

Of course, colonisers, adventurers and travellers also provoked a response within the territories and cultures they explored: this is the other, more neglected history of culture shock. In Virginia, for example, the Native Americans ascribed supernatural powers to the first European settlers, being unable to comprehend how their weaponry and instruments functioned. In the south Pacific, particularly in Melanesia and New Guinea, the arrival of English and French colonisers and the American military led to the creation of native cargo cults. These religious movements sprang from the belief that cargo (the panoply of Western consumer goods) would provide their islands with all their needs, leading to prosperity equal to that of their white providers. Formed in the 1940s, the John Frum movement of Vanuatu continues to prophesy that American soldiers will return to bring social and economic development – making use of songs learnt from American servicemen as hymns, army memorabilia as relics. And the anxiety and uncertainty roused by the Western other go deeper still. According to the psychiatrist and postcolonial theorist Frantz Fanon, the history of colonial domination was of rendering the oppressed 'an alien in his own country', forcing him to live 'in a state of absolute depersonalisation'.

This debilitating loss of identity is an experience far removed from the sense in which the social anthropologist Kalervo Oberg first employed the term 'culture shock' in the 1960s. For the expatriate Americans that Oberg studied, culture shock was an occupational disease, a side effect of sudden transplantation that might lead to varying degrees of psychological strain. As real as these anxieties and confusions were, they hardly compare with the self-estrangement that colonialism routinely enforced on its subjects. Even when its civilising mission assumed an apparently benign air, as with the importation of noble savages such as Omai into English society, one can only wonder how this human cargo was affected by the culture it was paraded before.

A Constant Craving

When it came to medical matters, the novelist William Burroughs considered himself 'rarely if ever wrong'. After undergoing treatment for a long-standing addiction to morphine in the early 1950s, Burroughs wrote to the editor of the *British Journal of Addiction* arguing that the term had lost 'any useful precision of meaning'. Neither cocaine nor alcohol, hashish nor most illicit drugs were, argued Burroughs, addictive. Only morphine and the barbiturates could, he insisted, give rise to 'metabolic dependence'. For this reason, his 'Letter from a Master Addict to Dangerous Drugs' insisted that:

> psychological treatment is not only useless it is contraindicated. Statistically, the people who become addicted to morphine are those who have access to it: doctors, nurses, anyone in contact with black market sources. In Persia, where opium is sold without control in opium shops, 70 percent of the population is addicted. So we should psycho-analyse several million Persians to find out what deep conflicts and anxieties have driven them to the use of opium? I think not. According to my experience most addicts are not neurotic and do not need psychotherapy.

With more than twenty years' apprenticeship to a pharmacopoeia of drugs, Burroughs intimately understood the 'algebra of need', the intense craving that transports the morphine addict into a netherworld in which time slows, the world recedes and the mind is transfixed by its own inertia. At the end of his 'junk line' in Tangiers, Burroughs recalled that he 'had not taken a bath in a year nor changed my clothes or removed them except to stick a needle every hour in the fibrous grey wooden flesh of addiction. Empty ampoule boxes and garbage piled up to the ceiling . . . I could look at the end of my shoe for eight hours. If a friend came to visit – and they rarely did since who or what was left to visit – I sat there . . . If he had died on the spot I would have sat there looking at my shoe waiting to go through his pockets'.

The conclusions that Burroughs drew from his insights into addiction were sometimes extremely wayward. Burroughs believed, for instance, that schizophrenia, in as far as it was also a disease of a 'disordered metabolism', might be cured by a treatment parallel to those being developed in the treatment of morphine addiction. (First, heroin should be prescribed until an addiction was established; then a withdrawal treatment with apomorphine should conclude the treatment.) Yet his scepticism regarding the way in which addiction was being 'used to indicate anything one is used to or wants' was prescient. In the past fifty years, a host of behavioural compulsions, from shopping to sex, have taken their place alongside drug and alcohol addictions. While some psychologists have certainly welcomed this democratisation, the notion of addiction has become an easy refuge for transgressions, deviancies and life problems that are inconsistent with the most minimal definition of a disease. The addict identity, of course, provides certain immunities. Therein lies its attraction.

Craving is a treacherous impulse: it denies, distorts, disguises and ultimately legitimates itself. Craving plays tricks on the mind, giving rise to an almost boundless capacity for self-deception. In *Understanding the Alcoholic's Mind* (1988), Arnold M. Ludwig gives numerous examples of the 'ingenious booby traps and inadvertent pitfalls' through which the recovering or abstinent alcoholic is outwitted by his craving:

> After several years of abstinence, one man got religion and began taking Communion with wine, regarding it as safe since it was the body of Christ. Within several weeks, he was drinking heavily again . . . On his way home from work, one individual figured that the snarled traffic ahead indicated an accident, so he took a long detour, which carried him several miles out of his way. By

accident, he happened to turn on the street of a once-favorite bar that he had not frequented in years. Noting that his radiator seemed to be overheating, he thought it best to turn off the engine and just pass some time inside while it cooled off. Instead of the intended soft drink, he ordered a beer . . . One man swore he ordered ginger ale on the plane, but the stewardess brought champagne . . . One individual developed a persistent cough after he took up smoking again. Rather than cut-back on his two-to-three-pack-a-day habit, he began to rely on an elixir of terpin hydrate as a palliative for the cough – an elixir that is forty percent alcohol. The cough, naturally, continued.

From a psychological perspective, cravings are patterns of thinking, or 'private self-statements, a type of nonvocal inner speech that usually, but not always, serves as a mediator between intentions and needs'. Because these thought processes are so familiar to the 'addicted' individual, Ludwig dubs them 'scripts'. Scripts are the excuses through which a craving seeks to fulfil itself. In all Ludwig identifies nine overlapping scripts that dispose the alcoholic to drinking. These include the escape script (which promises release from tension, anxiety, disappointment and unhappiness), the socialisation script (which promises ease in social situations), the self-control script (used to deny problem drinking) and the no-control script (in which the alcoholic acknowledges his impotence). The cognitive techniques that can be used to counter-act these scripts are all aimed at circumventing the message the 'addict' sends himself. The pithy mantras favoured by Alcoholics Anonymous (ONE DAY AT A TIME. THIS TOO WILL PASS. AVOID THE FIRST DRINK) have exactly the same functions. They are counterscripts through which the alcoholic tries to intercept himself.

The genealogy of the concept of addiction can be traced back to eighteenth-century medicine. The medicalisation of alcoholism, the excesses of which had for so long been attributed to weaknesses of character, began with Benjamin Rush, who would go on to be claimed as the founder of the Temperance Movement. In 1784, Rush's *Inquiry into the Effects of Ardent Spirits upon the Human Body and*

Mind set out both to diagnose the major symptoms of addiction to spirits, 'the great destroyer', and to advocate the establishment of 'sober houses' for treatment. At the heart of Rush's pamphlet was the belief that the consumption of spirits (as opposed to wine or beer) eroded free agency, moving inexorably from habit to absolute necessity. As one drunkard confided to Rush: 'Were a keg of rum in one corner of the room, and were a cannon constantly discharging balls between me and it, I could not refrain from passing before that cannon.'

Britain's gin plague had brought the issue of drunkenness to the fore in the first half of the eighteenth century, but the 'multitudes of dropsical consumptive people under the effect of spirituous liquors' were not, despite being clearly habituated, perceived as addicts. William Hogarth's *Gin Lane* depicted squalor and distress, poverty and ruin, as the outward effects of the gin plague, but drunkenness was perceived as vice, sin or weakness of character. A century later, when George Cruikshank portrayed the evils of intemperance in drawings such as *The Drunkard's Daughter*, *The Bottle* and *The Gin Trap*, the concept of alcoholism had only just been defined by the Swedish physician Magnus Huss. In this first incarnation, alcoholism was theorised as a degenerative disease. The theory of degeneration explained psychopathy and criminality in terms of the moral and physical failings that were exacerbated as they passed from generation to generation.

After the nature of alcoholism (and its cyclical cousin, dipsomania) had been examined by physicians such as Rush and Huss, 'hashishism', 'cocainism' and 'morphinomania' would be considered as 'diseases of the will'. The first case of ether addiction, reported in 1847 by F. T. Wintle, anticipated themes that European psychiatry would more fully explore in relation to morphine and cocaine addiction:

I have known great cerebral derangement produced in a highly talented and intellectual individual by too freely inhaling ether. The gentleman had a strange delusion that he could expand the powers of his mind *ad infinitum* if he could obtain a free supply of ether, and he pursued this delusion so earnestly that his mind became disordered, and, in fact, he suffered paroxysms very nearly allied to delirium tremens. At first he was speedily restored by being deprived of ether, but as often he was set at large, his delusion returned, he flew to the chemist for his admired drug, and again became deranged, requiring to be under surveillance; the attacks increased in violence and duration, until his mind was so impaired that it was necessary to place him under physical restraint.

The discussion and treatment of 'morbid craving' for morphine and cocaine in the 1870s and 1880s laid the foundations of the disease model of addiction. The first morphine and cocaine addicts were invariably doctors and patients who initially turned to these drugs for pain relief. In the 1880s, before discovering the talking cure, Freud championed cocaine as a cure for morphinism. His friend and patient, Ernst von Fleischl, died while being weaned from morphine on to cocaine. In America, the renowned surgeon W. H. Alsted was one of the first reported cocaine addicts. Alsted, by contrast, turned to morphine as a cure for cocaine. As these substances became more popularly available, the addict came to be seen as a public danger. In 1914, the *New York Times* quoted one doctor who pronounced 'Negro cocaine fiends' a 'southern menace', white women being allegedly being the targets of their frenzies. Prohibition was urged on the grounds of alcohol's capacity to 'make a brute out of a negro, causing him to commit unnatural crimes'. As whites were deemed 'further evolved', they were considered to exercise some measure of control over all drugs.

It was now that addiction began to be examined from a psychological perspective. In his 1913 *General Psychopathology*, Karl Jaspers asserted that 'alcoholics, morphinists, etc, who are addicts, carry with them a psychic readiness and that they can replace one craving with another but never become radically free from any because the cause of the craving cannot be abolished'. Although Jaspers and others agreed that 'every sort of human interest could degenerate into a craving', medicine and psychiatry would subsequently draw stricter boundaries. In 1934, the American

Psychiatric Association officially recognised addiction to alcohol or drugs as bona fide mental illnesses. Two decades on, as Burroughs fired off his polemic on the mythology of addiction, the American Medical Association had only just endorsed alcoholism as a disease. As the notion of the addictive personality began to take hold, WHO's Expert Committee on Addiction-producing Drugs proclaimed that 'psychological dependency was the most powerful of all factors involved in chronic intoxication with psychotropic drugs . . . even in the cases of most intense craving and compulsive abuse'. The motivation of the drug user, the context in which the drug was used, was now paramount.

Most epidemiological studies confirm that addiction is primarily a psychological and social rather than physiological phenomenon. In the case of cocaine, which in the 1980s assumed heroin's mantle as 'a chemical that would lock people into perpetual usage', patterns of usage indicate that the vast majority of users consumed the drug on fewer than ten occasions, while only 3 per cent were 'clinically addicted'. These findings turn the physiological view of addiction on its head. 'If addiction is not identified with any chemical or biological process,' writes Stanton Peele, a prominent critic of biological theories of addiction, 'then it can occur with a wide range of involvements in addition to drug use, such as love and gambling . . . Each type of addictive involvement, moreover, does not require a separate theory of addiction.'

The growing array of behavioural addictions raises serious issues. How many members of Workaholics Anonymous or Helpers Anonymous have experienced the feverish craving of a delirious alcoholic? Are all addictions truly equivalent? These questions nevertheless miss one important point: addiction and dependency are not, as Burroughs would have maintained, simply medical issues. The proliferation of support groups for addictions and pseudo-addictions has created a cultural network in which emotional confession and spiritual renewal are encouraged. The problems these groups address are those of life, for which friendship and community have so often proved the most effective 'cures'.

Mystical Maladies

Twice-Born Men

The book of Acts in the New Testament records many examples of conversion to the early Christian church, including that of Simon the Magus, the Ethiopian eunuch, the Philippian jailor and Saint Paul himself. All these spiritual initiations have one common denominator: they are essentially presented as miracles of heavenly intervention. Even the conversion of Saint Paul on the road to Damascus, which is given in three separate accounts, fails to provide any sense of conversion as a human process. This absence of psychological detail is particularly puzzling in the case of Paul. Why, after all, would a Pharisee and zealous persecutor of the Christians *suddenly* become their leading apostle?

According to Acts, Paul was nearing Damascus, 'still breathing threats against the disciples of the Lord', when a heavenly light caused him and his companions to fall to the ground. A voice spoke, asking, 'Saul, Saul, why do you persecute me?' When Paul asked who was speaking, he was told: 'I am Jesus, whom you are persecuting, but rise and enter the city, and you will be told what you are to do.' Now, 'Saul arose from the ground; and when his eyes opened, he could see nothing; so they led him by the hand and brought him into Damascus. And for three days he was without sight, and neither ate nor drank.'

Paul's own letters fail to mention the subsequent cure, baptism and instruction in Damascus which are reported in the biblical accounts. The immediate aftermath of this momentous conversion is sketchy in the extreme. From Damascus, Paul is said to have withdrawn into Upper Arabia, where, in solitude, he reflected on his bizarre reversal of belief. Then, instead of travelling to Jerusalem, where he might have joined with other members of the

Christian community, Paul seems to have decided that he had been chosen as Christ's emissary to the Gentiles. Preaching the promise of salvation, constructing a theology that envisioned the world as degraded, evil and sin-infested, Paul eventually embarked on a series of missionary journeys. Covering thousands of miles in the eastern corner of the Mediterranean, he claimed many converts, who adopted his ascetic principles. Conversion did not, however, usher Paul into a life of quiet serenity. Paul's letters describe periods of personal angst, self-castigation, violent outburst and rampant egotism. On three occasions, he asked God to relieve him of some unspecified burden or affliction: the 'thorn in his side'.

In the late nineteenth century, as medical science began to identify the Catholic saints as degenerates, Paul was retroactively diagnosed as suffering from hysteria, epilepsy, migraine, ophthalmia and erysipelas. But it was the philosopher Friedrich Nietzsche who offered the most vociferous attack on Saint Paul and the saintly ideals he represented. 'The *morbid*', Nietzsche writes in his *Genealogy of Morals*, 'are our greatest peril . . . it is the *weakest*, who are undermining the vitality of the race, poisoning our thrust in life, and putting humanity in question.' This corruption of Christ's teaching was, for Nietzsche, a direct result of Saint Paul and his teachings. 'The life, the example, the teaching, the death, the meaning and the right of the entire Gospel – nothing was left once this hate-obsessed false-coiner had grasped what he alone could make use of.'

The psychologist and philosopher William James was a little more charitable towards Saint Paul and the saintly impulses in general. Although recognising that purity, devoutness and asceticism all had their 'daft' excesses, James's seminal study, *The Varieties of Religious Experience* (1902), distinguished itself in two important regards. First, James regarded the psychological experience of conversion as the bedrock of theology and all its ecclesiastical outbuildings. Second, whatever the motives and reasons for conversion, its fruits were to be measured by human standards. What, asked James, are the private and public benefits of saintliness? This was his non-metaphysical yardstick.

James considered the kind of sudden conversion experienced by Saint Paul as peculiar to a certain temperament. The individuals most likely to undergo these conversions were those possessing 'a large region in which mental work can go on subliminally, and from which invasive experiences, abruptly upsetting the equilibrium of the primary consciousness, may come'. James cites a study of evangelical conversion conducted by George Coe in the 1890s, which found that each and every one of a group of seventy evangelists had previously experienced some form of automatism or religious dream before their conversion. When these subjects were tested under hypnosis, they were also found to be highly suggestible. The only possible explanation for Saint Paul's conversion was that he had been subliminally travelling to Damascus for far longer than he realised: he had been internally deliberating and rehearsing his volte-face, oblivious to the inner crisis that had incubated within him.

In his 1957 book *Battle for the Mind*, the psychiatrist William Sargant offered a radically different explanation for sudden conversion based on the many parallels between political indoctrination, religious conversion and medical and psychiatric treatment. The sudden religious conversions described in Acts were, Sargant suggested, very similar to cases of abreaction (a technique used in the treatment of combat neuroses in both World Wars) described by army physicians. Utilising large doses of barbiturates, abreaction sought to create a state of overwhelming fear, bringing subjects to the point of collapse:

The terror exhibited . . . is electrifying to watch. The body becomes increasingly tense and rigid; the eyes widen and the pupils dilate, while the skin becomes covered with a fine perspiration . . . . Breathing becomes incredibly rapid or shallow. The intensity of emotion sometimes becomes more than they can bear; and frequently at the height of the reaction, there is a collapse and the patient falls back in bed. . . . [Eventually] The stuperous become alert, the mute can talk, the deaf can hear, the paralysed can move, and terror-stricken psychotics become well-organised individuals.

255

Sargant maintained that the above effects are essentially identical to the 'violent agonies' experienced by the Methodist preacher John Wesley. After thirty years of inspiring the fear of damnation, Wesley was convinced that 'sanctification' could only be successful if it were sudden and dramatic. When he canvassed more than 650 London Methodists, he found 'everyone of these (without a single exception) has declared that his deliverance from sin was instantaneous; that the change was wrought in a moment'.

In the case of Saint Paul, Sargant's overtly Pavlovian theory of conversion suggests that anger rather than fear triggered the same process. Paul's collapse on the road to Damascus was the product of exhaustion exacerbated by a period of fasting. It was this state of acute anxiety that opened him to Christian message. Saint Paul's experiences are 'consonant with modern physiological observation'. The mystery of sudden conversion was, Sargant concluded, that of the body pushing the mind to its limits.

Three centuries after Paul, Saint Augustine's Christian conversion was of a very different kind. Augustine eventually embraced the teachings of Saint Paul, but his passage into the Catholic church was that of a man consciously struggling with ideas and doctrines, searching for a truth by which he might live. More than any other Christian saint, Augustine embodies James's definition of conversion as 'the process, gradual or sudden, by which a self hitherto divided and consciously wrong, inferior and unhappy becomes unified and consciously right, superior and happy in consequence of its firmer hold upon religious realities'. Augustine is a relentlessly modern witness. His conversion speaks to us in a way that Paul's cannot. Reduced to pithy telegraphese, Augustine's conversion might read: AN EXTENDED PERIOD OF MORAL DOUBT AND INTELLECTUAL UNCER-TAINTY . . . A SEARCH FOR GUIDING PRINCIPLES . . . THE REJECTION OF OLD BELIEFS . . . AN APPRENTICE-SHIP TO SCRIPTURE . . . A FINAL SURRENDERING. Here we have the template that so many of Christianity's twice-born have subsequently followed.

Too much has been made of the moral and sexual aspects of Augustine's conversion. To imagine Augustine as a debauched libertine turning his back on vice and folly, as old-school theologians were given to, is misleading. When, at the age of thirty-two, Augustine left Carthage to teach in Rome, he was falling away from Manicheism (which sought to supplement scripture with natural philosophy) and grappling with Neo-platonism and the Christian mysteries. Arriving in Milan, Augustine felt that he was becoming a 'phrase salesman' who told lies to the 'connoisseurs of lying'. After immersing himself in the Epistles of Paul, Augustine was, as Garry Wills notes in his recent biography, given instruction 'in a series of conversion accounts' that offered a tentative blueprint for his eventual conversion in the garden of his friend Alypius. The account of these events that Augustine later furnished in his *Confessions* has been much copied. Augustine describes himself 'thrashing about with stymied effort', seeking to recover the will that was denied him. Leaving Alypius, he sits beneath a tree and hears a voice, 'Tolle lege, tolle lege' – 'Pick up and read, pick up and read'. Taking this as instruction to read from the Bible, he turns at random to the words 'Be clothed in Jesus Christ'. After reading this sentence, Augustine notes, 'light was flooding my heart with assurance, and every shadow of doubt evanesced'. On surrendering himself to God, Augustine became hugely prolific. He produced four dialogues in as many months. Over the next forty or so years of his life, there was rarely any point at which he was not engaged in writing the books, sermons, pamphlets and letters for which he is now justly famed.

Paul, Saint Augustine, John Wesley – all were converts who went on to preach, calling on others to follow their example. The urge to proselytise is, however, not always associated with conversion. There is also an open-minded version of conversion which rejects the singular and resists the Final Answer. Such was the experience that William James underwent as a young medical student at Harvard. Disillusioned with the prospect of becoming a physician, James had not yet discovered his passion for psychology and philosophy. His health suffered. He was unable to study. Uncertain of his future, James was struck down with a feeling of dread and self-despair which, at its very worst, made him fearful of the dark and reluctant to be alone. '[T]he fear was so powerful and

invasive,' wrote James, 'that if I had not clung to scripture like texts
. . . I think I should have grown really insane.'

Philosophy, not scripture, saved him. On reading the French
philosopher Charles Renouvier on free will, he at last began to
experience 'a rebirth of the moral life'. Besides giving James a new
perspective on the relationship between mind and body,
Renouvier's pluralism, his advocacy of personal liberty, helped
him become 'free from the monolithic superstition under which I
had grown up'. His insight was almost the exact reverse of that
experienced by Augustine, who discovered that 'free will was the
cause of our doing ill'. James, the self-styled 'Methodist, minus a
Saviour' remained open minded to the end. Eschewing dogma
and scepticism, he declared himself 'willing to accept any theory if
the facts lend themselves best to it'.

Many of the most famous Christian converts, including Saint
Paul and Saint Augustine, distinguished themselves as important
writers of autobiography, theology and philosophy. Likewise, a
'creative malady' of the type described by James has launched the
work of many prominent thinkers, including Freud and Jung. But
the twice-born are not immune to hubris. There is a large library
– or oversized bunker – to be filled with the self-hagiographies, the
cod philosophy and the clumsy verse of the Church of the Lesser
Illuminati.

From this other history of conversion, take William Topaz
McGonagall, who is today remembered as the worst ever British
poet. In 1877, McGonagall, a weaver with little schooling, received
divine inspiration. 'Write, Write,' he imagined a voice impelling
him. Unencumbered by talent or aptitude, McGonagall applied
himself to the task as best he could. He wrote of the railway lines
and bridges of Edinburgh and Dundee. He mourned various
maritime disasters. Whatever his subject, McGonagall's meter was
wayward, his doggerel was torturously contrived, his register
unintentionally comic. Sending his work to Queen Victoria, he
petitioned unsuccessfully for a meeting with her. Still, he never
doubted his qualifications for the position of Poet Laureate. The
office was his by right, if not appointment. Conversion: a
treacherous muse.

Paths to Ecstasy

In 1927, the French Nobel Prize-winning novelist and biographer Romain Rolland was sent a copy of the *The Future of an Illusion* (0000), the essay in which Freud proposed that each and every religious movement was a displaced 'defence against childish helplessness'. Rolland shared some of Freud's misgivings about the role and function of modern religions, yet he was also certain that his friend had failed to understand the 'true source of religious sentiments'. 'There was', Rolland pointed out in a letter which Freud later paraphrased, 'a peculiar feeling, which he [Rolland] himself is never without, which he finds confirmed in many others. . . . a sensation of "eternity", a feeling as of something, limitless, unbounded – as it were "oceanic".' This feeling was, Rolland thought, 'the source of religious energy which is seized upon by various churches, directed by them into particular channels, and doubtless exhausted by them'.

Freud conceded that Rolland's letter caused him 'no small difficulty'. Although he was lacking in firsthand experience of the 'oceanic feeling', he was prepared to accept that the 'modifications of mental life, such as trances and ecstasies' were widely attested. As ever, it was the interpretation given to these experiences that he considered fallacious. The oceanic feeling, he maintained, was a temporary breakdown of the ego that was, like all religious attitudes, essentially the revival of a primary, infantile narcissism.

Freud was not the first to detect a morbid nostalgia behind the mystical sensibility. The pathology of ecstasy was, as previously noted, a popular subject for late nineteenth-century writers. Freud's mentor, the great neurologist Charcot, argued that the saints and mystics were hysterics – the pathognomic signs of

259

hysteria were even dubbed 'stigmata'. Charcot's one-time pupil Pierre Janet pointed to a neurotic condition, psychaesthenia, which appeared to make sense of the ecstasies and abjections of both the Christian mystics and his own patients. But it was with the Hungarian-born physician Max Nordau and his book *Degeneration* (1892) that Christian mysticism was most emphatically dismissed as a pathological stain.

As psychoanalysis traced the oceanic back to the amniotic cocoon of the mother–infant relationship, religious scholarship took a different turn and began to systematically catalogue the emotions and sensations, insights and intimations which were considered the universal mainspring of religious ecstasy. This focus on religious or mystical *experience* over doctrine, belief or underlying pathology provided a vital corrective to the diagnostic reductionism of Charcot, Janet and Nordau. That the major contributors to this field – Richard Bucke, William James, Rudolph Otto – all had a close rapport with the oceanic was no coincidence.

It was during a visit to London that the Canadian psychiatrist Richard Bucke first became attuned to the secret symphony of ecstasy. He was thirty-five years of age, and the 'cloud' that unexpectedly consumed him as he took a cab across the city was to have a lasting impact on both his personal and professional life:

I was in a state of quiet, almost passive enjoyment, not actually thinking, but letting ideas, images and emotions flow of themselves, as it were, through my mind. All at once, without warning of any kind, I found myself wrapped up in a flame-colored cloud. For an instant I thought of fire, an immense conflagration somewhere close by in that great city; the next, I knew that the fire was within myself. Directly afterward there came upon me a sense of exultation, of immense joyousness accompanied or immediately followed by an intellectual illumination impossible to describe. Among other things, I did not merely come to believe, but I saw that the universe is not composed of dead matter, but is, on the contrary, a living Presence: I became conscious in myself of eternal life. It was not a conviction that I would have eternal life, but a consciousness that I possessed eternal life then; I saw that all men are immortal . . . that the foundation principle of the world, of all the worlds, is what we call love, and that the happiness of each and all is in the long run absolutely certain. The vision lasted a few seconds and was gone; but the memory of it and the sense of the reality that it taught has remained during the quarter of a century that has since elapsed. I knew that what the vision showed was true. . . . That view, that conviction, has never, even during periods of deepest depression, been lost.

Almost all of the elements described by Bucke echo descriptions of ecstasies described in other times and cultures. First, ecstasy begins typically with a state of mental passivity, a disengagement from the here and now. What Bucke describes as 'not actually thinking' is, for example, advocated in the fourteenth-century mystical treatise *The Cloud of Unknowing*, which advises: 'forget all the creatures that ever God made and the works of them, so that thy thought or thy desire be not directed or stretched to any of them.' For the Indian yogi, it is through an even more systematic extermination of the self that the bliss of *samadhi* is achieved. Secondly, the sensation of internal fire described by Bucke finds direct parallel with the powers of 'magical' or 'psychic heat' that are cultivated in Asiatic shamanism and yoga, as well as the 'pleasant fire' described by medieval Christian mystics in the West. Other actual physical sensations include tumescence and levitation. These are not tropes – they are actual physical sensations. Thirdly, although the joy of ecstasy may be mingled with, even overshadowed by, a sense of terror or too-muchness, the unveiling of a universe united by some higher principle provides, as Bucke testifies, its intellectual core. Lastly, and perhaps most importantly, the door that ecstasy ópens is left ajar. At the time of his experience, Bucke was superintendent of Hamilton's Asylum in Ontario. His 'few seconds' were enough to convince him of a moral dimension to life of which he was previously unaware. Professionally, this led him to shun the use of drugs and physical restraint in treating the mentally ill; privately, it inclined him towards the nature mysticism of Walt Whitman, and he became a lifelong disciple of the poet and his philosophy.

Bucke was well aware that transports such as his had been

repeatedly experienced by Christian mystics when penetrating the mysteries of the Holy Trinity – Saint Ignatius claimed that in one hour of meditation he had learnt 'more truths about heavenly things than all the teachings of all the doctors put together could have taught'; Jacob Boehme took a quarter of an hour to grasp 'more than if I had been many years at university'; quicker still, Saint Teresa took but one instant to see 'how all things are seen and contained in God'. Yet the nature and frequency of ecstatic revelation in modern and secular contexts remained largely undocumented. Bucke took this as his task. After twenty-five years of collecting and cataloguing, in his 1901 anthology *Cosmic Consciousness: a Study in the Evolution of the Human Mind*, he argued that humankind had awoken to a second level of self-consciousness. A great mystical leap was, he predicted, about to take place. The highest realms of cosmic consciousness, once the preserve of Jesus, Buddha and Mohammed, were about to be breached. A New Age was under way.

In *The Varieties of Religious Experience*, William James set out to reclaim the words 'mysticism' and 'mystical' from disrepute. Too often, James remarked, these words were 'used as mere terms of reproach, to throw at any opinion which we regard as vague and vast and sentimental, and without a base in either facts or logic'. Unlike Freud, James believed that 'personal religious experience has its roots and centre in mystical states of consciousness'; unlike Bucke, he was a remarkably acute psychologist, able to trace the contours of mysticism in its higher and lower, diabolic and drunken, forms. Ecstasy had, he proposed, two chief characteristics. First, all mystical states elude definition: 'No one can make clear to another who has never had a certain feeling, in what quality or worth it consists.' Second, mystical ecstasy is noetic, 'full of significance and importance, all inarticulate though they remain'.

James also spoke from experience. In the early 1880s, a series of self-experiments with nitrous oxide convinced him that 'rational consciousness as we call it is but one special type of consciousness, whilst all about it, parted from it by the filmiest of screens, there lies potential forms of consciousness entirely different'. At the heart of ecstasy, anaesthetic or otherwise, was a sense of the real inclusivity that lay beneath the conflict and contradictoriness of everyday life. 'We pass into mystical states from out of ordinary consciousness as from a smallness to a vastness, and at the same time as from an unrest to a rest. We feel them as reconciling, unifying states.'

Twenty years after James, the religious historian Rudolph Otto also proposed that at the core of mystical ecstasy, from animism to the god-centred theophanies of developed religion, there was an intimation of overarching oneness. In his unlikely bestseller *The Idea of the Holy* (1917), Otto employed the phrase *mysterium tremendum et fascinas* to describe this overwhelming experience of unity. The *mysterium* is the realm of the transcendental, the 'wholly other', which the mystic enters with feelings of awe and terror. The numinous, the cosmic, the oceanic – every form of mystical ecstasy – contained, in varying degrees, the same manifestation of the vastness of God or the universe, a revelation of dependency and interconnectedness. Many scholars have echoed this assertion, arguing that the so-called higher and lower religions differ only in the means and techniques through which they commune with the sacred. This is particularly evident in Mircea Eliade's work on shamanism, which demonstrated that the most archaic techniques of ecstasy 'have the same precision and nobility as the experiences of the great mystics of East and West'.

It is through ecstasy that the shaman is able to confront the sacred (on behalf of others), to depart his body, to ascend to the sky or descend into the underworld. While music and dance once acted as conduits to shamanic ecstasy in its most 'spontaneous' and 'organic' forms, for Eliade the use of narcotics represented the first 'distortion' and aberration of this ancient experience, especially in Siberia and Central Asia. 'Intoxication by mushrooms also produces contact with the spirits, but in a passive and crude way . . . Intoxication is a mechanical and corrupt method of reproducing ecstasy.' Each adjective is telling. This is exactly the language employed by religious commentators who sought to deny the authenticity of the 'instant mysticism' that came to be associated with mescaline in the 1950s and with LSD and other related drugs in the 1960s.

Eliade may or may not have been right to regard the use of plant drugs as a later supplement to shamanism, but the grounds for discounting intoxication as a sham ecstasy are, from a psychological perspective, unclear. In terms of the phenomenology of ecstasy – the feelings, sensations and thoughts of which it is composed – what is there to distinguish the ecstasies of mysticism and intoxication? Walter Pahnke's 'Good Friday Experiment', dubbed the 'Miracle of Marsh Chapel' by East Coast leader writers, attempted to address this question in quantitative terms. His triple-blind experiment took place at a small, private chapel in Harvard, in 1962. Twenty seminary students were divided into groups of four. Each group was assigned a guide and given identical capsules – some containing 30 milligrams of the psychedelic drug psilocybin, the others nicotinic acid, a substance which had only minor physical effects – before listening to a three-hour devotional service. Every individual was subsequently interviewed and required to provide a report of their experiences. Follow-up questionnaires were employed to assess the lasting effects of the experience. Using this information, Pahnke found that the subjects who received psilocybin experienced phenomena that were apparently indistinguishable from those described in the literature of mysticism, particularly as regarding the sense of unity and transcendence, illumination and ineffability. All nine categories of experience that Pahnke investigated, bar the 'sense of sacredness', were far more pronounced in the students who were given psilocybin rather than the placebo.

Naturally, few theologians were prepared to accept Pahnke's claim 'that it appears possible to experience mystical consciousness (*samadhi* in Hinduism, *satori* in Zen Buddhism, the beatific vision in Christianity) with the help of a drug on a free Saturday afternoon'. And his sweeping conclusion, which echoed Huxley's more elegant speculations on the subject, certainly requires qualification.

The major psychedelic drugs are generally capable of inducing experiences that have most in common with what is called *extrovertive mysticism*, that is, with ecstasy that is roused via contemplation of the human or physical world. But introvertive or inner-directed mysticism, usually achieved by shutting down awareness of the sensate world through concentration, visualisation and heightened focus upon parts of the body, is altogether more rarely reported. The introvertive, anaesthetic experience described by James and others is perhaps far closer to the 'higher' mysticism of Buddhist and Hindu ecstasy. Where psychedelics such as LSD, mescaline and psilocybin are associated with such ecstasies, it is usually by acting as an as an adjunct and amplifier to meditation. This, for instance, was the case with the philosopher Alan Watts, who failed to experience anything approaching ecstasy on first taking LSD. It was only through subsequent experiments that he managed to go deeper, to penetrate the interior he went on to describe in *The Joyous Cosmology*:

> I trace myself back through the labyrinth of my brain . . . Back through the tunnels – through the various status and survival strategies of everyday life, through the interminable passages which we remember in dreams – all the streets we have ever travelled, the corridors of schools, the winding pathways between the legs of tables and chairs where we crawled as a child, the tight and bloody exit from the womb, the fountianous surge through the channel of the penis, the timeless wandering through ducts and spongy caverns. Down and back through ever narrowing tubes to the point where the passage itself is the travel – a thin string of molecules . . . Remembering back and back through endless whirling dances in astronomically proportioned spaces which surround the original nucleus of the world . . . I feel, with a peace so deep that it sings to be shared with all the world, that at last I belong, that I have returned to the home behind home.

The Inuit shaman who drops to the bottom of the sea so that he may truly become himself, the Hindu sadhu who seeks to escape the karmic cycle, the Sufi dervish who seeks the divine through the act of remembrance – all of the them, like Watts, seem to recover some kind of 'ancient identity'. The technologies and uses of ecstasy are manifold, the authority accorded its experts varies, but it is difficult to ignore the correspondences that all these higher transports – through personal history into the vast cosmic beyond – share. To quote one Sufi mystic: 'The lights are many, but the light is one.'

Mental Radio

In the curtained darkness of drawing rooms, women mediums and sensitives – and their more flamboyant 'secondary personages' – discovered a station and prominence that was so often denied them in Victorian society. The séance, whether conducted to commune with the other world, to tap the subliminal self or merely to entertain, was a pre-eminently feminine affair. The Fox sisters, Kate and Maggie, were the first celebrities of spiritualism. When they set the spirits rapping and knocking in Rochester, New York State, they seemed to awaken the dormant powers of a whole psychic sisterhood, holding a door open to Cora Hatch, Emma Hardinge, to the Misses Moor and Dunsmore, to the Bay sisters . . .

After spiritualism migrated across the Atlantic, leaving a trail of churches and home circles in its wake, the phenomena with which it was associated – apparitions, levitations, materialisations, clairvoyance and thought-transference – became the subject of investigation by the Society for Psychical Research (SPR), founded in 1882. One of the first cases investigated by the SPR committee on thought-transference was that of the Creery sisters, four young girls from Buxton in Derbyshire. With their father, the Reverend A. M. Creery, and a maidservant, the children had begun homespun trials in thought-transference in October 1880. Following the rules of the then popular 'willing game', one person left the room for a short period, while the remaining group fixed their attention on some object which the absent person then had to name. The results were, according to the Reverend Creery, quite exceptional:

After a few trials the successes preponderated so much over the failures that we were all convinced there was something very wonderful coming under our notice. Night after night, for several months, we spent an hour or two each evening in varying conditions of the experiments, and choosing new subjects for thought-transference. We began by selecting the simplest objects in the room; then chose the names of towns, of people, dates, cards out of a pack, lines from different poems, in fact any things or ideas that those present could keep steadily before their minds; and when the children were in good humour and excited by the wonderful nature of their successful guessing, they very seldom made a mistake. I have seen seventeen cards, chosen by myself, named right in succession, without any mistake.

Only forty years earlier, another Northern clergyman, Hugh M'neile, had protested that all mesmeric phenomena, including thought-transference – a phenomenon which mesmerism had investigated by placing subject and operator *'en rapport'* or by inducing a 'community of sensation' – were the devil's own work. But thought-transference had at the same time been repeatedly linked to a morbid and unhealthy temperament. The case of James Tilly Matthews, as described by John Haslam, director of the Bethlem Hospital, in 1810, is perhaps the earliest example of a clinical description of thought-transference. Matthews was a London tea merchant who, in the early 1790s, as England looked set for war with France, embroiled himself in attempts to broker peace. Imprisoned in Paris for three years, Matthews returned to England and began another one-man mission, accusing Lord Liverpool, the Home Secretary, of treason. Matthews's public rebuke of Lord Liverpool led him directly to the Bethlem Hospital, where he eventually confided in Haslam, describing how an 'Air Loom' (a fanciful bricolage of pneumatic chemistry, mesmerism and fermentation, controlled by a shadowy gang of 'pickpockets or private distillers') was able to remotely overpower his reasoning and speech. The connections between illness and thought-transference were soon discussed more widely. In George Eliot's short story of 1859, 'The Lifted Veil', for example, the angina-suffering Latimer experiences a 'diseased participation in other people's consciousness', his illness making others' thoughts and feelings all too audible.

For a cleric such as Creery to be now engaged in experiments that tested the *natural* capacity for thought-transference suggested that mesmerism and spiritualism had at least given the phenomenon a modicum of respectability. The SPR's frontline of Cambridge intellectuals, Frederic Myers, Edmund Gurney, Henry Sidgwick and William Barrett, would move towards explaining telepathy as a subconscious or subliminal process, but this did not preclude some speculation on the material (or the 'metetherial') plane on which telepathic communication might take place. Either way, thought-transference was being rehabilitated.

It was to William Barrett, Professor of Physics at the Royal College of Science in Dublin, that the Reverend Creery wrote expressing his conviction of his daughters' psychical talents. In 1882, the year in which the SPR's Frederic Myers coined the word 'telepathy', the Creery sisters appeared to have reached the height of their powers. William Barrett and various members of the SPR all undertook trials (mainly guessing hidden cards and names), but Barrett's results were far and away the most impressive. In April of the same year, he undertook 382 trials with the Creerys and reported that '127 were successes on the first attempt, 56 on the second'. Among these, Barrett counted two runs of eight consecutive cards and names, the odds of the former being in excess of 140 million to one. Barrett claimed that these experiments made collusion impossible, yet later experiments revealed that the sisters had in fact utilised a system of communication. It is impossible to ascertain whether the Creerys' earliest successes were also fraudulent, whether the sisters only began to collude once their 'powers' were in decline or, indeed, if some 'experimenter effect' was at work. These issues are important ones for parapsychology, but the historian has other equally pertinent questions to ask. Why was the practice and theory of telepathy beginning to arouse so much interest in the late nineteenth and early twentieth centuries? What were the social and intellectual conditions in which mental mediumship prospered?

The decline of the hypnotic séance, the context in which thought-transference had been first observed, was certainly the most decisive factor in the rise of telepathy. Since the 1780s, mesmerised subjects had been thought able to receive 'impressions', or to experience a 'community of sensation' with persons near and far. By the 1860s, as medical and public interest in hypnosis was declining, its attendant phenomena began to relocate, finding a safe house in the spiritualist movement. Gurney and Myers both took a keen interest in hypnosis, having acted as observers to many experiments, including those of Charcot and Liebault; however, neither of them considered the hypnotic trance a necessary condition for psychic powers to emerge. Their compendium of 'crisis apparitions', *Phantasms of the Living* (1886), documented 702 cases of hallucinations 'generated in the percipient by the receipt of a *telepathic* "message" from the dying agent'. Telepathy was thus beginning to provide an explanatory buttress for other psychic phenomena.

In the first decades of the twentieth century, psychical research formed an extramural wing of mainstream psychology. The involvement of noted psychologists such as William James and William McDougall provided intellectual validation for psychical research, which at this time relied so heavily on well-heeled amateurs and weekend hobbyists. As Alan Gauld notes, it was only when psychology became increasingly experimental that psychical research went into academic exile. When this academic sponsorship was removed, there was a conspicuous demise in the number of telepathic mediums. And it was not only orthodox psychology that allowed parapsychology to founder in the doldrums of disbelief: another scientific *bête noire*, psychoanalysis, eventually refused to lend its support.

The relationship between psychoanalysis and parapsychology was for many years unconsummated. Freud's famous remarks on the 'the black tide of mud – of occultism', addressed to Jung in 1910, are, nevertheless, too often highlighted as evidence of a highly sceptical relationship with psychical research. 'What Freud seemed to mean by occultism', Jung reflected, 'was virtually everything that philosophy and religion, including the science of parapsychology, had learned about the psyche'. But Jung's remark is misleading, especially in relation to telepathy. From 1911, Freud took an active interest in the SPR. Having touched on the subject of telepathy in his early work on dreams, and having later conducted informal experiments with friends and colleagues, he retained a wavering and ambivalent attitude towards psychical evidence.

In Freud's 1921 conference paper 'Psychoanalysis and Telepathy', the true source of this uncertainty appears to be skirted. Here Freud begins by suggesting that a rapprochement of occultism and psychoanalysis was both 'plausible and promising', but then makes a sharp U-turn. 'The overwhelming majority of occultists are not motivated by a thirst for knowledge . . . On the contrary, they are believers who want to find new proofs.' If the analyst was to adopt this attitude when tending to his own investigations in the unconscious, he would, Freud insisted, without any hint of irony, 'lose that unbiased, impartial attitude, which, up to now, was an essential part of his analytic armour and equipment'.

The jeopardising of analytic sang-froid was not, however, the most important reason for Freud's reticence towards psychical research. Psychoanalysis had gained a good deal of respectability – Freud was not about to expose his empire of the unconscious to allegations of credulousness and irrationality. In a much misquoted letter to Hereward Carrington, an American psychical researcher who had repeated exposed spiritualist trickery, Freud confided that: 'If I were at the beginning rather than the end of a scientific career, as I am today, I might possibly choose just this field of study – in spite of all difficulties.' But this was not his last word on the subject. Freud's attitude towards telepathy – despite, apparently, having no personal or professional experience of the phenomenon – was becoming less doubtful. A 1922 paper on telepathy in dreams was, on the advice of his British disciple and hagiographer Ernest Jones, heavily edited before publication. This was not the only occasion on which Jones would be called upon to police the boundaries between psychoanalysis and para-psychology. Three years later, after reading Gilbert Murray's reports on telepathic experiments, Freud announced himself 'ready to give up my opposition to the existence of thought-transference . . . I should even be prepared to lend the support of psychoanalysis to the matter of telepathy'. Jones, the recipient of this letter, quickly dispatched a circular warning initiates of the dangers of such a move.

There was no shortage of corresponding reports among other analysts. When the psychoanalyst Jan Ehrenwald published *Telepathy and Medical Psychology* in 1947, providing still more detailed evidence, the subject nevertheless remained a controversial one for psychoanalysts. Ehrenwald argued that the true extent of 'telepathic leakage' could easily elude analysts, especially those who were unaware of their personal blind spots. Telepathy was, he insisted, a bona fide form of unconscious transmission of material, usually generated by the therapist's own interests and pre-occupations. Ehrenwald also noted the marked tendency for patients to dream 'Freudian', 'Rankian', 'Adlerian' and 'Jungian' dreams for their respective analysts and suggested that a kind of 'doctrinal compliance' was at work.

When psychical research did eventually begin to make inroads into American universities in the 1930s, the study of spontaneous telepathy, clinical or otherwise, was sidelined in favour of laboratory testing and statistical analysis in the general population. Gifted subjects did emerge, but the focus remained quantitative. This transition, from psychical research to parapsychology, was largely due to the efforts of J. B. Rhine, a botanist turned psychologist whose previous investigations of spiritualist phenomena had led the spiritualist and one-time SPR member Arthur Conan Doyle to pronounce him 'a monumental ass'. When, at the invitation of William McDougall, Rhine established his laboratory at Duke University, he concentrated his efforts on devising controlled experiments that would eliminate the possibility of sensory cues and maximise statistical accuracy. Much of his early laboratory work was centred on studies of clairvoyance and precognition using the newly designed Zener cards – based on five symbols: a star, three vertical wavy lines, a plus sign, a circle and a square – but it was not until the late 1930s that Rhine began to test for 'Pure Telepathy'. These experiments confirmed what an earlier generation of psychical researchers had observed. First, 'the decline effect' was commonplace: extended high scoring in telepathy experiments would almost invariably soon drop to chance level. Second, boredom, tiredness and introspection produced poor results: subjects appeared to perform best when they were relaxed and motivated.

As much as Rhine's extensive research helped to develop a conceptual framework and experimental protocol for parapsychology, placing it on a surer footing with mainstream science, its remit was narrowly empirical. The investigation of laboratory telepathy (via card-guessing) did little to advance an understanding of telepathy in its natural and spontaneous forms. Many experimenters who claimed previous experiences found the laboratory an alien and inhibiting environment, its techniques too restrictive. When the aviator Sir Hubert Wilkins and Harold Sherman carried out a well-documented series of sixty-eight telepathy tests between 1937 and 1938, the tests with the Zener cards proved the least successful. As Wilkins later noted, 'it is the highly emotional or exciting thoughts that are most apt to get through, and to make an impression on another mind'.

With the British SPR adopting the methodology and protocol Rhine had developed, spontaneous accounts of telepathy became, as Rosalind Heywood recalls in her paranormal memoirs, 'quite out of fashion as evidence of its existence'. It was not until the very early 1950s that Dr Louisa Rhine, J. B.'s wife and co-researcher, began to survey and report on spontaneous ESP experiences and that a second generation of parapyschologists began, in parallel, to study the general psychology of telepathy – personality types, emotionality and arousal, the role of fantasy, beliefs and motivations, etc. The most emphatic finding claimed by these latter studies was a correlation between extroversion and above-chance telepathy. However, as if to prove the tenuous nature of statistical analysis, a 1964 study on the effect of time of day on performance suggested that extroverts performed better in the afternoon, introverts better in the morning.

The empirical approach also ignored another body of evidence.

From the very beginnings of psychical research in the 1880s, the wider historical and anthropological evidence for telepathy was thought to be extensive. The folklorist Andrew Lang, president of the SPR in the 1890s, had sought to bring about a synthesis of psychological and ethnological perspectives in the study of telepathy and other so-called 'magical' powers and beliefs, but his suggestions had only provided ammunition for opponents of the SPR. One of the most vehement of the SPR's critics, Edward Clodd, whose antipathy to psychical research almost equalled that of the eminent physiologist Hermann von Helmholtz (who once declared that he would not accept any evidence for telepathy, even if advanced by all the members of the scientific academy), argued that Lang's proposal showed that 'telepathic energy' and 'subliminal consciousness' were nothing more than primitive spiritualism in modern dress.

The assumption that telepathy is widely documented in historical and anthropological archives remains widespread. In a recent interview, Rupert Sheldrake, a British researcher who has conducted research into animal–human telepathy, claimed: 'Modern, urban humans of the educated type are not very good [at telepathy]. Educated people, if they believe in telepathy, feel they can't admit it in public. People in traditional, non-Western societies are far better at these things, at least according to anecdotal accounts.' Sheldrake's explanation of the imputed demise of telepathy, as a consequence of the rise of 'simpler, more direct and more reliable technological means of achieving distant communication', extends beyond the parapsychological community. In William Golding's 1955 novel *The Inheritors*, the Neanderthals are, for instance, seen to communicate through the direct transmission of 'pictures'. But where exactly is the pre-technological evidence of telepathy?

When the classical historian and psychical researcher E. R. Dodds took stock of the facts in the 1920s, he claimed that 'telepathic action is as old as history and as wide as the world'. As an indication of this ubiquity, Dodds pointed, in the random fashion of one apparently faced with a surfeit of historical records, to Maori apparitions of husbands presumed dead; to the visions of

Cornelius (who distantly saw Caesar triumph at Pharsalia); to Pliny's description of visionary trances among the Greeks; and to many more recent apparitions of the kind catalogued by Gurney and his co-workers in *Phantasms of the Living*. What is notable about Dodds's back catalogue is that only one of the phenomena he mentions involves *the remote perception of the mental state of another person*. The events Dodds lists are generally instances of precognition and clairvoyance 'which the modern psychical researcher would ascribe to telepathic action'. This is interpolation, not history.

The claims made for telepathy as a vestige of a primitive W*eltanschauung* need to be interrogated closely. If a renowned classicist such as Dodds failed to provide one single pre-modern example of telepathic experience, then telepathy (whether genuine, fraudulent or imagined) might perhaps be better examined as a response to technological innovations that have collapsed spatial and temporal boundaries, allowing us to be remotely present to each other. The 'willing game' that the Creerys and other Victorian families participated in was certainly not the first popular experiment in telepathy. As far back as 1696, readers of the Dutch publication *Vallemont's Physique Occulte* were being invited to try out a 'curious and well-tried secret' called a 'sympathetic compass'. Comprising a pair of boxed lodestone compasses the outer rims of which contained the letters of the alphabet, the sympathetic compass allowed one to 'communicate with a distant friend, and impart to him one's intentions instantaneously or almost instantaneously'.

Speaking in Tongues

Soon after the resurrection of Christ, the disciples found their grief mysteriously lifted as 'they were all filled with the Holy Spirit and began to speak in other tongues'. As 'devout men from every nation under heaven' came to witness these ecstatic outpourings, these pilgrims were perplexed to hear the Galileans speaking in their own tongues, while the disciples themselves were unable to comprehend the words they spoke. In his first letter to the Corinthians, Paul explained that the gift of tongues took different forms: 'To one its gives through the Spirit the utterance of Wisdom, and to another the utterance of knowledge . . . to another the gift of healing . . . the working of miracles.' The power to interpret these utterances could, furthermore, only be visited by the Spirit.

The practice of glossolalia, or speaking in tongues, was relatively common within the early church. By the second century AD, it was subject to its first revival as the Montanist movement, seeking to return to the essence of Christianity, embraced this form of ecstatic worship as a direct communion with the Holy Spirit. Since then, other evangelical and charismatic movements have periodically adopted this form of communal worship. It is today most associated with the American Pentecostal movement, where speaking in tongues is perceived as a sign of divine grace.

Glossolalia should not, however, be considered a uniquely Christian phenomenon. Felicitias D. Goodman's analysis of glossolalia as a type of senseless speech with characteristic vocalisations (alien and high-pitched sounds which suddenly increase in volume, hyperventilation and pronounced glottal constrictions) and stereotyped patterns of stress and duration lends it a more general connection with the trance state. Irrespective of the language and culture of the ecstatic speaker, Goodman regards glossolalia as a symptom of dissociation (a state of divided consciousness, in which there may be no awareness of thoughts and actions) and hyperarousal of the body's nervous system. Although their respective speech patterns are often dissimilar, Goodman claims that Christian glossolalia is closely related to the babblings of schizophrenics and, more obliquely, to the 'animal languages' of shamanism.

Other anthropologists and sociologists have denied this implied connection to the trance state. Most notably, William Samarin has argued that the charismatic speech observed among Pentecostal congregations is essentially a learned behaviour. Far from requiring an abandonment of will, 'the tongue speaker is most often a sophisticated user of speech, selecting this and that variable with considerable delicacy'. This is consistent with the reports of some charismatic speakers who claim to have an active and mindful engagement with the Spirit throughout, but it does not apply to all outbursts of glossolalia, especially those that have not been subject to 'driving' by a minister, congregation or other third party. These spontaneous or self-induced instances of ecstatic speech are clearly linked to trance states. One laboratory study found that the EEG profile of a natural speaker in tongues showed bursts of spikelike activity emanating from one or both of the temporal lobes. No signs of any altered activity were observed in a Pentecostal-trained speaker in tongues.

Whether glossolalia is at root a social or a mental phenomenon, or a combination of both, it has consistently led speakers and spectators alike to read meaning into its half-sung, half-grunted utterances. The need to equate these vocalisations with speech takes various forms. The reaction that Saint Paul reported among the first observers of the apostle's speaking in tongues – all of whom mistakenly thought their own language being spoken – is not uncommon.

The case of 'Albert Le Baron', reported in the *Proceedings of the Society for Psychical Research* in 1896, was typical. At the age of thirty-nine, Le Baron (the pseudonym for a minor American writer whose vocal automatisms were studied and recorded by William James and Richard Hodgson) was undergoing a minor breakdown. Summering with members of an 'esoteric camp' who had direct experience of glossolalia, Le Baron began suddenly to speak in excitable phrases that appeared to emanate from outside his consciousness. The episode was short lived, but more were to follow. Soon, his thinking and temperament were completely transformed. In the words of one anonymous correspondent, 'Where he was formerly despondent, he is now optimistic, and at peace with himself.'

Le Baron believed that he had unwittingly mastered an ancient or remote language. Consequently, he kept a journal of this phonetically transcribed tongue and dedicated much of his time and energy to locating its source. Having studied Coptic, Romany and Dravidian, he sent out specimen transcripts to various linguists. Slowly and reluctantly disabused of his conviction, he eventually came to recognise that, in the words of William James, 'the whole thing was a decidedly rudimentary form of motor automatism'.

Le Baron's search for the language that lay behind his trance utterances was not unprecedented. A full century before his case was discussed in print, Coleridge's *Biographia Literaria* report that various German physicians and physiologists had investigated the case of a young illiterate woman who, while seized by a nervous fever, had begun to speak a convoluted mixture of Latin, Greek and Hebrew. These 'ravings' were transcribed and studied, but little connection could be found between individual phrases:

> In the town, in which she was resident for many years as a servant in different families, no solution presented itself. The young physician [who had initially attended to her], however, determined to trace her past life step by step; for the patient herself was incapable of returning a rational answer. He at length succeeded in discovering the place where her parents had lived . . . [it transpired that] the patient had been charitably taken by an old Protestant pastor at nine years old, and had remained with him for some years . . . it appeared that it had been the old man's custom

to for years to walk up and down a passage house into which the kitchen door opened, and to read to himself with a loud voice out of his favourite books . . . he was a very learned man and a great Hebraist. Among the books were found a collection of rabbinical writings, together with several of the Greek and Latin fathers; and the physician succeeded in identifying so many passages with those taken down at the young woman's bedside that no doubt could remain in any rational mind concerning the true impression name on her nervous system.

Instances of xenoglossia – the mistaken recognition of a foreign language – are still to be found in contemporary reports. One minister's 'foreign' outpourings were recognised as both Polish and Arabic; another Pentecostal convert reported singing and speaking in 'Greek and Latin, and Chinese and other languages I had never heard'. The subject of an LSD experiment who thought his strange, glossolalia-like pronouncements to be vestiges of a lost *ursprache*, the original language of mankind, echoed the lasting belief that there exists a primordial language which, when ecstatically revived, speaks to the animal and spirit world.

Cosmic Luv

Accounts of alien abduction first appeared in the 1950s, almost a full decade after the first modern UFO sighting (by American pilot Kenneth Arnold in the Cascade Mountains in Washington) triggered a wave of virtual visitations across the world. One of the first reported cases of UFO abduction was that of Antonio Villas Boas, a Brazilian farmer who, in 1957, reported having been captured by three silver-suited creatures who emerged from a dish-shaped craft with red and green flashing lights. After having been carried on board the craft, Villas Boas claimed that his diminutive abductors, all less than five feet tall, conversed to each other in doglike barks and animal grunts, undressed him and submitted him to a physical examination. Twice seduced by a naked humanoid, the dazed farmer was taken on a tour of the craft before being released.

Unlike previous contactees such as George King, who adventured out of body, Villas Boas's abduction was above all a physical ordeal. His four-hour misadventure left him exhausted, with strange marks across his hands and limbs. In this and other respects, his story – reported the day after the Russians sent Sputnik 1 into orbit – proved a dress rehearsal for later alien abductions. The theme of the sexual encounter and the extra-terrestrial mission to reproduce would, however, only emerge as the true theme of the abduction experience in the 1960s and 1970s, when ufologists and regression therapists began to assume their roles as narrative detectives and amplifiers. When the sexual narrative established itself, Villas Boas would, much later, add further details to his story that concurred with it.

The lodestar for modern abduction experiences is that of Betty and Barney Hill, whose story was first reported in the Boston press in 1965. Driving back to New Hampshire from Canada, husband and wife were trailed by a hovering disc with fins and flashing lights. For several minutes they stopped to watch the craft through binoculars, spying 'crew members behind glass' who were also observing them. On returning home, they realised that they could not account for two hours of missing time and that their return journey was thirty-five miles less than their outward. Ten days after reporting the sighting – but not the figures behind the portholes – Betty began to have nightmares. Before being referred to Boston psychiatrist Benjamin Simon, both the Hills were interviewed by air force intelligence officers and UFO investigators, all of whom were interested in verifying the nature of the craft. Over several months, Dr Simon assisted the Hills in recovering memories of a 'pregnancy test' by way of a machine composed of needles. Eventually, Betty also recalled conversations and astronomical maps, bypassing the 'post-hypnotic block' that the aliens had employed. (After the Hill story broke, an amateur astronomer called Marjorie Fish studied Betty's drawings of the star system and identified the alien abductors as natives of the star system Zeta Reticuli.)

Born in the 1950s, in the first heady days of manned space exploration, as scientists first sought to tune into extraterrestrial radio signals and pop culture was suffused with planet-eyed, intergalactic anticipation, the alien abduction is a child of its time. Space science and sci-fi clearly provided many of the stage props for the first wave of abductees. In the case of the Hills, various aspects of their abduction present, as Michel Meurger notes in a recent essay, 'strong affinities with scenes from visual science fiction in movies or TV programmes'. The gynaecological instrument that Betty Hill describes, for example, appears to be a rehash of the alien machinery which was a conspicuous feature of 1930s sci-fi.

The folk science of ufology, which now controls and polices the demi-monde of the alien abduction, claims that up to 3000 persons a day are abducted by aliens in America. The individual details of alien abduction may vary to the extent that aliens and their modes of transport and communication sometimes assume different forms, but the basic plot almost always centres on some form of bodily intervention (mindscan, gynaecological examination, embryo extraction, psychosurgical implant, sperm collection or insemination) for the creation of new offspring. Attempts to retrieve material from the spacecraft are always thwarted, although the abductee may retain visible signs of his ordeal – cosmic stigmata. More importantly, what unites these abduction narratives is their collective production. They are co-authored stories, assisted memories, which rely on the involvement of therapists and ufologists. As Elaine Showalter notes in her study of their hysterical production and transmission, it is now more or less impossible to disentangle the alien abduction from ufology: 'Only when abductees talked with ufologists who knew the meta-narratives did patterns emerge. All the abductees had lost their memories and had to be treated with hypnosis – an obstacle, or perhaps an advantage, for researchers.'

The diversity that was once characteristic of the accounts of early UFO contactees was, when managed by hypnosis and ufology, shaped into a folk narrative. Once appearing dressed in silver suits or wrapped in cellophane, the unstyled aliens of old have donned a standard uniform. And aside from the uniform, there is a stock physiognomy: grey-skinned, dome-headed and bug-eyed. This consistency of narrative is, however, only achieved through the wholesale rejection of some stories, and the manipulation and censorship of others. When, for instance, an abductee's report diverges from the typical UFO narrative, a therapist may view it as a screen memory, perhaps implanted by aliens to prevent true recollection of events. And when ufologists claim that almost no abductee fails to describe in great detail the dark, almond shaped eyes of the alien 'greys' or that '[the] pattern [of abduction motifs] is an indication that something real – whatever it may be – is happening', this uniformity is never innocent. It is actively fashioned by unwitting oversight or deliberate exclusion.

Even within the New Age rank and file, alien abductees have been regarded with a certain amount of derision and mistrust.

Harvard Professor of Psychiatry John Mack has, however, lent a degree of respectability to their stories. From his clinical experience of treating more than seventy abductees, Mack has sided with his patients, to defend the reality of their experiences. Mack's reliance on regression hypnosis, and his insistence that it clarifies more than it distorts, does nevertheless cast a lingering shadow on the abduction experience. The same applies to Whitley Strieber, whose bestselling account of his alien abduction, *Communion: a True Story* (1987), reads, by his own admission, as a successor to his previous works of fiction.

As much as these practices indicate that the alien abduction scenario is shaped and rubber-stamped to order, there is also much to suggest that alien abduction belongs to a more free-floating and long-running narrative. There are many similarities between abduction stories, captivity narratives of early American settlers and tales of medical body-snatching. Further back in history, the visions of prophets such as Ezekiel (whose descriptions of heavenly throne-chariots and strange cherubim have led to him being claimed as a kind of honorary patron of ufology) and assorted seers suggest that UFOs and possibly even abductions had a place in ancient folklore and religion. More recently, some accounts of near-death experiences have parallels with alien abductions.

The correspondences between alien abduction and religious conversion are also numerous. Just as blazing lights, physical sensations of electricity, the intimation of a higher presence and a sense of tremendous awe are reported in both, long-lasting trans-formations and an entrée into a new-found faith and community, not to mention possible publication of a spiritual autobiography, are equally commonplace. And if, as Max Steur suggests, the methods used by the UFO network to verify alien encounters are the same as those used by the Catholic Church to verify miracles, there is also a common internal hierarchy – contactees who claim voluntary contact with aliens play second fiddle to abductees, who are genuinely 'spontaneous' mystics. All the trademarks of an alternative religion can, in short, be found in the alien abduction. Even the economic and social background of abductees – a study by the British UFO society BUFORA suggests that they are often 'status inconsistent', holding jobs that fall short of their educational and social background – is reminiscent of the great mystics of the sixteenth and seventeenth centuries, who often emerged in economically depressed regions.

While a literary and sociological analysis of the alien abduction account provides valuable insights into its narrative tics and devices, its modes of production and circulation, this approach leaves the nature and veracity of the abduction *experience* on hold. As much as we may doubt the grand narrative, there is still some experience, however elusive, which is being rewritten. Given that the vast majority of abductions occur under the cover of sleep, there is good evidence to suggest that many abductions occur during false awakening. (A common feature of this half-dreaming state is, as previously noted, the experience of sleep paralysis, in which subjects sense an incubus-like presence enter the room and seize their bodies. These sensations tally with accounts of capture and restraint in alien abduction and may be embellished through hypnosis or otherwise.) Waking abductions that involve a period of 'missing time', sometimes running into days, on the other hand, suggest a fugue state in which there may also be genuine amnesia. More unusual experiences of collective abduction, such as that described by Betty and Barney Hill, are perhaps a transient form of *folie à deux*. Lastly, it is notable that experiences of levitation (or of being lifted up and away), of alien mindscan (a kind of hypnotic telepathy performed by the aliens), of implantation and mechanisation, are all familiar in other mystical and psychopathological experiences.

It is, then, quite possible that many 'memories' of alien abduction are assimilations and reworkings of these primary experiences. Some alien abductees are no doubt hoaxers and attention seekers, but the vast majority cannot be simply dismissed as fraudulent. The fact that most abductees genuinely believe their stories is confirmed by polygraph tests – the so-called 'lie detector' may not live up to its name, but it is still a reasonably reliable indicator of truth-telling.

The historian of religion I. P. Couliano suggests that all

otherworldly narratives converge not because they have been culturally transmitted, but because they are based on desires and impulses that are part of a universal cognitive and cultural make-up. The extraterrestrial is, in this sense, one form which the perennial Other assumes – angels, fairies, spirits and other shadowy forms having all, at some time, been of comparable importance. Drug visions, modern and primitive, open a similar portal. Central to the excursions undertaken by the *ayahuasca* shamans of the Amazon, for example, is the experience of travelling to distant and unfamiliar villages, towns and cities inhabited by white people. While this encounter with whites is echoed in the Bwiti cult of Gabon – who employ a powerful hallucinogen, iboga, in their initiation ceremony – and elsewhere in Africa, such narratives are also typical of modern drug visions. The Chilean psychotherapist Claudio Naranjo found that blacks appeared only to the white Chileans who took harmaline (an active compound of the *ayahuasca* drink). When the novelist William Burroughs took *ayahuasca* in the 1950s, his experiences confirmed that the drug's visions were a type of 'space time travel' through the 'blood and substance of many races, Negro, Polynesian, Mountain Mongol, Desert Nomad, Polyglot Near East, Indian, new races as yet unconceived and unborn'.

Of the other drugs known to conjure foreign lands and alien inhabitants, special mention should be made of the psilocybin mushroom, which has, over the past twenty years or so, become a subcultural conduit to an alien world which echoes that described by UFO abductees. Terence McKenna, late high priest of the 'shrooms, has made much of this parallel. 'There is a general futuristic, science fiction quality to the psilocybin experience that seems to originate from the same place as the modern myth of the UFO . . . The issue of contact with the extraterrestrial for a large number of people has been broached by mushrooms.' While the keynote of both the psilocybin-fuelled and classic alien encounter is often highly erotic (McKenna writes of 'alien LUV'), there is nowhere near the same narrative consensus among mushroom eaters. The classic 'greys' described by alien abductees here give way to a parade of alluring sirens, anthropomorphs and fantasy creatures. The mushroom community makes no attempt to standardise these avatars. This is a natural religion, a cosmic gnosticism that deals direct, cutting out the brokers and middlemen to who alien abductees too often turn.

Hunger

'The most effective and upsetting drug, bitterest and most ferocious,' writes the historian Piero Camporesi, 'has always been hunger, creator of unfathomable disturbances of mind and imagination.' Despite these potent effects, historians, psychologists and anthropologists have often neglected the psychological impact of hunger and starvation. The frenzies, manias and deliriums of the Middle Ages are as likely to have been stimulated by famine or drought as they were disease or pestilence. And just as hunger was feared, so were the hungry. 'During such outright starvation,' wrote Jean de Léry in his account of a voyage across the Atlantic in 1540, 'the body becomes exhausted, nature swoons, the senses are alienated, the spirit fades away, and this not only makes people ferocious but provokes a kind of madness.' This madness was always unpredictable. Hunger led to rape, murder and suicide, but it might also be punctuated by periods of euphoria, vitality and fevered imaginings.

These experiences are perhaps the same extremes visited on the early Christian mystics, who turned to fasting and other mortifications as a way of surrendering themselves to God. The 'temptations' that so many of the medieval saints described as inspiring constant horror were, like those of Saint Anthony, a maelstrom of irrational impulses and haunting ideas that had to be resisted. Such inner turmoil has, as Aldous Huxley observed, been intimately linked to fasting and malnutrition:

Much of what the earlier visionaries experienced was terrifying. To use the language of Christian theology, the devil revealed himself more frequently than did God. In an age when vitamins were deficient and a belief in Satan universal, this was not surprising. The mental distress, associated with even mild cases of pellagra and scurvy, was deepened by fears of damnation and a conviction that the powers of evil were omnipresent. This distress was apt to tinge with its own dark colouring through a cerebral valve whose efficiency had been impaired by underfeeding. But in spite of their preoccupations with eternal punishment and in spite of their deficiency disease, spiritually minded ascetics often saw heaven . . . a glimpse of beatitude. Mortification of the body may produce a host of undesirable symptoms; but it may also open a door into a transcendental world.

The ways in which vitamin deficiency can mimic the symptoms of mental illness have only belatedly been recognised by medics and scientists. Pellagra, for example, was identified as a disease produced by dietary deprivation as late as 1937. Aside from the physical symptoms, pellagra causes confusion and amnesia. To plug the gaps of memory, pellagra sufferers confabulate, inventing stories of their whereabouts and activities. In its most severe form, pellagra caused depression, paranoia and permanent psychosis. All these effects are due to a deficit of nicotinic acid, a B complex vitamin.

Looking back on the early nineteenth-century literature on fasting and self-starvation, it is surprising to discover how many physicians claimed that the human body could be nourished and sustained by air alone. Although the French chemist Antoine Lavoisier had shown that food was turned into energy through a combustion process in the mid-eighteenth century, the nutritional value of air provided an enduring explanation for a tradition of miraculous fasting which was now reaching its heyday. The miraculous seven-year fast of Maria van Dijk in 1770s Netherlands, the two-year fast of Maria Kienker in Germany in the 1800s and the seven-year fast of Anne Moore of Tutbury – all, despite being quite rightly decried as impostors, were lent some credence by medical claims that the body could absorb nutrition through respiration or, as some mesmerists later claimed, by the ingestion of 'magnetic fluids'.

Despite the demise of both theories, feats of prolonged fasting continued to be reported in the medical journals. The notorious case of twelve-year-old Sarah Jacob, a.k.a. the 'Welsh Fasting Girl', brought the whole question of food abstinence under the clinical spotlight. After supposedly fasting for two years, Sarah was subjected to a round-the-clock watch, designed to rule out the possibility of deceit. The *Lancet* poured cold water on the idea, upbraiding the vicar of Llanfihangel-ar-Arth and the girl's family for giving credence to 'a most extra-ordinary case'. When, after nine days, Sarah died on 11 December 1869, a chorus of medical voices expressed indignation at the 'cruel demonstration' to which she had been subjected. A *Lancet* editorial regarded its scepticism as now vindicated:

> From the first moment that we heard of this so-called miracle, we did not hesitate to characterise it as a gross imposition. Every scientific man knew that it was a palpable absurdity, and in contravention of all known laws and experience, to suppose that the temperature and development of tissue could have been maintained without any waster or change of substance. The only medical aspect of the case of any interest ought to have been the cure of the child, and this would have been mainly induced by moral means easily accomplished in the wards of a hospital, whither she ought to have been removed long ago.

Most of the commentators agreed that Sarah's 'diseased volition' was a common form of hysteria, but she would soon be would be retroactively diagnosed as a tragic case of anorexia nervosa. This medical reassessment of self-starvation did not, however, lead to any significant study of the *psychological* effects of hunger and malnutrition.

For obvious reasons, experimental psychologists have neglected mental effects of hunger. The only major study of 'semi-starvation', the 'Minnesota Experiment' of the late 1940s, found that that the principal 'symptoms' of semi-starvation over a period of six months (without, it should be stressed, the declining levels of hygiene and sanitation that would usually occur in famine) were lethargy, irritability and depression. Of late, it is only in the field of medical anthropology that we find the experience of hunger reclaimed. Nancy Scheper-Hughes, an anthropologist who has studied the illnesses of the impoverished sugarcane workers of the Brazilian Alto, argues that the common affliction of *nervos* (a folk idiom used throughout North and South America, the Mediterranean and the Middle East to describe feelings of stress, tiredness and anxiety) is the discourse through which symptoms that are often the direct result of hunger are expressed and treated in these areas. This medicalisation of hunger, its transformation into 'breakdown', claims Scheper-Hughes, is a way of neutering political protest by providing workers with 'a safe way to express and register their discontent'.

It is likely that the effects of undernourishment are elsewhere confused with disease and pathology. Misunderstanding of the psychology of hunger may also pervade current perceptions of eating disorders such as anorexia nervosa which are commonly seen as having their roots in modern obsessions around the body and sexuality. As complicated and overdetermined as anorexia is, it is at the very least productive of a state of mind that may bear parallel with the self-denials of Christian mystics. Anorexics often experience perceptual distortions and dissociative experiences. Like all fasting, anorexia is a constant struggle with impulse, a drive for self-mastery that may in abjection find some kind of peace.

Of Lights and Tunnels

On 12 December 1705, John Smith, a burglar and highwayman, was hanged at Tyburn, at the north-eastern corner of London's Hyde Park. As his body dangled from the Tree of Death, a messenger arrived with a belated reprieve. The rope was cut and Smith was taken indoors, where, to the amazement of the gathered onlookers, he revived. Asked what it was like to die, Smith later explained that he had felt his 'spirits in a strange commotion violently rising upwards; which having forced my way to my head . . . saw a great blaze of glaring light, which seemed to go out at my eyes with a flash, and then I lost all sense of pain'.

With their death-defying stories featured in publications such as the *New Wonderful Magazine*, the 'half-hanged' were minor celebrities of their day. Once the gallows began to employ a trap door and extended drop – immediately breaking the spinal cord – the hanged would, however, have no tales to tell. From the mid-eighteenth century onwards, principal witness to near death instead came from the almost drowned. When the psychologists Albert Heim and Charles Feré reported accounts of these near-death survivors in the late 1880s, spiritualists such as Madame Blavatsky, the founder of theosophy, quickly claimed such experiences as evidence of 'the ultimate ectasis' in her *Secret Doctrine*:

[A]s we approach the end . . . horizons of vaster, profounder knowledge are drawn on, bursting upon our mental vision, and becoming with every hour plainer to our inner eye. Otherwise, how account for those bright flashes of memory, or prophetic insight that comes as often to the enfeebled grandsire, as to the youth who is passing away? The nearer some approach death, the brighter becomes their long lost memory and the more correct the previsions. The unfoldment of the inner faculties increases as the life-blood becomes more stagnant.

By the early 1970s, when Raymond Moody embarked on his pioneering study of near-death experiences, *Life after Life*, modern medical intervention had revived countless individuals from illness and accident. Interviewing 150 survivors, Moody found remarkable similarities in their accounts. A ringing or buzzing sound was often heard as the dying person felt herself travelling bodilessly, at high speed, down a dark tunnel. At the end of the tunnel, the dying person might be met by a 'Being of Light', with whom she could enter into silent communication. Spirits of deceased family and friends might appear, or the patient might experience the 'Life Review', a comprehensive replay of her life to date. The experience was almost always serene and tranquil, to the point that many reported reluctance to return to their bodies. The effects of a near-death experience (NDE) were, according to Moody's research, always powerful and lasting.

When Atlanta cardiologist Michael B. Sabom began to investigate the NDE more methodically, he was initially sceptical of Moody's claims, stating that individuals who undergo these 'death experiences suffer from a hypoxic state, during which they tried to deal psychologically with the anxieties provoked by medical procedure'. After he had interviewed more than one hundred returnees, Sabom recanted. Distinguishing the first stages of near-death, in which patients 'observed' themselves and efforts to revive them, often from a detached or elevated position, from its visionary resolution, he suggested that no adequate psychological explanation could be offered. Leaning towards 'alternative, perhaps less traditional, explanations', positing 'some sort of mind brain split', Sabom rejected explanation of the NDE as a subconscious phenomenon. These were certainly not delusions or dreams. Near-death experiences were, he maintained, full-blown voyages of the soul.

Sabom's research did more than corroborate Raymond Moody's outline of NDE. His rejection of a psychological or medical model helped to foster the Aquarian sensibility that still sustains much of the research and interest in near-death, especially in the United States, where almost 15 million people have, according to one vastly inflated estimate, undergone an NDE. As much as subsequent research has adapted Moody's and Sabom's findings, putting forward countless other typologies and variations, it has consistently endorsed NDE as an initiation into a quasi-religious movement. While not all researchers claim NDE as an otherworldly initiation, the eagerness with which some have endorsed the unfounded claims that it 'expands and enhances faculties not normally available to us', allowing 'access to more of the electromagnetic spectrum' indicates that it has become a repository for a good deal of ersatz science.

The visions experienced on near-death are, however, by no means unique to clinical resuscitation. Many of the same emotions, sensations and insights have been reported in mystical and drug-induced experiences. Ketamine, a dissociative anaesthetic, is, for example, one of a number of substances that can reproduce all the features associated with the NDE. (These effects are generally attributed to the action of ketamine on the brain's NMDA receptors, which have a key role in cognitive processing, memory and perception.) Ketamine users are often convinced that they have died. As with many other anaesthetic and dissociative drugs, ketamine induces a sense of disembodied travel, often through a tunnel or hole. And just as near-death survivors are able to describe the details of their resuscitation, ketamine 'can permit sufficient sensory input to allow accounts of procedures during which the patient appeared wholly unconscious'.

Antiquity also furnishes accounts of near-death. In the *Republic*, Plato recounts the story of a soldier, Er, who, after being wounded and left for dead, travels to the middle of the universe, where he sees souls in transit between heaven and hell, and learns the secrets of transmigration. The Venerable Bede, writing in the eighth century AD, tells of a devout man from Northumberland, Drythelm, who, 'to the consternation of those weeping around the body', returned to life in 696. To those 'willing to take his words to heart and grow in holiness', the man described how an angel in a shining robe had guided him. After being taken to a hellish underworld the flames of which were full of human souls, Drythelm travelled through valleys and meadows before coming into a lightness 'greater than the brightness of daylight or of the sun's rays at noon'. Later medieval visionaries, whose writings were repeatedly embellished, often described the same tour, paying particular reference to hell's 'narrowing bridge'.

More genuine parallels with today's near-death experience are contained in the *Tibetan Book of the Dead*, the six bardos of which provide specific and detailed guidance to the dying. More relevantly, the Himalayas had until recently a living tradition of *deloks*, ordinary villagers who having returned from the dead were able to repeat their journey, passing messages to, or requesting information from, the deceased. The powers employed by *deloks* bring to mind the spirit journeys of the Amazonian and Arctic healers who act as conduits between the worlds of the living and the dead. As psychopomps, escorts to the souls of the dead, shamans undertake a journey into regions they have navigated. The death and resurrection that many shamans undergo as part of their initiation is clearly a kind of near-death experience in all but name.

There are, of course, differences between the shamanic journey and the NDE, past and present. Each is to a large extent coloured by conventions and belief. From a clinical perspective, all NDEs nevertheless represent a particular form of dissociation or psychological self-detachment that is an adaptive response to trauma, distress and sensory deprivation. While a number of writers have interpreted the light and tunnel experience as a memory of birth, or as passage into an actual beyond, a more convincing explanation of this visionary motif is as an effect of heightened stimulation of the central nervous system and the production of light on the retina. Many of the elements that are 'universally' characteristic of the NDE, from geometric forms to the 'life review', do not require metaphysical explanation: they are best explained in terms of a secret heritage called 'the body'.

The Song of Solitude

Across the New World and the Siberian Arctic, the would-be shaman or seer was once required to leave his home and family to prepare for ecstatic initiation in seclusion. In the initiation of a shaman among the Ammasalik Inuits, the neophyte would, for example, be instructed how to isolate himself by an old grave or lake, where he would rub two stones together while waiting for his helping spirits to reveal themselves. The ordeals and rituals of shamanic initiation have differed widely across different cultures, but exile of some sort seems to have always been essential for obtaining powers of divination or healing. When all other techniques failed, isolation provided a last opportunity. An Iglulik Inuit gave the polar explorer Knud Rasmussen this account of her eventual transformation into an *angakok*:

> Then I sought solitude, and here I soon became very melancholy. I would sometimes fall to weeping, and feel unhappy without knowing why. Then, for no reason, all would suddenly be changed, and I felt a great inexplicable joy, a joy so powerful that I could not restrain it, but had to break into song, a mighty song, with only room for one word: joy . . . And then in the midst of mysterious and overwhelming delight I became a shaman, not knowing myself how it came about. I could see and hear in a totally different way.

Echoing one of the features that Vladimir Propp has recognised as a near-universal theme in world folklore, the initiation of the shamanic or magical 'hero' first requires him to be absented from his society. But unlike the heroes of folklore, the successful shaman can never fully return from his magical quest. The bestowal of visionary or psychic powers implies a permanent break with society. As much as he serves his people, he is always partly elsewhere, in contact with the spirit world.

While Christianity and the monotheistic religions have always had an ambivalent and uneasy relationship with the ritualised solitude of primitive religion, the Christian saints and mystics still bear witness to the revelations of ascetic isolation at its most protracted. The example of Saint Anthony, who is reputed to have lived without human contact for twenty years, was followed by other anchorites, who withdrew to the desert to endure solitude and self-mortification, which would enable them to commune with the divine and attain Christian oneness. In the fourth century AD, when the influence of these desert fathers spread to the West, the urge to contemplative isolation would be at once accommodated and diluted within monastic orders.

At some point in the eighteenth century, isolation underwent another form of institutionalisation. Rejecting the casual brutalities of incarceration, the penitentiaries built by the Pennsylvania Quakers attempted to use isolation to induce spiritual conversion, providing a space for silent reflection and Bible reading. Driven by this moral imperative, the modern prison became, in the words of Michel Foucault, 'a machine for altering minds'. Its effects were only slowly recognised as more damaging than illuminating. Isolation caused restlessness, insomnia, inability to concentrate, memory failure, delirium, self-mutilation and, in many cases, suicide.

The first laboratory reports of the effects of sensory isolation came from McGill University, Canada, where, in 1954, D. O. Hebb and his colleagues placed student volunteers in a semi-soundproof cubicle, with translucent goggles that prevented patterned vision and gloves that impaired tactile sensation. Kept in these conditions for two to three days, fed but allowed limited communication, almost all of the twenty-nine subjects experienced profound alterations in their thinking and perception. In twenty-five cases, visual imagery proved the most dramatic manifestation of sensory isolation. Beyond the amorphous or geometric filigrees that were seen by almost all the subjects, some of these visions involved complex imagery such as 'a procession of squirrels with sacks over their shoulders, moving purposefully across a snowfield'. In one case, these images were vivid enough to lead one volunteer to believe that they were being projected onto his goggles by the experimenters. Other significant effects produced by the experiment included drastic and bizarre alterations to the body schema and out-of-body experiences.

When John Lilly adapted these techniques at the US National Institute of Mental Health in Maryland, he was able to achieve comparable effects within a few hours. Lying suspended in a 'tranquillity tank' filled with salt water, in a sound- and lightproof room, Lilly reported that 'other people apparently joined me in this dark silent environment. I could actually see them, feel them, and hear them. At other times, I went through dreamlike sequences . . . in which I watched what was happening. At other times I apparently tuned in on networks of communication that are normally below our levels of awareness, networks of civilisations way beyond ours.' When Lilly combined sensory isolation with LSD, in a series of now famous experiments, these effects were magnified to the extent that he was able to move within himself, to explore his internal organs and nervous system, to travel to other planets and make contact with other life forms.

The mental phenomena that Lilly and other experimenters were able to induce through prolonged spells of sensory isolation were comparable to those described by explorers, astronauts and prisoners. In a review of the hallucinatory experiences of hostage survivors, the psychiatrist Ronald K. Siegel found that eight out of thirty interviewees had experienced hallucinations directly paralleling those reported in sensory deprivation, moving from the abstractly geometric to the fully realised. That isolation and life-threatening stress provide sufficient conditions for such hallucinations has also been borne out by accounts of solo explorers. Sailing around the world in the 1890s, the yachtsman Joshua Slocum found that the 'dismal fog' of loneliness was able to revive his memory with startling acuity. 'The wonderful, the insignificant, the commonplace – all appeared before my mental vision in magical succession. Pages of my history were recalled which had been so long forgotten that they seemed to belong to a previous existence. I heard all the voices of my past laughing, crying, telling what I had heard them tell in many corners of the earth.'

Less intense forms of social isolation have also proved able to fire the imagination, stirring thoughts and feelings that are entirely novel. When Henry Thoreau set up home in the woods of Massachusetts in the 1840s, his two-year experiment in self-sufficiency produced moments of 'slight insanity' which were quickly tempered by an intimation of the numinous presence of nature at its most beneficent. 'Every little pine needle', he wrote of one nature epiphany, 'expanded and swelled with sympathy, and befriended me. I was so distinctly aware of the presence of something kindred to me, even in scenes which we are accustomed to call wild and dreary . . . that I thought no place could ever be strange to me again.' Animism is the comfort, the religion, the song of the solitary.

Acknowledgements

Bill Broady, Colin Campbell, Mike Jay, Francesco Melechi, Michael Neve, Derroll Palmer, Giorgio Samorini and Ronald Sandison all provided tip-offs, comments or encouragement for which I am extremely grateful. A visiting fellowship in the Department of Sociology, University of York, facilitated much of the research and writing. For commissions which have, over the years, allowed me to explore some of the many areas I've covered in this book, thanks to Bob Rickard at the *Fortean Times*, Greg Neale at *BBC History Magazine*, Anna Vaux at the *Times Literary Supplement* and Gareth Evans at *Entropy*. Staff at Baildon Library, the Reading Room of the British Library at Boston Spa, the Wellcome Institute Library and the inter-library loans desk at York University Library – all helped me to obtain out-of-the-way books and journals. Finally, thanks to my agent, Lavinia Trevor, for getting me started.

Bibliography

The Schizophrenic Sentence

While there is no shortage of secondary literature on Daniel Paul Schreber, much of it is testimony to the fatuity of armchair psychoanalysis. Morton Schatzman's *Soul Murder* (Harmondsworth: Allen Lane, 1973) makes a convincing argument for a more direct connection between Schreber's insanity and his father's system of child pedagogy.

Thomas Hennell's *The Witnesses* (New York: University Books, 1967) is unfortunately long out of print.

Nancy Andreasen, an English professor turned psychiatrist, has examined the nature of schizophrenic language in a series of articles, including 'Thought, Language and Communication Disorders: I', *Archives of General Psychiatry*, vol. 36, 1979, p. 1318, and 'Thought, Language and Communication Disorders: II', pp. 1325–30 of the same volume.

Beyond the case study of 'Joseph' the inveterate writer, Lauren Slater's *Welcome to My Country* (Harmondsworth: Penguin, 1996) has some moving portraits of catatonic schizophrenia and acute depression.

Hearts of Stone

Stanley W. Jackson's *Melancholia and Depression: From Hippocratic to Modern Times* (New Haven and London: Yale University Press, 1986) is the most complete and scholarly history of depression through the ages. Chapter 5 of Edward Shorter's *From the Mind into the Body: The Cultural Origins of Psychosomatic Illness* (New York: Free Press, 1994) highlights the changing physical symptoms of depression.

Robert Burton's often-quoted, little-read *Anatomy of Melancholy* (*New York Review of Books*, New York, 2001) is said to have been the only book that took Johnson out of bed two hours sooner than he wished to rise.

William Styron's memoir *Darkness Visible* (London: Jonathan Cape, 1991) endorses the work of the social historian Howard Kirchner, whose book *Self-Destruction in the Promised Land* (New Brunswick: Rutger University Press, 1989) examines the role of 'incomplete mourning' in American suicide.

For a summary account of Arthur Kleinman's extensive research into neurasthenia and its place in Chinese culture, see chapter 6 of his book *The Illness Narratives: Suffering, Healing and the Human Condition* (New York: Basic Books, 1988).

Andrew Solomon's *Noonday Demon* (London: Chatto & Windus, 2001) is by a long way the best of a recent crop of books on depression.

The Theatre of the Possessed

Aldous Huxley's *The Devils of Loudun* (Harmondsworth: Penguin, 1971) is the most accessible introduction to Grandier, Sister Jeanne and the leading protagonists of this late medieval drama. Michel de Certeau's *The Possession at Loudun* (Chicago and London: University of Chicago Press, 2000) draws on a much greater range of medical reports, court proceedings and private letters to examine the social forces which converged at Loudun, a town that was caught between Protestantism and Catholicism. De Certeau is a testing writer, but his rampant subclauses are an indispensable guide to all aspects of sixteenth- and seventeenth-century religious life.

The case of Mary Reynolds is discussed by Michael Kenny in *The Passion of Ansel Bourne: Multiple Personality in American Culture* (Washington and London: Smithsonian Institution Press, 1986).

Freud's case history of Christoph Haizmann, 'A Seventeenth Century Demonological Neurosis', appears in *Art and Literature*, vol. 14 of the Pelican Freud Library (Harmondsworth: Penguin, 1987). Roy Porter's observations on Haizmann's possession are from *A Social History of Madness* (New York: Weidenfeld and Nicolson, 1987).

Multiple Minds

Henri F. Ellenberger's *The Discovery of the Unconscious* (New York: Basic Books, 1970) discusses the early psychiatric history of multiple personality.

Ian Hacking gives a subtle and sophisticated reading of the multiple personality movement in *Rewriting the Soul: Multiple Personality and the Sciences of Memory* (Princeton: Princeton University Press, 1995).

Written on the Body

There is an extensive and ever-growing body of scholarship on the medical history of hysteria. Elaine Showalter's *Hystories: Hysterical Epidemics and Modern Culture* (London: Picador, 1997) is a very readable polemic which runs from Charcot to modern 'epidemics' of chronic fatigue and Gulf War syndrome. The seriously interested might want to look at Mark Micale's fine study of the 'cultures of hysteria', *Approaching Hysteria* (Princeton: Princeton University Press, 1995), which extends into poetry, fiction and the arts.

For Freud's case study of Dora, see *Case Histories 1*, vol. 8 of the Pelican Freud Library (Harmondsworth: Penguin, 1977).

Morton Prince's psychological who-is-it, *The Dissociation of a Personality* (Oxford: Oxford University Press, 1978) is a combination of unconsummated love affair and therapeutic thriller. Although Prince was not quite as 'stupid' as the Freudians claimed, his search for the Beauchamp family is often blinkered and wayward.

Breton and Aragon both studied medicine. Their 1928 editorial on the fiftieth anniversary of hysteria is reprinted in Franklin Rosemont (ed.), *André Breton: What Is Surrealism?* (London: Pluto Press, 1978).

One-Track Minds

Kusama's dot art is lavishly illustrated in *Yayoi Kusama* (London: Phaidon, 2000). Her reflections on her art and illness are taken from an interview with Akira Tatehata, published in the same volume.

The case history of Mademoiselle F is from J. E. D. Esquirol's *Mental Maladies* (New York and London: Hafner Publishing Company, 1965). Eugene Taylor's *William James on Exceptional Mental States* (New York: Charles Scribner's Sons, 1983) cites the case of 'Georgette', whose doubting mania was originally examined by Valentin Magnan.

Samuel Johnson lived in more or less permanent fear of the madhouse. Beyond the well-chronicled 'particularities', James Boswell's *The Life of Johnson* (Harmondsworth: Penguin, 1986) contains various references to the 'vile melancholy' that he apparently inherited from his father.

True Delusions

Louis A. Sass's *Madness and Modernism* (Cambridge, Mass.: Harvard University Press, 1996) and *The Paradoxes of Delusion: Wittgenstein, Schreber, and the Schizophrenic Mind* (Ithaca and London: Cornell University Press, 1994) are dense but rewarding studies of delusory thinking and its affinities with modern art and philosophy.

For some lively case studies of paranoia, see Ronald K. Siegel's *Whispers: the Voices of Paranoia* (New York: Touchstone, 1994).

Victor Tausk's paper 'On the Origins of the Influencing Machine in Schizophrenia' is reprinted in Jonathan Cray and Sanford

Kwinter (eds), *Incorporations* (New York: Zone, 1992). Mike Jay's recent book *The Air Loom Gang: Mesmerism, Revolution and the Visionary Madness of James Tilly Matthews* (London: Bantam Press, 2003) uncovers the social and political background to Matthews's delusions of thought control via mesmeric machinery.

The German-born artist and writer Unica Zurn first came to prominence in Paris through her automatic drawings and anagram poems. *The Man of Jasmine* (London: Atlas, 1994) and *The House of Illnesses* (London: Atlas, 1993) include point-blank accounts of the hallucinations, delusions and 'miracles' to which she was subject in her later years.

Manic Sunlight

Raymond Roussel is one of the few literary figures to have eluded the attention of Kay Redfield Jamison, whose seminal study *Touched with Fire* (New York: Free Press Paperbacks, 1994) covers the pantheon of manic-depressive writers, composers and artists. I have drawn heavily from Mark Ford's excellent biography, *Raymond Roussel and the Republic of Dreams* (London: Faber, 2001), which contains excerpts of Pierre Janet's case study of Roussel, and much more besides. François Caradec's *Raymond Roussel* (London: Atlas, 2001) provides some supplementary information on Roussel's manic episode and its lasting effects.

Thomas C. Caramagno's *The Flight of the Mind: Virginia Woolf's Art and Manic-Depressive Illness* (Berkeley and Los Angeles: University of California Press, 1992) is an exemplary study in literary pathology.

Hearing Voices

Poet–painter Henri Michaux brought a unique and unwavering intelligence to his self-experimentation with various drugs. As John Ashberry observed, Michaux was 'hardly a painter, hardly even a writer, but a conscience – the most sensitive substance yet discovered for registering the fluctuating anguish of day-to-day, minute-to-minute living'. Michaux's accounts of his intimacies with mescaline, cannabis, psilocybin and LSD are to be found in *Miserable Miracle* (San Francisco: City Lights, 1967), *Infinite Turbulence* (London: Calder and Boyars, 1964), *Light through Darkness* (New York: Orion Press, 1963) and *The Major Ordeals of the Mind, and the Countless Minor Ones* (New York: Harcourt Brace Jovanovich, 1974).

The 1890 census of hallucinations was conducted by the London SPR, in conjuction with the International Congress of Psychology. See H. Sidgwick, A. Johnson, F. W. H. Myers et al., 'Report on the Census of Hallucinations', *Proceedings of the Society for Psychical Research*, vol. 10, 1894, pp. 25–422. The inflated findings of Edmund Parish, a critic of the SPR census, are contained in *Hallucinations and Illusions* (London: Scott, 1897). For a summary of the 1947 Mass Observation study, see D. J. West, 'A Mass-Observation Questionnaire on Hallucinations', *Journal of the Society for Psychical Research*, vol. 35, 1948, pp. 187–96. The most thorough modern study of auditory hallucinations is A. Y. Tien's 'Distributions of Hallucinations in the Population', *Social Psychiatry and Psychiatric Epidemiology*, vol. 26, 1991, pp. 287–92.

Richard Bentall's quote on 'self-talk' is from his essay 'Why There Will Never Be a Convincing Theory of Schizophrenia', in Steven Rose's *From Brains to Consciousness?* (Harmondsworth: Penguin, 1999). Louise C. James and Philip K. McGuire's study of 'Verbal Self-monitoring and Auditory Hallucinations' was reported in *The Lancet*, vol. 353, 6 February 1999, p. 469.

Experimental Delirium

Z. J. Lipowski's *Delirium: Acute Confusional States* (New York and Oxford: Oxford University Press, 1990), the only clinical history of delirium, overlooks the hashish experiments which J. J. Moreau de Tours reports in *Hashish and Mental Illness* (New York: Raven Press, 1973).

Forbes Winslow's account of belladonna poisoning is from Mordecai Cooke's 1860 book *The Seven Sisters of Sleep* (Rochester, Vermont: Park Street Press, 1997).

Huston Smith points out the spiritual significance of typhoid and other delirious illnesses in 'Do Drugs Have Religious Import: A Thirty-Five-Year Retrospective', in Thomas B. Robert (ed.), *Psychoactive Sacramentals* (San Francisco: Council on Spiritual Practices, 2001).

The Impersonators

The case of Madame M originally appeared in J. Capgras and J. Reboul-Lachaux's 1923 paper 'L'Illusion des "sosies" dans un délire systématisé'. Hadyn D. Ellis, Janet Whiteley and Jean-Pierre Luauté have translated and discussed this article in 'Delusional Misidentification', *History of Psychiatry*, vol. 5, 1994, pp. 117–48. In his comprehensive survey 'The Syndrome of Capgras', *British Journal of Psychiatry*, vol. 130, 1977, pp. 556–64, G. N. Christodoulou suggests that Magnan and Bessière had both previously 'described a condition corresponding to the syndrome without thinking of giving it a name'.

The case of Arthur is from V. S. Ramachandran's *Phantoms in the Brain*, (London: Fourth Estate, 1999); the Capgras patient who admitted herself to hospital so that she could 'prove to my husband that I'm not crazy' is reported by E. L. Merrin and P. M. Silderfarb in 'The Capgras Phenomenon', *Archives of General Psychiatry*, vol. 33, 1976, pp. 965–8. The brief transcript of a psychiatric interview with a Capgras patient is from Philip Gerrans's 'Refining the Explanation of Cotard's Delusion', *Mind and Language*, vol. 15, 2000, pp. 111–22.

See Me Now

The patient's account of epileptic autoscopy is taken from N. Lukianowicz's 'Autoscopic Phenomena', *AMA Archives of Neurology and Psychology*, vol. 80, 1958, pp. 199–220. A full description of Dr Harry Asher's misadventures under LSD is reprinted in Antonio Melechi (ed.), *Mindscapes: An Anthology of Drug Writings* (Bradford: Mono, 1998) pp. 239–251.

Research on bodily transformations under LSD is reported in C. Savage's 'Variations in Ego Feeling Induced by D-Lysergic Acid Diethylamide', *The Psychoanalytical Review*, vol. 42, no. 1, 1955, pp. 1–16. Savage found that 'feeling for the legs and genitals disappear first, then the arms and trunk', with only a vestige of sensation retained finally in the lips and face. These findings corroborate Wilder Penfield's research into the 'homunculus', which found that the hands and mouth occupied an excessive share of this sensory map. See Penfield and Theodore Rasmussen's *The Cerebral Cortex of Man* (New York: Macmillan, 1950).

The Divine Seizure

For a comprehensive history of epilepsy up to the late nineteenth century, see the second edition of Owsei Temkin's *The Falling Sickness: A History of Epilepsy from the Greeks to the Beginnings of Modern Neurology* (Baltimore: Johns Hopkins University Press, 1971).

W. Penfield and P. Perot discuss 'experiential seizures' provoked by electrical stimulation of the temporal lobe in epileptic patients in 'The Brain's Record of Visual and Auditory Experience', *Brain*, vol. 86, 1963, pp. 595–696.

Michael Persinger draws dubious conclusions from his experiments in electrical stimulation of the temporal lobe in *Neuropsychological Bases of God Beliefs* (New York: Praeger, 1987).

Mechanical Boys

The various neurological, cognitive and genetic theories of autism
are covered in Uta Frith *Autism: Explaining the Enigma* (London:
Blackwell, 1989), which provides a very good introduction to
autism research. Frith (ed.) *Autism and Asperger Syndrome*
(Cambridge: Cambridge University Press, 1991) includes translations of Hans Asperger's early clinical studies.
Leo Kanner's work appeared in a number of paediatric and
psychiatric journals in the 1940s and 1950s. His first and most
substantial article was 'Autistic Disturbances of Affective
Contact', *Nervous Child*, vol. 2, 1943, pp. 217–50.
Bettelheim offered readers of his 1955 book, *Truants from Life*,
lessons 'On Writing Case Histories'. His first case study of 'Joey:
The Mechanical Boy' appeared in *Scientific American*, vol. 200,
parts 3–4, 1959, pp. 116–27. I have not been able to confirm the
rumour that Joey provided the science-fiction writer Philip K.
Dick with the prototype of Manfred for his novel *Martian Time-
Slip* (1964).
Margaret Dewey notes the autistic tendency to assimilate other
people's ideas in an essay in Uta Frith (ed.) *Autism and Asperger's
Syndrome*.
Lorna Wing's influential paper 'Asperger's Syndrome: A Clinical
Account' can be found in *Psychological Medicine*, vol. 11, 1981, pp.
115–29.
Some of Andy Warhol's manifold peculiarities are described in Bob
Collacello's biography *Holy Terror* (New York: HarperCollins,
1991).

A Literary Headache

Caro Lippman's speculations on the migrainous inspiration for
Alice's adventures appeared in 'Certain Hallucinations Peculiar
to Migraine', *Journal of Nervous and Mental Disorder*, vol. 116, 1952,
pp. 346–51. J. Todd expanded the possible causes to include fever
and intoxication in 'The syndrome of Alice in Wonderland',

Canadian Medical Journal, Vol. 73, 1955, pp. 701–4. In his essay 'Wonderland Revisited', in Antonio Melechi (ed.), *Psychedelia Britannica* (London: Turnaround, 1997), Michael Carmichael peeps into Dodgson's medicine cabinet and library to suggest a psychoactive basis for Alice's hallucinatory escapades.

Oliver Sacks's *Migraine* (Berkeley and Los Angeles: University of California Press, 1986) remains the best introduction to the symptomology and clinical treatment of migraine. Sacks here reiterates Singer's earlier conjectures on Hildegard's 'migrainous visions', pointing to the fortifications, scintillations and scotomas that are apparently elaborated in her *Scivias* and *Liber Divinorum Operum Simplicis Hominis*. This, however, gives the erroneous impression that such phosphene-based visions are unique to migraine, which they are clearly not. I would suggest that Hildegard's malady is less certain than Sacks suggests.

Michael Ferrari's suspicions on the influence of the migraine aura (without headache) in Picasso's *Weeping Woman* and other works from the late 1930s and 1940s were reported at the Headache World 2000 Conference in London.

The first detailed nosographic study of the migraine aura, reported by M. B. Russell and J. Olesen in *Brain*, vol. 119, no. 2, 1996, pp. 355–61, surveyed a sample of 4000 and found that a total of 163 experienced attacks of migraine aura with and without headache.

Carnival of the Senses

Nabokov's reflections on his hereditary *audition colorée* can be found in his autobiography *Speak, Memory* (Harmondsworth: Penguin, 1996), alongside some interesting asides on hypnagogic imagery and scarlet fever.

Richard E. Cytowic outlines his theory of synaesthesia as 'a normal brain process . . . that reach[es] consciousness in only a handful' in the *The Man Who Tasted Shapes* (London: Abacus, 1996).

Kevin T. Dann's *False Colors Brightly Seen* (New Haven: Yale

University Press, 1998) examines the history of synaesthesia in both its literary and laboratory habitats. For a breakneck survey of the subject, see my 'Senses and Sensibility', *Fortean Times*, no. 113, 1998, pp. 28–31.

Seeing Stars

For Brion Gysin's account of the history of the dreamachine (and the reflections of some of its lesser initiates), see Paul Cecil's *Flickers of the Dreamachine* (London: Codex, 1996).

Gerardo Reichell-Dolmatoff's *Shamanism and Art of the Eastern Tukanoan Indians* (Leiden and New York: E. J. Brill, 1987) is a short, illustrated monograph on the phosphene-inspired arts and crafts of the Tukanoans, who inhabit the central regions of the Colombian northwest Amazon.

Purkinje's visionary experiments are outlined in Z. Votava, 'Purkyne's Pioneer Contribution to Neuro-Psychopharmacology', *Acta Facultatis Medicae Universitatis Brunens*, vol. 40, 1971, pp. 47–56. A short report on Max Knoll's experiments at the Institut für Technische Elektronik in Munich can be found in *Nature*, 5 December 1959, pp. 1823–4.

For S. Weir Mitchell's account of his peyote visions, see 'Remarks on the Effects of *Anhelonium Lewinii*', *British Medical Journal*, 5 December 1896, pp. 1625–9; Havelock Ellis's corresponding observations are taken from 'Mescal: A Study of a Divine Plant', *Popular Science Monthly*, vol. 61, 1902, pp. 52–71.

For Gautier's account of his hashish fantasia, see J. J. Moreau's *Hashish and Mental Illness* (1973). Michael Herner's *ayahuasca* visions can be found in his book, *The Way of the Shoman* (San Francisco: HarperSanFrancisco, 1990).

Hugh Trevor-Roper described the hallucinations of Charles Bonnet syndrome in Candida Crewe's 'Now I Know All about Ghosts', *Daily Telegraph*, 8 April 2002. Martin G. Coles examines the cognitive and visual status of thirteen Charles Bonnet patients in 'Charles Bonnet Hallucinations: A Case Series', *Canadian Journal of Psychiatry*, vol. 137, 1992, pp. 267–70.

From Here to Oblivion

Thirty years before his fugue travels to Norristown, Ansel Bourne was subject to another life-changing experience. While walking to Westerly, Rhode Island, he lost his powers of speech, sight and hearing, and fell into a 'deep, bottomless and shoreless sepulchre', which led, through ensuing illness, to conversion to the Evangelical church. Chapter 2 of Michael G. Kenny's *The Passion of Ansel Bourne* (Washington: Smithsonian Institution Press, 1986) provides an excellent introduction to Bourne in the context of American preoccupation with multiple personality.

Ian Hacking examines the case history of Albert Dadas, the first diagnosed fugeur and a patient of Philippe Tissié, in his illuminating book *Mad Travellers: Reflections on the Reality of Transient Mental Illnesses* (London: Free Association, 1999). According to Hacking, lack of British and American interest in hysterical fugue can be partly explained by the absence of standing army conscripts, who generally provided French and German physicians with their staple cases.

The case history of Greg F appears in Oliver Sacks's *An Anthropologist on Mars* (London: Picador, 1995).

Temps Perdu

The medical history of nostalgia has been retraced in George Rosen's important essay 'Nostalgia: A "Forgotten Psychological Disorder"', *Psychological Medicine*, vol. 5, part 4, 1975, pp. 340–54. Michael Roth's short paper 'Time of Nostalgia', *Time and Society*, vol. 1, no. 2, 1992, pp. 271–86, approaches the affliction from a different perspective, arguing that: 'Nostalgia, as a disease, as a subject for study, and as a way of returning to the dead [in the writing of history], was a protest against progress.'

Aubert-Roche's case of nostalgia is referred to in J. J. Moreau's *Hashish and Mental Illness* (1973).

For a discussion of the nature of childhood recollection in the work of various nineteenth-century writers and artists, including

Darwin, Ruskin, Pater and Stevenson, see Anne C. Colley's *Nostalgia and Recollection in Victorian Culture* (London: Palgrave Macmillan, 1998).

Proust's nostalgic transports are discussed in George D. Painter's meticulous biography *Proust* (Harmondsworth: Penguin, 1983).

The Strangely Familiar

Dickens's description of *déjà vu* in *David Copperfield* prefigures an experience which he succumbed to some years later: 'I suddenly (the temperature being then most violent) found an icy coolness come upon me, accompanied with a general stagnation of the blood, a numbness of the extremities, great bewilderment of the mind, and a vague sensation of wonder. I was walking at the time, and, on looking about me, found that I was in the frigid shadow of Burlington Hotel. Then I recollected to have experienced the same sensations once before precisely in that spot. A curious case, don't you think?' In his biography *Dickens* (London: Vintage, 2002), Peter Ackroyd injects a note of supernatural suspense into the episode, adding that his own 'assiduous research has yielded no earthly clue to the source of his sensation'.

Dr Jensen's remarks on *déjà vu* are quoted in Anne Harrington's *Medicine, Mind, and the Double Brain* (Princeton: Princeton University Press, 1989).

Bergson's paper 'Memory of the Present and False Recognition' is reprinted in *Mind-Energy* (London: Macmillan, 1920).

I am indebted to German Berrios's encyclopaedic *History of Mental Symptoms* (Cambridge: Cambridge University Press, 1996) for drawing my attention to the case of Louis.

H. Bannister and O. L. Zangwill's paper on 'Experimentally Induced Visual Paramnesias' appeared in the *British Journal of Psychology*, vol. 32, no. 1, 1941, pp. 30–51.

For Robert Efron's updated theory of hemispheric delay, see 'Temporal Perception, Aphasia and *Déjà Vu*', *Brain*, vol. 86, 1963, pp. 403–24.

Total Recall

For the full history of Solomon Shereshevski, see Aleksandr Luria's *Mind of a Mnemonist* (New York: Basic Books, 1968). Chapters 5 and 12 of Darold A. Trelfert's *Extraordinary People* (London: Bantam, 1989) discuss other cases of savant memory, some of which have been linked specifically to brain injury or autism.

Dr Mesmer's Invisible Cure

Of the recent scholarly works on mesmerism and hypnotism, two books stand out: Alan Gauld's *A History of Hypnotism* (Cambridge: Cambridge University Press, 1995) and Alison Winter's *Mesmerized* (Chicago: University of Chicago Press, 1998). While Gauld's exhaustive survey spans three centuries, taking in Europe and America, Winter focuses on Victorian Britain, tracing mesmerism's gradual passage from would-be science to theatrical marvel.

Derek Forrest's *Hypnotism: A History* (London: Penguin, 2000) is the best of the popular histories. Forrest has an excellent chapter on John Elliotson and the O'Key sisters.

For a pacy and generally reliable biography of Mesmer, see Vincent Buranelli's *The Wizard from Vienna* (London: The Scientific Book Club, 1977).

There is, as yet, no full-length biography of James Braid. A. E. Waite's (ed.) *Braid on Hypnotism* does, however, have a fairly lengthy biographical introduction to the Manchester surgeon.

John F. Kihlstrom is today's leading researcher on hypnotic amnesia and dissociation. His paper 'Hypnosis, Memory, and Amnesia', *Philosophical Transactions of the Royal Society: Biological Sciences*, vol. 352, 1997, pp. 1727–32, contains a useful summary of some his experimental findings. For a more general overview of recent issues and preoccupation in hypnosis research, see Erika Fromm and Michael R. Nash's *Contemporary Hypnosis Research* (New York: Guilford Press, 1992).

The Automatic Hand

There is, as I have indicated, no comprehensive history of either inspirational or automatic writing. For two particularly useful surveys of psychological research into automatic writing in the nineteenth and early twentieth centuries, including those of Gurney, James and Jeret see Wilma Koutstaal's 'Skirting the Abyss: A History of Experimental Explorations of Automatic Writing in Psychology', *Journal of the History of the Behavioural Sciences*, vol. 28, 1992, pp. 5–27, and Sonu Shamdasani's 'Automatic Writing and the Discovery of the Unconscious', *Reality*, vol. 54, 1993, pp. 100–31. See also Shamdasani's excellent introduction to Théodore Flournoy's *From India to the Planet Mars* (Princeton: Princeton University Press, 1994).

Florence Theobold's and Louisa Lowe's adventures in automatic authorship are described in Alex Owen's *The Darkened Room* (Philadelphia: University of Pennsylvania, 1990), from which I have drawn heavily.

Thanks to David Maclagan to drawing my attention to the much-neglected doodle. See his 'Solitude and Communication: Beyond the Doodle', *Raw Vision*, Summer 1990, pp. 34–9.

Mind Fog

Edward Hunter's *Brainwashing* (New York: Pyramid Books, 1961) claims to provide a true history of brainwashing techniques employed during the Korean War. For a more sober examination of methods of Chinese methods of ideological conversion, see Robert Jay Lifton's *Thought Reform and the Psychology of Totalism* (London: Victor Gollancz, 1962).

My essay, 'Truth in Small Doses', *Fortean Times*, no. 137, 2000, pp. 40–4, briefly examines the pseudo-scientific roots of the truth drug and recruitment pill.

Library of Dreams

Robert L. Van De Castle's *Our Dreaming Mind* (New York: Ballantine Books, 1994) provides a good overview of the history of dream theory and research. Norman Mackenzie's *Dreams and Dreaming* (London: Aldus, 1965) covers less ground, but offers a rather better survey of the medieval and romantic periods. For the nineteenth-century roots of the Freudian dream revolution, see Henri F. Ellenberger's indispensable *The Discovery of the Unconscious* (New York: Basic Books, 1970).

Aristotle's essays 'On Memory and Reminiscence', 'On Dreams', and 'On Prophesying By Dreams' can be found in *The Works of Aristotle*, vol. one. (Chicago: Encyclopaedia Brittanica, 1992).

Chapter 8 of Nancy G. Siraisi's biography of the Renaissance physician and prophet Girolamo Cardano, *The Clock and the Mirror* (Princeton: Princeton University Press, 1997), contains an excellent discussion of the ideas that Cardano expounded in his *Synesiorum Somniorum Libri*.

William Hazlitt's 'Dreaming' is reprinted in *Selected Writings* (Harmondsworth: Penguin, 1970)

Eugene Aserinsky and Nathan Kleitman's landmark article on dreaming and rapid-eye movement, 'Regularly Occurring Periods of Eye Motility and Concurrent Phenomena during Sleep', was published in *Science*, vol. 118, 1953, pp. 273–4. For an insider's summary of the subsequent wave of REM research in American sleep laboratories, see William C. Dement's *Some Must Watch while Some Must Sleep* (San Francisco: W. H. Freeman, 1974). Alan Hobson's activation-synthesis theory of dreaming is outlined in the latter chapters of *The Dreaming Brain* (London: Penguin, 1990). Harry T. Hunt's classification of dream types can be found in *The Multiplicity of Dreams* (New Haven: Yale University Press, 1989).

The Night Shift

Almost every early nineteenth-century work on psychology

included some discussion of natural or magnetic somnambulism. See, for example, John Abercrombie's brief amble, via dreaming and heading towards insanity, in *Inquiries Concerning the Intellectual Powers and the Investigation of Truth* (New York: J. & J. Harper, 1834).

Paolo Zacchias was physician to Pope Innocent X. As well as discussing sleepwalking, the compendious *Questionum Medico-Legalium* holds forth on subjects such as poisoning, suicide, madness, sorcery and popular superstitions.

Justinus Kerner's case history of Friedericke Hauffe is, according to Henri Ellenberger, 'the first monograph devoted to an individual patient in the field of dynamic psychiatry'. An English translation by Catherine Crowe appeared under the title *The Seeress of Prevorst* (London, 1845). Just as Hauffe anticipated the rise of German spiritualism, American somnambulists such as Rachel Baker, Miss L. Bracket and Andrew Davies Jackson played their part in the emergence of the spiritualist movement in North America.

Roger Broughton has supported a defence case of sleepwalking in at least two murder trials, but his own research confirms that sleepwalkers *rarely* engage in complex activities. Where purposeful actions are undertaken, they are usually related to unfinished tasks.

Lucid Dreaming

Nicholas Fry's English translation of Hervey de Saint-Denys's *Dreams and How to Guide Them* (London: Duckworth, 1982) is only marginally easier to track down than the French original, *Les rêves et les noyens de les dirigers*.

Alfred Maury, a daytime archaeologist, was, like Hervey, a relative amateur in the field of dream research. His 1861 book *Le Sommeil et les rêves* attempted to provide somatic explanations for the content of his recorded dreams. Maury investigated his thesis by having his assistant apply various stimuli (a feather to his lips, drops of water to his face, cologne to his nose) while he slept.

Hervey later extended these olfactory experiments, attempting to gauge the effect of different perfumes on his dreams.

My misgivings regarding the way in which Stephen LaBerge's Lucidity Institute has promoted lucid dreaming does not extend to LaBerge's more scholarly activities. His book *Lucid Dreaming* (New York: Ballantine, 1986) is highly recommended.

The Undercover Assassin

The extract from Paul Eluard's dream diary, *Donner à voir*, is reprinted in Guido Almansi and Claude Béguin's *Theatre of Dreams: An Anthology of Literary Dreams* (London: Picador, 1986). For another literary treatment of sleep paralysis, see Thomas Hardy's *Wessex Tales*.

David J. Hufford draws the connection between sleep paralysis and Newfoundland Old Hag in *The Terror That Comes in the Night* (Philadelphia: University of Pennsylvania, 1982).

Running Wild

The 1891 report on Imam Mamat is quoted by Joseph Westermeyer in his essay 'Amok', in Claude T. H. Friedmann and Robert A. Faguet's *Extraordinary Disorders of Human Behaviour* (New York and London: Plenum Press, 1992). For a wide-ranging discussion of *amok*, its history, pathology and cultural foundations, see Ronald C. Simons and Charles C. Hughes's *The Culture-bound Syndromes* (Dordecht: D. Reidel Publishing Company, 1985).

Ernst Von Bibra was the nineteenth-century pharmacologist who, in his 1847 book *Plant Intoxicants* (Rochester, Vermont: Healing Arts Press, 1995), feigned knowledge of hashish and opium stirring an '*amok* frenzy' in the feckless Malay.

Sheuk-Tak Cheng's paper 'A Critical Review of Chinese Koro' was presented at the International Congress of Psychology, Madrid, July 1994.

Northern Flights

A. A. Brill's essay 'Pibloktoq or Hysteria among Peary's Eskimos' was published in the *Journal of Nervous and Mental Disorders*, vol. 40, 1913, pp. 514–20. See also Seymour Parker's 'Eskimo Psychopathology in the Context of Eskimo Personality', *American Anthropologist*, vol. 64, 1962, pp. 76–96, and Edward F. Foulk's 'The Transformation of Arctic Hysteria', in Ronald C. Simons and Charles C. Hughes's *The Culture-bound Syndromes* (Dordecht: D. Reidel Publishing Company, 1985).
The work of Knud Rasmussen and other Arctic ethnographers on the hysterical aspects of shamanism are discussed in Mircea Eliade's *Shamanism* (Harmondsworth: Penguin Arkana, 1988).

A Chinese Conundrum?

The earliest medical writings on *koro* are discussed in Beng Yeong Ng and Ee Heok Kua's 'Koro in Ancient Chinese History', *History of Psychiatry*, vol. 7, 1996, pp. 563–70.
For an important nonmedical perspective on epidemic *koro*, see Robert E. Bartholomew's 'The Medicalization of Exotic Deviance: A Sociological Perspective on Epidemic Koro', *Transcultural Psychiatry*, vol. 35, no. 1, 1988, pp. 5–38.
J. Guy Edwards notes that elements of *koro* can be found in other cultures and periods in his essay 'The *Koro* Pattern of Depersonalization', in Ronald C. Simons and Charles C. Hughes (1985).
The case of 'Koro in a Londoner' was reported in K. Barret's letter to *The Lancet*, vol. 2, 1978, p. 1319.

Fits and Starts

George Beard's report on 'Experiments with the "Jumpers" or "Jumping Frenchmen" of Maine' appeared in the *Journal of Nervous and Mental Disease*, vol. 7, 1880, pp. 487–90. According to

Gilles de la Tourette, Beard was one of a number of physicians who failed to realise 'that *Jumping* in Maine, *Latah* in Malaysia and *Myriachit* as observed by American officers in Siberia were one and the same condition' – namely pseudo-chorea. Beard was, however, adamant that the jumpers betrayed no evidence of hysteria.

Ronald Simons has extended his research on the startle response and maintained his claims for a neurophysiological explanation of *latah* in *Boo!: Culture, Experience and the Startle Reflex* (New York: Oxford University Press, 1996).

For Robert Bartholomew's ethnographic and historical survey of *latah*, see *Exotic Deviance* (Boulder: University Press of Colorado, 2000).

The Beast Within

Paulus Aegineta's writings on lycanthropy can be found in F. Adams (ed.), *The Seven Books of Paulus Aegineta*, vol. 1 (London: Sydenham Society, 1844).

For further information on Peter Strubbe, Jean Grenier and medieval cases of lycanthropy, see C. F. Otten (ed.), *A Lycanthropy Reader: Werewolves in Western Culture* (New York: Syracuse University Press, 1986) and H. Sidky, *Witchcraft, Lycanthropy, Drugs, and Disease* (New York: Peter Lang, 1997).

The testimony of the modern-day lycanthrope is taken from Michel Benezec, Jacques De Witte, Jean Jacques Etcheparre and Marc Bourgeois's letter 'A Lycanthropic Murder', *American Journal of Psychiatry*, vol. 146, no. 7, 1989, p. 942. For two other modern psychiatric cases of lycanthropy, see P. M. Jackson, 'Another Case of Lycanthropy', *American Journal of Psychiatry*, vol. 135, 1978, pp. 134–5; P. G. Coll, G. O'Sullivan and P. J. Browne, 'Lycanthropy Lives On', *British Journal of Psychiatry*, vol. 147, 1985, pp. 201–2.

Carlo Ginzburg argues that werewolfism was originally a form of Eurasian shamanism in *Ecstasies* (Harmondsworth: Penguin, 1992).

E is for Ergot

The symptomological affinities between convulsive ergotism and demonic possession have been vastly exaggerated. For a pertinent critique of the ergotism hypothesis in relation to Salem, see Nicholas P. Spanos and Jack Gottlieb's 'Ergotism and the Salem Village Witch Trials', *Science*, vol. 194, 1976, pp. 1390–4.

For the full story of Pont-Saint-Esprit, see John G. Fuller's *The Day of St. Anthony's Fire* (New York: Macmillan, 1868).

For well-founded speculations on ergot's role in the Eleusinian mysteries, see Gordon Wasson, Albert Hofmann and Carl A. O. Ruck's *Road to Eleusis* (New York: Harcourt Brace Jovanovich, 1978).

Cannibalism: Its Uses and Abuses

Carleton Gajdusek's 'Unconventional Viruses and the Origin and Disappearance of Kuru' appeared in *Science*, vol. 197, 1977, pp. 943–60.

William Arens appears to have been slightly too emphatic in denying *all* firsthand evidence of ritual cannibalism in his *The Man-eating Myth* (New York: Oxford University Press, 1979). Another review of the ethnographic literature, Peggy Reeve Sanday's *Divine Hunger* (Cambridge: Cambridge University Press, 1986), points to at least one reliable eyewitness description: this testimony of 1879, from a native of the Cook Islands turned missionary, observes (in unflinchingly visceral detail) the cannibal feast that followed a battle in New Caledonia.

Lou Marano's '*Windigo* Psychosis: The Anatomy of Emic-Etic Confusion' was first published in *Current Anthropology*, vol. 23, 1982, pp. 385–412. The essay can be found reprinted in Simons and Hughes (1985).

Return of the Zombi

The 'walking zombie syndrome' never found its way beyond the narrow confines of the American hypnotherapy community, where it was considered a particularly acute form of 'accidental hypnosis'. Ray O. Sexton and Richard C. Maddox's 'The Walking Zombie Syndrome in Depressive Disorders', *Journal of the Tennessee Medical Association*, vol. 72, no. 12, 1979, pp. 886–9, can claim the dubious honour of first alerting the medical community to this syndrome.

For Wade Davis's first investigations of Haitian zombi powders, see 'The Ethnobiology of the Haitian Zombi', *Journal of Ethnopharmacology*, vol. 9, part 1, 1983, pp. 85–104. Davis responded to the critics of his hastily conceived tetrodoxin hypothesis – and ensuing charges of deliberately withholding negative data – by ceding greater emphasis to the 'set and setting' of zombification.

Roland Littlewood and Chavanne Douyon's 'Clinical Findings in Three Cases of Zombification' was published in *The Lancet*, vol. 35, 1997, pp. 1094–6.

Fear is the Key

Montaigne's reflections on the ways in which the body betrays fears and desires without intellectual 'consent' can be found in 'On the Power of the Imagination', in his *Essays* (Harmondsworth: Penguin, 1983).

Crosscultural research conducted by Paul Ekman and Wallace V. Friesen points to a certain amount of confusion in distinguishing the nonverbal expression of surprise and fear, particularly in non-Western societies. See their *Unmasking the Face* (Englewood Cliffs: Prentice Hall, 1975).

Freud's 1909 study of Little Hans, 'Analysis of a Phobia in a Five-Year-Old Boy', can be found in *Case Histories 1*, vol. 8, Pelican Freud Library (Harmondsworth: Penguin, 1977). For J. B. Watson and Rosalie Rayner's classic experiment with Albert B, see 'Conditioned Emotional Responses', *Journal of Experimental Psychology*, vol. 38, 1920, pp. 1–14.

Joseph LeDoux examines the neural substrates of the emotions, and the fear system in particular, in *The Emotional Brain* (New York: Simon & Schuster, 1996). LeDoux's call for 'a more harmonious integration of reason and passion' echoes Antonio Damasio's thesis in *Descartes' Error: Emotion, Reason, and the Human Brain* (London: Picador, 1994).

A Tale from the Vault

In his essay 'The Stockholm Syndrome: Law Enforcement Policy and Hostage Behaviour', in F. M. Ocberg and D. A. Soskis's *Victims of Terrorism* (Boulder: Westview Press, 1982), Thomas Strentz suggests that 'identification with the aggressor', as described by Anna Freud, does not entirely explain the development of hostage affection for their captor. Instead, Strentz views the traumatic dependency fostered by the hostage scenario as 'a regression to a more elementary level of development'. To my mind, both these interpretations take a good analogy rather too literally.

The story of Patty Hearst's abduction and indoctrination has been buried under an avalanche of conspiracy theories on mind control and brainwashing. For Hearst's own story, see *Every Secret Thing* (New York: Doubleday, 1981).

Jeffrey Masson's claims regarding the circumstances under which Freud abandoned his seduction theory have been challenged by a number of Freudian scholars, including Mikkel Borch-Jacobsen. See his essay 'Neurotica: Freud and the Seduction Theory', *October*, vol. 16, pp. 15–43.

A Secret Called Shame

Howard French's article on the double lives of Tokyo's jobless appeared in the *Guardian*, 20 December 2000.

The modern genealogy of 'shame', 'repugnance' and 'disgust' is discussed in Norbert Elias's history of manners, *The Civilizing Process* (London: Blackwell, 2000).

For an analysis of shame in the writings of Kierkegaard, Hawthorne, Eliot and some twentieth-century writers, see Joseph Adamson and Hilary Clark (eds), *Scenes of Shame* (New York: SUNY, 1988)

De Amore

Denis de Rougemont's *Love in the Western World* (Princeton: Princeton University Press, 1983) and C. S. Lewis's *The Allegory of Love: A Study in Medieval Tradition* (Oxford: Oxford University Press, 1968) make consonant claims for passionate love's medieval coinage.

L. Takeo Doi discusses the psychology of *amae* in '*Amae*: A Key Concept for Understanding Japanese Personality Structure', in R. J. Smith and R. K. Beardsley (eds), *Japanese Culture* (London: Methuen, 1963). In his recent book *Emotion* (Oxford: Oxford University Press, 2000), Dylan Evans resists the notion that *amae* is peculiarly Japanese: 'People all over the world experience this emotion, but only some of them have a word for it.'

Freud's observations on the parallels between hypnosis and being in love can be found in his 1921 essay 'Group Psychology and the Analysis of the Ego', reprinted in vol. 12 of the Pelican Freud Library, *Civilization, Society and Religion* (Harmondsworth: Penguin, 1985).

Esquirol incorporated 'erotic monomania' in his clinical taxonomy of 1838, *Mental Maladies* (New York: Hafner Publishing Company, 1965).

In Search of the Sublime

Thanks to Frances Ferguson's *Solitude and the Sublime* (New York Routledge, 1992) for the anecdote about Samuel Taylor

Coleridge's effusive lady traveller, I have presumed the incident dates back to the late 1790s, when Coleridge was to be found afoot in north Wales.

Culture Shocks

For a good general study of the Western encounters with alien cultures and civilisations, see Andrew Sinclair's *The Savage* (London: Weidenfeld and Nicolson, 1977.)

Columbus's observations on the 'marvellously timorous' Caribs encountered on the journey into the New World can be found in *The Journal of Christopher Columbus* (London: Anthony Blond, 1968).

The social psychologist Kalervo Oberg coined the term 'culture shock' in an eponymous essay in *Practical Anthropology*, vol. 7, 1960, pp. 177–82. There is now a wide body of psychological literature on the crosscultural experience of tourists, sojourners, immigrants and refugees, mostly dry and empirical in nature. Coleen Ward et al. (eds.), *The Psychology of Culture Shock* (London: Routledge, 2002), reviews the field.

Frantz Fanon married Marxism and psychoanalysis to understand the black experience of colonial oppression in *Black Skin, White Masks* (London: Pluto, 1991).

A Constant Craving

Burroughs's 'Letter from a Master Addict to Dangerous Drugs' is reprinted in the appendix to *Naked Lunch* (London: Paladin, 1986).

For critiques of the biological concept of addiction, see John Booth Davies, *The Myth of Addiction* (Amsterdam: Harwood Academic Publishers, 1997); Stanton Peele et al., *The Truth about Addiction and Recovery* (New York: Simon and Schuster, 1991); Thomas Szasz, *Ceremonial Chemistry* (New York: Doubleday, 1974).

Twice-Born Men

For biographies of Saint Paul, see Michael Grant's *Saint Paul* (London: Fount Paperbacks, 1978) and E. P. Sander's *Paul* (Oxford: Oxford University Press, 1992).

The intellectual background that Garry Wills furnishes when describing Saint Augustine's conversion in *St Augustine* (London: Weidenfeld and Nicolson, 1999) debunks the emphasis previous generations of theologians and psychologists have to given to Augustine's supposed 'sex-complex'.

The testimony of the unnamed Frenchman in William James's *Varieties of Religious Experience* (Harmondsworth: Penguin, 1985) was in fact the author's own account of acute depression in the early 1870s. Elizabeth Hardwick's (ed.) *Selected Letters of William James* (New York: Anchor Books, 1993) includes some letters to Charles Renouvier, to whom James gave credit of indirect cure.

The notion of a creative illness belongs to Henri Ellenberger's *Discovery of the Unconscious* (New York: Basic Books, 1970). George Pickering has also investigated the role of psychological illness in the lives and minds of Charles Darwin, Florence Nightingale, Sigmund Freud and others in *Creative Malady* (New York: Delta Books, 1976).

William Topaz McGonagall's poetry has been rescued from obscurity in a number of anthologies. He is the worthy recipient of a four-star rating in Nick Page's *In Search of the World's Worst Writers* (London: HarperCollins, 2000).

Paths to Ecstasy

Freud's remarks on religious ecstasy are from *Civilization and Its Discontents* and can be found in vol. 12 of the Freud Pelican Library, *Civilization, Society and Religion* (Harmondsworth: Penguin, 1985).

Richard M. Bucke describes his experience of ecstasy and its impact on his life in section one of his anthology *Cosmic Consciousness* (Philadelphia: Innes, 1905).

Pahnke never published a definitive account of his Harvard experiments with psilocybin. For a summary of the so-called 'Good Friday Experiment', see his essay 'LSD and the Religious Experience', in Richard C. Debold and Russell C. Leaf (eds), *LSD, Man and Society* (London: Faber, 1969). For a long-term follow-up, see Rick Doblin's 'Pahnke's Good Friday Experiment', in Thomas B. Roberts (ed.), *Psychoactive Sacramentals* (San Francisco: Council of Spiritual Practices, 2001).

Mental Radio

Summaries of the SPR experiments with the Creery family and other subjects can be found in appendix A of Alan Gauld's *The Founders of Psychical Research* (New York: Schocken Books, 1968). For the original findings, see *Proceedings of the Society for Psychical Research*, vol. 1, 1882, pp. 19–30, and, for the eventual detection of fraud, vol. 5, pp. 269–70. It is interesting to note that Myers, Gurney and Sidgwick declined to publish the details of the other 'startling successes' that followed these initial investigations. Barrett, by contrast, never entirely lost his faith in the Creery sisters. Many years later, he still lamented the fact that positive data relative to their experiments in thought-transference was squandered.

Raymond Van Over (ed.), *Psychology and Extrasensory Perception* (New York: Mentor Books, 1972), includes a number of important papers on the relationship between psychoanalysis and telepathy, including essays by Freud, Helene Deutsch and Jan Ehrenwald.

J. B. Rhine's 1934 book *Extra-Sensory Perception* (Brookline Village: Braden Press, 1983) provides the first full-length report on the trials and tests undertaken at Duke University.

E. R. Dodds, a past president of the SPR, purports to review experimental and spontaneous cases of telepathy in 'The Evidence for Telepathy: An Historical Survey', *Psychic Research Quarterly*, October 1920, pp. 131–49. In fairness to Dodds, his paper does, at the very least, provide some clues to understanding the conceptual history of thought-transference. His paper rightly points out that 'the nuns of Loudun were thought to obey orders transmitted mentally'. Theologians of the day were in fact routinely astonished by the ways in which 'the Devil divines the thoughts of the Exorcist without the latter's manifesting them by signs and words'.

Speaking in Tongues

There is a wealth of Pentecostal literature on tongue speaking. Over the past few decades, the spiritual credentials of the phenomenon have been questioned. A number of Pentecostal commentators are now prepared to concede the 'natural mechanisms' which give rise to glossolalia.

Beyond the Pentecostal church, outbreaks of tongue speaking have occurred among Presbyterians, Methodists, Baptists and Lutherans, and in various nonreligious settings. The best general survey of glossolalia is still George Cutten's *Speaking with Tongues* (New Haven: Yale University Press, 1927). For a very useful crosscultural analysis of the vocal components of tongue speaking, see Felicitias D. Goodman's *Speaking in Tongues* (Chicago: University of Chicago Press, 1974).

William James reported the adventures of Albert Le Baron in 'A Case of Psychic Automatism, including "Speaking with Tongues" ', *Proceedings of the Society for Psychical Research*, vol. 12, 1896, pp. 277–9.

Cosmic Luv

For one recent addition to the corpus of abduction confessionals, see Angela Thompson Smith's *Diary of an Abduction* (Charlottesville: Hampton Road Publishing, 1999).

On the social construction of the abduction experience, see Michael Lieb's *Children of Ezekiel* (Durham, NC: Duke

University Press, 1999); Elaine Showalter's *Hystories* (London: Picador, 1997); and Michele Meurger's essay 'Surgeons from Outside', *Fortean Studies*, vol. 3, 1996, pp. 308–21.

On the mythological aspects of the UFO experience, see Jacques Vallee's *Dimensions* (London: Souvenir Press, 1996); Keith Thompson's *Angels and Aliens: UFOs and the Mythic Imagination* (New York: Random House, 1991); and Ioan P. Couliano's *Out of This World: Otherworldly Experiences from Gilgamesh to Albert Einstein* (Boston: Shambala, 1991).

John E. Mack has lent credence to the reality of UFO abductions in a number of bestsellers, including *Abduction: Human Encounters with Aliens* (New York: Simon and Schuster, 1992) and *Passport to the Cosmos: Human Transformation and Alien Encounters* (London: Thorsons, 2000). The Harvard Medical Board investigated Mack's controversial research in the early 1990s. They found faults with his methodology and findings, but resisted pressure to remove him from his post. Of late, Mack has become increasingly impervious to criticism and debate. The Committee for the Scientific Investigation of Claims of the Paranormal, which has been less than even-handed in its criticisms of Mack, should take some responsibility for his exile.

Max Steur draws attention to the procedures that are common to the Vatican's compilation of miracles and the UFO community's investigation of abductions in 'Miracles and Alien Abduction', Centre for Philosophy of Natural and Social Science, Discussion Paper 38, 1999.

Burroughs's visions of 'space time travel' can be found in *The Yage Letters* (San Francisco: City Lights, 1975).

Terence McKenna discusses the connections between mushroom intoxication and UFO abduction in *The Archaic Revival: Speculations on Psychedelic Mushrooms, the Amazon, Virtual Reality, Ufos, Evolution, Shamanism, the Rebirth of the Goddess, and the End of History* (San Francisco: HarperSanFrancisco, 1991).

Hunger

Piero Camporesi draws attention to the role that hunger might have played in the 'collective vertigo' of the Middle Ages in *The Bread of Dreams: Food and Fantasy in Modern Europe* (London: Polity Press, 1989). By conquering hunger, Camporesi argues that Western society has destroyed a sensibility that was 'fundamentally irrational and visionary'.

Details of 'The Minnesota Experiment' and earlier wartime studies of starvation can be found in volume 2 of A. Keys et al., *The Biology of Human Starvation* (Minnesota: University of Minnesota Press, 1950).

On *nervos* among the malnourished cane workers of the Brazilian shantytown of Alto do Cruzeiro, see Nancy Scheper-Hughes, 'The Madness of Hunger', *Culture, Medicine, Psychiatry*, vol. 12, 1990, pp. 429–58.

Huxley's quotation is from his 1956 essay 'Heaven and Hell', in *The Doors of Perception and Heaven and Hell* (London: Panther Books, 1985).

Of Lights and Tunnels

Michael B. Sabom's findings on the NDE can be found in *Recollections of Death* (London: Corgi, 1982).

For a caustic and amusing critique of the International Association of Near Death Studies and the so-called 'Moody-Ringers', see Harold Bloom's *Omens of Millennium* (London: Fourth Estate, 1996). Bloom is a noted literary scholar, who, à la Eliade, champions the *authentic* gnostic tradition – 'Nearly dying is our contemporary half-hearted evasion of gnosis and its vision of Resurrection' – while mocking its New Age traducers.

Karl Jansen discusses the action of ketamine in relation to the NDE in 'Using Ketamine to Induce the Near-Death Experience', *Yearbook of the Journal of Ethnomedicine*, 1995, pp. 55–79.

Sogyal Rinpoche notes the correspondences between the

experiences of the Tibetan *déloks* and the contemporary NDE in chapter 20 of *The Tibetan Book of Living and Dying* (London: Rider Books, 1992). Rinpoche writes that '*déloks* are people who seemingly "die" as a result of an illness, and find themselves traveling in the bardo'. The fact that it was commonplace to test the authenticity of the *déloks*' 'death' through a battery of physical tests suggests otherwise. Unlike the NDE, this 'death' may well have been an initiation-cum-cure, a purposeful malady, for those aspiring to mystical vocation.

The Song of Solitude

The Iglulik Inuit who found ecstasy in solitude is quoted in Mircea Eliade's *Shamanism: Archaic Techniques of Ecstasy* (Harmondsworth: Arkana, 1989).

For a brief summary of the methodology and results of D. O. Hebb's experiments in sensory isolation, see Woodburn Heron's 'The Pathology of Boredom', *Scientific American*, vol. 196, 1956, pp. 52–6.

John Lilly's heroic self-experiments with sensory deprivation and LSD are described in *The Centre of the Cyclone* (London: Paladin, 1974).

Ronald K. Siegel's study of 'Hostage Hallucinations: Visual Imagery Induced by Isolation and Life-threatening Stress' appeared in the *Journal of Nervous and Mental Disease*, vol. 172, no. 5, 1984, pp. 264–72.

Various passages in Joshua Slocum's memoir *Sailing around the World* (London: Pan Books, 1950) describe his periodic 'drifting into loneliness'.

Thoreau retreated to the shore of Walden Pond, Massachusetts, in 1847. *Walden* (London: Everyman, 1996) is an account of his two-year experiment in self-sufficiency.

Index

331

childhood 85
delusions 42, 44, 46
glossolalia 277
paranoias 220
symptoms 6–7, 9
vocal hallucinations 55–60
voice recognition 59–60
schizophrenic language 9–10
schizophrenic writing 9–11
Schneider, Kurt 55
Schreber, Daniel Paul 3–8, 44,
229, 300
Schreiber, Flora Rheta 29
science fiction, alien abduction
281
scurvy 288
séances 267–75
mesmeric 131–32
second self 71–75
sensory
isolation 296–97
perception 95–97
Sexton, Ray O. 321
shamanism
abduction 285
Arctic hysteria 186, 187
cerebral cleansing 150
ecstasy 261, 263, 264
initiation 295
lucid dreaming 174
near-death experiences 294
zoomorphic 200
Shamdasani, Sonu 314
shame 226–29
and civilizing process 227
distinguished from guilt 226–27
mechanism of denial 227
physical expression 228
psychological aspects 228–29
shame-based disorders 227

unacknowledged 227
Sheldrake, Rupert 274
Shelley, Percy Bysshe 71, 72
Shereshevski 122
Sheuk-Tak Cheng 317
Shorter, Edward 301
Showalter, Elaine 190, 302, 328
Sidgwick, H. 305
Sidky, H. 319
Siegel, Ronald K. 297, 303, 330
Silderfarb, P.M. 306
Sim, James 16
Simons, Ronald C. 193–94, 317,
318, 319
Sinclair, Andrew 324
Singapore, outbreak of *koro*
189–90
Siraisi, Nancy G. 315
Slater, Lauren 10, 300
sleep
abductions 284
cycles 160–62
night terror 219–20
nightmares 175–78
non-dreaming sleep 220
paralysis 175–78
sleepwalking 163–67
see also dreaming, REM
Slocum, Joshua 297–98, 330
Smart, Christopher 12
Smith, Angela Thompson 327
Smith, Hélène 144–46
Smith, Huston 306
Smith, John 291
Smith, R.J. 323
social interaction, autistic
children 84
social isolation 295–98
Society for Psychical Research 57,
141, 170, 267, 270, 305

345